Iowa Interstate Railroad: History Through the Miles

Barton Jennings

Iowa Interstate Railroad: History Through the Miles
Copyright © 2017 by Barton Jennings

All rights reserved. This book may not be duplicated or transmitted in any way, or stored in an information retrieval system, without the express written consent of the publisher, except in the form of brief excerpts or quotations for the purpose of review. Making copies of this book, or any portion, for any purpose other than your own, is a violation of United States copyright laws.

Publisher's Cataloging-in-Publication Data
Jennings, Barton

Iowa Interstate Railroad: History Through the Miles
314p.; 21cm.
ISBN: 978-0-9849866-7-5

Library of Congress Control Number: 2017913443

First Edition

Front cover photo by Barton Jennings
Back cover photo by Sarah Jennings

Please send comments or corrections to sarah@techscribes.com

TechScribes, Inc.
PO Box 620
Avon, IL 61415
www.techscribes.com

Printed in the United States of America

for my parents,
who have always been puzzled by my love of trains

Other books by this author:

Arkansas & Missouri Railroad: History Through the Miles
Alaska Railroad: History Through the Miles

Contents

Map 6
Preface 8
Acknowledgments 9
Iowa Interstate Route History 11
Iowa Interstate History 15
Iowa Interstate Route Guides 29
Blue Island Subdivision
    Blue Island (Illinois) to Silvis (Illinois) 31
Iowa City Subdivision
    Silvis (Illinois) to South Amana (Iowa) 107
Newton Subdivision
    South Amana (Iowa) to Des Moines (IA) 147
Council Bluffs Subdivision
    Des Moines (Iowa) to Council Bluffs (Iowa) 181
Peoria Subdivision
    Bureau Junction (Illinois) to Peoria (Illinois) 241
Milan Branch
    Rock Island (Illinois) to Milan (Illinois) 269
Prairie City Line
    Altoona (Iowa) to Mitchellville Station (Iowa) 279
Grimes Line
    Des Moines (Iowa) to Grimes (Iowa) 283
Atlantic Spur
    Atlantic Junction (Iowa) to Harlan (Iowa) 289
Hancock Spur
    Hancock Junction (Iowa) to Oakland (Iowa) 293
Iowa Interstate – Cedar Rapids Interchange
    Yocum Connection (Iowa) to Cedar Rapids (Iowa) 297
Hills Line
    Iowa City (Iowa) to Hills (Iowa) 309
About the Author 313

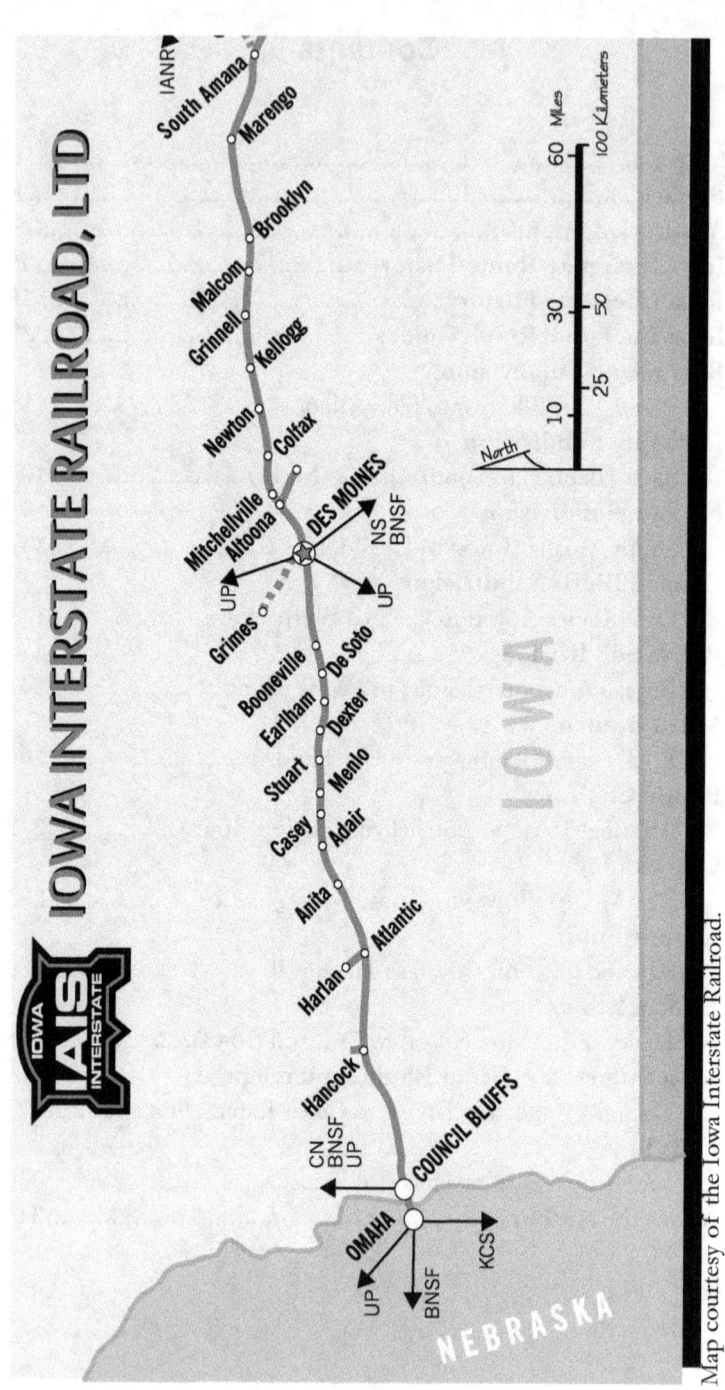

Map courtesy of the Iowa Interstate Railroad.

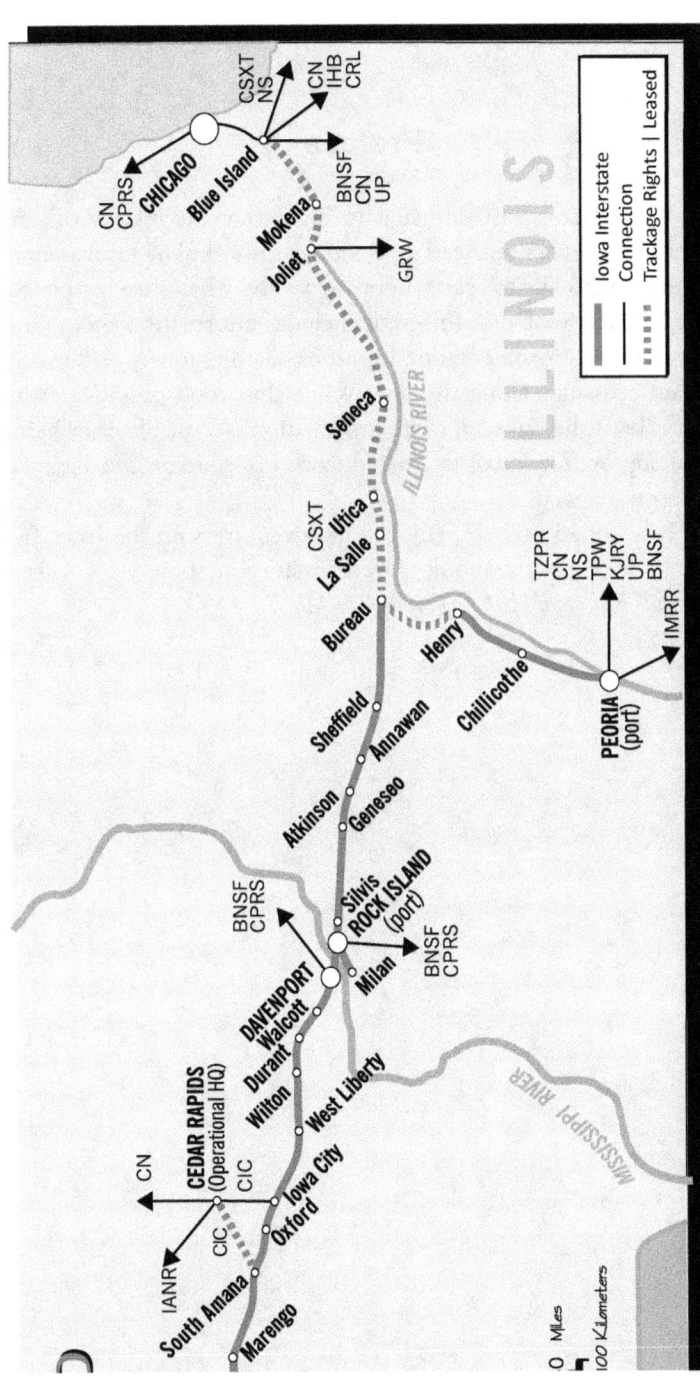

Map courtesy of the Iowa Interstate Railroad.

Preface

This guide is not designed to be a complete history of the Iowa Interstate, but instead it provides a great deal of information for those who like to ask "where are we and what once happened here?" Because of this, the guide includes information about current as well as former station locations, historic towns, and major stream crossings along the line. While this book provides great detail about the railroad, more information is available elsewhere, including on *The Unofficial Iowa Interstate Photo Archive and Railfan's Guide* on the web.

It is hoped that you enjoy your adventure with the Iowa Interstate and that this book is of assistance in some ways – *Iowa Interstate Railroad: History Through the Miles*.

Acknowledgments

For almost two decades, various groups have operated excursion passenger trains over various parts of the Iowa Interstate. These groups include local fire departments, rail enthusiast groups, and professional organizations. Recently, the railroad has operated several trips a year to benefit local fire departments and to assist them in acquiring needed equipment and supplies. This route description was first written in 2011-2012 for a series of passenger train charters, sponsored by different organizations, over various parts of the railroad. It has been updated since with several other visits to the company. Much of the information comes from internal railroad records, government and public records, railroad workers, and conversations with old and new friends. A number of these sources are listed in this book. In particular, Henry Posner, Mick Burkart, Jerry Lipka, Greg Mitchell, and many of the employees of the Iowa Interstate deserve a thank you for their help by reviewing and commenting on this book.

IAIS 714 at Atlantic, Iowa. Photo by Sarah Jennings.

Iowa Interstate Route History

The rail route of the Iowa Interstate has a significant history, some of which is included in school textbooks. The line was built from east to west during a period of significant change. It included a Supreme Court case, early land grant law, a Civil War, a historic train robbery, and the transcontinental railroad. This route guide provides the history of the line station by station, from east to west.

The east end of the route started as the Rock Island & La Salle Railroad Company, incorporated on February 27, 1847. On February 7, 1851, the charter was amended, creating the Chicago & Rock Island, chartered by the Illinois legislature to build from Chicago to the Mississippi River at Rock Island. Construction started on October 1, 1851, and the line and first train reached Joliet a year later on October 10, 1852. The railroad was completed with trains running in late February of 1854. In 1853, the Mississippi & Missouri (M&M) was incorporated to build from the Mississippi River at Davenport across Iowa to the Missouri River. Construction initially took place quickly, with track reaching Wilton, and the branch to Muscatine, by November 20, 1855. The railroad reached Iowa City on December 31, 1855, the last day to qualify for a $50,000 bonus. While the M&M was building west, a bridge was built across the Mississippi River, a bridge that would establish the rights of railroads to bridge over rivers nationwide, thanks to Abraham Lincoln and a Supreme Court case. Eventually, the track between Chicago and Iowa City would all be double track to support the numerous passenger and freight trains on the route.

In spite of a 774,000-acre land grant awarded by act of Congress on May 15, 1856, the Civil War slowed construction west of Iowa City, and by 1865, the railroad had extended only to Kellogg, about 75 miles further west. Trying to speed up the construction, the Chicago & Rock Island Railroad Company bought the stock of the Mississippi & Missouri in October 1865, and merged the companies on July 9, 1866, to create the Chicago, Rock Island & Pacific Rail Road Company. Construction did speed up with the line reaching Des Moines by 1867, but the railroad didn't reach Council Bluffs until May 11, 1869, a day after the Transcontinental Railroad was completed in Utah. The line became part of the core Rock Island system over time, providing a connection to the Union Pacific mainline at Omaha as well as providing the shortest connection to the Nebraska, Kansas, and Colorado parts of the Rock Island system. Between World War II and 1953, a large portion of the line between Atlantic and Council Bluffs was realigned as the Atlantic Cutoff.

The track between Bureau and Peoria was completed on November 9, 1854, as a part of the Illinois railroad boom of the 1850s. The railroad was built by the Peoria & Bureau Valley, and then immediately leased to the Chicago & Rock Island for operation. CSX acquired the northern part of this line in 1980 to serve the Goodrich chemical plant just north of Henry. The rest of the line to Peoria was saved by the Lincoln & Southern Railroad, owned by BF Goodrich, presumably to provide competitive pressure to keep CSX's prices in line.

In addition to these mainlines, the Iowa Interstate operates several short branch lines, all built by companies directly or indirectly tied to the Chicago, Rock Island & Pacific. More details about the history of these lines are provided with each route guide.

Rock Island Passenger Trains

As did most major railroads, the Rock Island once operated an extensive passenger service. The primary Rock Island routes included Chicago-Los Angeles, Chicago-Denver, Memphis-Tucumcari, and Minneapolis-Dallas. The route west of Chicago to Davenport was the eastern core of both the Denver and Los Angeles routes. At Davenport, the Golden State route to California turned to the southwest. This route, operating in competition with the Santa Fe Chiefs, was jointly operated with the Southern Pacific Railroad from 1902–1968. It was advertised as a "low altitude" crossing of the Continental Divide.

Heading west through Iowa City was the route of the *Rocky Mountain Rockets*. This route through Omaha and on to Colorado Springs and Denver benefitted from its connection with Union Pacific. Two trains on this route carried Iowa names: the *Des Moines Rocket* and the *Corn Belt Rocket*.

The *Des Moines Rocket*, #505 westbound and #506 eastbound, was inaugurated in September 1937 as a Chicago to Des Moines train. Its original run included a baggage-dinette, two chair cars, and a parlor-buffet-observation car. The train was always primarily a coach train, but by 1958, #505 had acquired a number of mail cars. Westbound #505 generally left Chicago with a dining car in the late afternoon with a Des Moines arrival shortly before midnight. Eastbound, #506 generally left Des Moines about 7:15am and arrived in Chicago just after lunch. By the Fall-Winter 1959-1960 public timetable, the *Des Moines Rocket* had been renumbered #5/#6. The Fall-Winter 1960-1961 public timetable had #6 as an overnight train from Des Moines to Chicago with only chair cars and no *Des Moines Rocket* name. By late 1967, train #5 had merged with #9 and train #6 had merged with #8, forming the *Quad City Rocket*.

In 1947, after upgrading parts of the route, the Rock Island introduced the *Corn Belt Rocket* between Chicago and Omaha. During the late 1950s, #9 operated sleeping cars from Chicago to Des Moines and Omaha as well as coaches. Train #10 was less glamorous, handling coaches as well as a Des Moines-Chicago parlor car and a Rock Island-Chicago dining car. During 1957, the *Corn Belt Rocket* departed Chicago at 10:00pm, passed through Iowa City at 2:43am, and arrived at Omaha at 8:15am. Eastbound, the train left Omaha at 11:30am and arrived at Chicago at 8:30pm, passing through Iowa City at 4:02pm. By the Spring-Summer 1963 public timetable, train #9 no longer carried the *Corn Belt Rocket* name, and #10 lost the name in the Spring-Summer 1965 public timetable. However, their schedules remained very similar to what they had been for almost two decades.

During the early 1960s, train #9 was known to carry a number of westbound New York Central express cars. For example, the Camerail Club reported that on April 30, 1965, #9 had three NYC express cars for Oakland, and one each for San Francisco, Salt Lake City, and Ogden. This train also included three mail cars and two RPOs for Des Moines, an express car for Oakland, one for Sacramento and another for San Francisco. Passengers had the use of two coaches and the 8 Duplex Roomettes-6 Roomettes-4 Double Bedroom sleeper "Granger."

The November 5, 1967, public timetable showed that train #9 had been cut back to a Chicago-Rock Island train but that #10 was the last Omaha-Chicago passenger service on the route. By July 1970, train #10 was gone and #5-9 was the evening Chicago-Rock Island *Quad City Rocket*. Too poor to join Amtrak in 1971, the railroad kept running the trains with the support of the State of Illinois. Starting soon after the creation of Amtrak, Illinois had to cover two-thirds of the losses experienced on the passenger trains to Rock Island and Peoria. This pattern continued until Illinois withdrew its subsidy and the trains made their final runs on December 31, 1978.

Sign on former Rock Island station, Atlantic, Iowa. Photo by Sarah Jennings.

Iowa Interstate History

On March 31, 1980, the Chicago, Rock Island & Pacific Railroad totally ceased train operations. Trustees for the railroad quickly sold off rail lines and equipment, and scrapped what couldn't be sold. On the route between Chicago and Omaha, Metra purchased the segment from Joliet through Blue Island to downtown Chicago's La Salle Street Station to protect its commuter service. Farther west, the International Mining Company (IMC), a subsidiary of the Chicago Pacific Corporation, a diversified holding company for the Chicago, Rock Island & Pacific Railroad, ended up high bidder for the section of track from Joliet (IL) to Bureau (IL). The Chessie System, now CSX, entered into a long-term lease with IMC to operate this section of track. The lease on what became known as CSX's New Rock Subdivision runs through 2030. On February 4, 2006, a sub-lease went into effect that gave IAIS control of everything west of Utica and down to Henry, restricting CSXT to Joliet-Utica.

For a while, the Davenport, Rock Island & Northwestern ran trains between the Quad Cities and Iowa City. Farther west, the Chicago & North Western operated between Dexter (IA) and Des Moines (IA) and on to Newton (IA). On the very west end of the line between Atlantic (IA) and Council Bluffs (IA), the Iowa Railroad Company (IARR), created on November 10, 1981, operated trains. On June 1, 1982, IARR entered a two-year lease for the whole line segment (with some exceptions) from Council Bluffs (IA) to Bureau (IL).

With a great deal of concern about the line's future, Heartland Rail Corporation was created by a number of shippers and area companies (Maytag Corporation, Pella Rolscreen, Iowa Electric Light & Power, Pioneer Hi-bred, the Alter Group, Cedar Rapids & Iowa City Railway, and several grain elevators) in 1983 and acquired the track and structures between Bureau and Council Bluffs for $31 million. Heartland assigned freight operations to the Iowa Interstate Railroad (IAIS), formed on May 17, 1984, by Dr. Paul Banner, Harry S. Meislahn (President), and Paul M. Victor, to conduct operations. All three of IAIS' founders had worked in the railroad industry. For example, both Meislahn and Banner were formerly with the Rock Island. The first Iowa Interstate train operated on November 4, 1984.

In 1985, the railroad negotiated trackage rights with Metra and CSX to reach Blue Island, the railroad's eastern terminus. In 1987, the IAIS expanded even more with the long-term lease of the Lincoln & Southern Railroad's (owned by B.F. Goodrich) trackage between Henry and Peoria, and an agreement with CSX to move trains between Henry and the IAIS' main line. Even with the company's growth, the railroad's future was uncertain. As the railroad described it: "rising costs, particularly financing costs, quickly led to mounting red ink, negative working capital, and a lack of cash. Vendors and creditors daily hounded the Company for payment. Creativity was the word of the day, and Illinois Central veteran Bill Duggan, as IAIS' VP-Engineering, held the railroad together on a shoestring budget."

In 1991, things changed when Heartland, the IAIS, and Railroad Development Corporation (RDC – an external investment concern headed by Henry Posner III and Robert A. Pietrandrea) reached an agreement to settle many of the financial issues. Heartland acquired all of the railroad's stock and RDC restructured IAIS' finances and provided long-term management to IAIS. RDC then acquired a 19.9% ownership interest in the IAIS with option rights to purchase the remaining interest. RDC's exercise of this option would automatically trigger an option to purchase the railroad lines and property of Heartland at fair market value. At this point, IAIS no longer existed as an independent entity separate from Heartland. With these changes, Fred Yocum was appointed President of the IAIS, a position he held until April 17, 1998. Additionally, in 1995, Archer Daniels Midland (ADM) took a majority equity interest in Heartland with the purchase of $5.5 million of new Heartland stock and buyout of other existing shares.

In July of 2001, RDC served notice it was exercising its purchase option rights to the IAIS and the properties associated with it. Determining the value of the railroad took some time, but on January 1, 2004, RDC acquired full ownership. Since that time, the railroad has carried out extensive capital programs to make up for past deficiencies, and has brought the track up to the 286,000-pound car weight industry standard.

Track work on the IAIS. Photo by Sarah Jennings.

In 2006 and 2007, the IAIS purchased the properties of the Lincoln & Southern (trackage from Henry to Peoria), Iowa Transfer (a dormant terminal switching company in Des Moines), and Council Bluffs Railway (CBGR – Council Bluffs yard). The IAIS further purchased land in Silvis to reinstall a portion of a yard facility that had been removed by the Rock Island. Recently, the Company has won two gold Harriman awards for safety. Besides track improvements, the railroad has acquired new locomotives. In 2008, 12 new GE AC 4400 horsepower, six-axle locomotives were also purchased by the IAIS, with more coming over the next few years. In the same year, the IAIS moved over 75,000 carloads of traffic (2.2 billion gross ton miles) on its system.

Today, the Iowa Interstate Chicago to Council Bluffs mainline consists of trackage rights over Metra and CSX, as well as four subdivisions. On the east end of the railroad, the Iowa Interstate runs on trackage rights over Metra trackage for the first 25 miles between Blue Island and Joliet, and then over CSX territory for the next 55 miles into Utica. The IAIS Blue Island Subdivision stretches from Utica (Milepost 95.0) to the Silvis rail yard (Milepost 171.9). Heading west, next is the Iowa City Subdivision, which consists of the tracks between Silvis (Milepost 173.4) and the new yard complex at South Amana (Milepost 259.2). The Newton Subdivision heads west from South Amana (Milepost 260.0) to the trackage rights over Union Pacific in Des Moines (Milepost 353.2). The westernmost part of the line is the Council Bluffs Subdivision, running from the west end of the Union Pacific trackage rights at Des Moines (Milepost 358.7) to Council Bluffs (Milepost 487.3).

Besides the mainline, there are a number of secondary lines. The Peoria Subdivision is the longest of these. It breaks off of the mainline at Bureau and heads south to Peoria. Several other branch lines also exist, primarily on the west end of the railroad. Additionally, the Iowa Interstate also operates over parts of the Cedar Rapids & Iowa City to reach the huge market at Cedar Rapids, Iowa.

Freight Train Operations

The following information covers the trains that generally operate on the Iowa Interstate Railroad. Many operate daily, some only on certain days, and others only as needed. Obviously, operations can and do change as needed, and this information is current as of the writing of this book.

Most Iowa Interstate trains use a simple name system where the first two letters represent the origin of the train, and the last two letters represent the destination. Trains based at a single location are assigned the switcher designation and use the two-letter base code followed by SW, or in a few cases the interchange railroad that they work with. Since new customers can quickly appear, additional trains will certainly be added in the future, and train schedules changed.

BICB – Blue Island-Council Bluffs

The BICB is the Iowa Interstate train that operates across the former Rock Island mainline from the Chicago area to Council Bluffs. Therefore, it operates from the east end of the railroad to the west end. This train, often known as "The Westbound" or "The West Train," operates seven days a week with the crew going on duty at Blue Island about 6:30pm. The crew then builds the train and departs Blue Island at the end of the Metra evening rush. It normally arrives in Silvis about 6:00am, with the local SISW (Silvis Switcher) crew working the train there. The BICB generally heads west after the arrival of the CBBI, often using the same crew out of South Amana. The BICB generally is handled on to Newton using the NTSW crew that brought the CBBI to South Amana, meaning a westbound trip at night. The train generally departs Newton shortly before sunrise and arrives in Council Bluffs in the late afternoon. It is not uncommon for the BICB to end at South Amana and be replaced by the SACB west of there when crews are unavailable, or when traffic volumes require.

CBBI – Council Bluffs-Blue Island

The CBBI, the eastbound train across the railroad, goes on duty at Council Bluffs seven days a week during the early afternoon. "The East Train" departs later in the afternoon and is worked at Newton about midnight, heading east to South Amana during the early morning hours, often arriving about sunrise. It then works east during the mid-morning to Silvis. It is planned to leave Silvis by about 5:00pm to make Blue Island before the morning Metra commuter rush.

BISI – Blue Island-Silvis

This train, which operates as needed over the east end of the railroad, is often known as "The Second Westbound." It typically departs Blue Island about midnight and handles an empty ethanol train from the Indiana Harbor Belt, CSX, or Norfolk Southern. The cars are headed to one of the ethanol plants along the line, such as Annawan, Cedar Rapids, Menlo or Council Bluffs.

SIBE – Silvis-Blue Island

This train covers the east end of the Iowa Interstate and is generally used to forward loaded ethanol unit trains to the Indiana Harbor Belt, CSX, or Norfolk Southern in Chicago. It normally departs Silvis about midnight when needed, which means it can be fighting the morning Metra rush east of Joliet.

SIBU – Silvis-Bureau

This train operates over the sixty miles of mainline east of Silvis. Operating Monday through Friday evening, often behind the CBBI, the SIBU forwards cars to Bureau for the BUSW jobs. The train also switches industries between Silvis and Bureau.

BUSI – Bureau-Silvis

This train is the reverse move of the SIBU. It again switches any customers between Bureau and Silvis that need service, and handles cars from the BUSW trains to Silvis.

PESI – Peoria-Silvis

This is generally an interchange train with Norfolk Southern, and often uses their black locomotives. The train can consist of almost any type of freight, but it generally consists of empty ethanol cars, or an entire empty ethanol train. It operates as needed.

SIPE – Silvis-Peoria

This train operates as needed, generally as a train for interchange with Norfolk Southern in Peoria. It often runs with Norfolk Southern power and commonly includes a loaded ethanol train or block of cars.

PECR – Peoria-Cedar Rapids Coal Train

This train operates as a loaded coal train, handed off from the Norfolk Southern Bloomington District in Peoria. Often using Norfolk Southern power to Silvis, it is headed to the ADM plant on the CIC in Cedar Rapids. The train operates as needed, but generally about once a week. The train is often used to shuttle IAIS locomotives from Silvis to South Amana.

CRPE – Cedar Rapids-Peoria Coal Train

This train is the empty PECR headed back to Norfolk Southern at Peoria. It operates as needed, but generally about once a week. Sometimes, the CRPE is combined with the CBBI at South Amana.

NSPEDM – Peoria-Des Moines Grain Train

This is the empty grain train, interchanged to the IAIS at Peoria from Norfolk Southern, that operates to Des Moines for loading. NS locomotives often operate on this train.

NSDMPE – Des Moines-Peoria Grain Train

This is a grain train loaded in Des Moines that operates to Norfolk Southern at Peoria. It operates as needed and generally uses NS power, although power from other railroads are often used.

SASI – South Amana-Silvis

The SASI/SISA is the out-and-back train west of Silvis. This mid-afternoon train runs seven days a week and moves eastbound cars that have been brought from Cedar Rapids. At Silvis, the train drops the cars for blocking to trains to Chicago, Peoria, and other eastern locations.

SISA – Silvis-South Amana

This is the westbound run of the turn from South Amana. It normally heads west about 10pm after having worked Silvis, and possibly picking up cars at the old Rock Island yard. The train often combines with the PECR coal train when that train is running.

SACR – South Amana-Cedar Rapids

This is the train that justified the construction of the South Amana yard. Operating seven days a week, this train heads north to the Smith-Dows Yard complex at Cedar Rapids to interchange with the Cedar Rapids & Iowa City. The SACR is often simply the SISA (Silvis to South Amana) train which turns north to Cedar Rapids just east of South Amana at Yocum Connection.

The train generally is heading north before sunrise, with the crew often called between 3am and 5am. When volumes are large, a second turn will run as soon as the first train returns as the CRSA.

CRSA – Cedar Rapids-South Amana

This train is the return run of the SACR. It departs Cedar Rapids after the SACR has completed its switching at Cedar Rapids. It takes its cars into South Amana Yard and sometimes returns back north for a second train of business from the Cedar Rapids & Iowa City.

SACB – South Amana-Council Bluffs

This train operates west of South Amana, either as a second train or as a replacement for the BICB. In some cases when traffic is heavy, the crew from Newton doesn't have the hours to handle the BICB. With the delay, the train is reworked and becomes the SACB.

BIIND – Blue Island Industrial Switcher

The train goes on duty at about 7:30am seven days a week. The train builds the BICB, pulls cars as needed from the Indiana Harbor Belt, and switches the few industries in the area.

BIIHB – Blue Island IHB Switcher

This train is a true interchange train, delivering blocks of cars from the CBBI and SIBI to the Indiana Harbor Belt, where they are broken up and handed off to several eastern railroads. The BIIHB then returns to Blue Island with blocks of cars from the IHB. It operates seven days a week and typically the crew goes on duty mid-morning.

BISW – Blue Island Switcher

This train operates as needed to relieve the BIIHB, to build the BISI, or to do local industry work. It generally goes on duty late afternoon to early evening.

BUSW – Bureau Switcher

There are actually two daily trains known as BUSW, also known as "The Bureau Rocket." There is a daytime BUSW that goes on duty about 9am, with a night train going on duty about 7pm. The train switches the area around Bureau as needed, generally east to LaSalle/Utica and west to Annawan/Silvis on the mainline. On the branch to Peoria, the BUSW goes as far as needed. This means Henry most days, and even on to Chillicothe and Peoria to handle local customers. The crews generally use the sidings and yard at Bureau to interchange cars with the CBBI and BICB.

SISW – Silvis Switcher

There can be as many as three SISW trains a day. The first crew normally goes on duty at 5am, seven days a week, and switches the inbound BICB. The crew also makes a transfer run to Rock Island Yard. The second SISW goes on duty at 8am, seven days a week, and switches the SASI and CBBI. This means the 5am crew is working the west end of the Silvis Yard while the 8am crew is working the east end of the yard. A third SISW normally operates Sunday through Thursday starting at 7pm and handles any work left at Silvis Yard.

RISW – Rock Island Switcher

This crew goes on duty in the late afternoon Sunday through Thursday. It handles customers on the Milan Branch, handles interchange with Canadian Pacific and switches customers in Davenport, and handles business in the Rock Island Yard where more interchange is conducted with BNSF and Canadian Pacific.

ICSW – Iowa City Switcher

Like many yards, there are often two switchers that serve this terminal. Operating Tuesday through Saturday, the 7am ICSW handles local customers and makes a round trip to South Amana. The late afternoon ICSW normally goes on duty at 4pm Monday through Friday and handles industries at Iowa City, Wilton and Durant.

SASW – South Amana Switcher

When needed, this train is often called at 11pm to handle work that the SACR and other trains don't complete. Tasks often include building the BICB, the CBBI, and working the South Amana Yard.

NTSW – Newton Switcher

There is a daytime NTSW that goes on duty at 9am Monday through Friday, and a nighttime crew that starts work about 6pm seven days a week. The daytime crew works the industries between Newton and Altoona. The night crew handles any additional work in the Newton area, and then often takes the CBBI east to South Amana and the BICB back.

DMSW – Des Moines Switcher

The crew for this train normally goes on duty about sunrise Sunday through Thursday. It works local customers in the Des Moines area, the Grimes Branch, and handles all interchange business in Des Moines.

ATSW – Atlantic Switcher

Nicknamed "The Rover," this train handles pretty much all local business on the mainline and branches west of Des Moines, and even heads as far east as Newton. It serves the remains of the Grimes and Prairie City branches, and often heads to Council Bluffs to swap cars. While most trips stay west of Des Moines, it sometimes interchanges cars with Norfolk Southern, BNSF, and Union Pacific in Des Moines. The crew normally goes on duty at 5pm on weekdays.

CBSW – Council Bluffs Switcher

A daily CBSW normally goes on duty before sunrise to switch the inbound BICB and/or SACB. The train also handles interchange work with Union Pacific and switches the intermodal ramp. The crew also begins building the eastbound CBBI while also serving local customers such as the Hancock elevator. A second CBSW goes on duty late afternoon and does any work that the morning crew hasn't completed. One common task is the evening interchange with Union Pacific.

Iowa Interstate Locomotives

While the locomotive fleet of the Iowa Interstate has included many different models, today it is dominated by three basic locomotive types, the SD38-2, the GP38-2, and the new ES44AC. The 22 GP38-2 locomotives (700-721), all built for Penn Central and later sold to Conrail and then Union Pacific, were acquired in 2004 to replace the many smaller and older locomotives such as SD20s, IC rebuilds GP8 and GP10, and even a few Alcos. The SD38-2 locomotives, numbered 150-153, were acquired starting in 2005 to handle the heavier mainline trains.

IAIS 704 switching at Milan, Illinois. Photo by Barton Jennings.

Finally, in 2008 and 2009, GE built 14 ES44AC (Evolution Series, 4400 HP, AC traction) locomotives (500-513) for the railroad to handle the heavier freight volumes, much of which comes from Cedar Rapids. All of IAIS's ES44ACs were built to CSX's ES-44AH "heavy" specification at 432,000 pounds, and includes the high traction software modifications. Note that locomotive 513 is painted in a Chicago, Rock Island & Pacific Railroad heritage scheme. Three more of these units (514-516) were bought in late 2014, with locomotive 516 painted in an Iowa Interstate version of the famous Rock Island red and yellow paint scheme.

IAIS 513 in heritage CRIP paint scheme, Iowa City, Iowa. Photo by Barton Jennings.

For the steam fan, Iowa Interstate also has two Chinese QJ 2-10-2 steamers on the property. The QJ (Qian Jin, meaning "advance") was once the most popular mainline steam locomotive in China, with more than 4700 built between 1964 and 1988. The more modern QJs used 12-wheel tenders and featured mechanical stokers, feedwater heaters, electric lights, and air horns.

QJs 6988 and 7081 were rebuilt to FRA standards and brought to the US by Railroad Development Corporation (their actual owners) to test the market for modern imported steam in the United States. IAIS 6988 was built in 1985 while 7081 was built in 1986, and both operated on the Jitong Railway until coming to the States. Steamer 6988 was altered in 2011 to look more American, with the change to a single headlight, the addition of a whistle, removal of the shroud around the exhaust stack, and changing all red parts to black.

Passenger Train Operations

Over the years, the Iowa Interstate has operated a number of passenger trains. Some of these have been operated for railroad industry meetings, historical societies, and for similar events. They have also been operated to help local fire departments raise funds for training and new equipment. Anyone able to ride one of these trips can consider themselves fortunate.

A large fleet of former STCUM (Societe de Transport de Montreal, or Montreal Urban Community Transit Corporation) commuter cars was the initial passenger fleet used by the railroad. Owned by IAIS owner Railroad Development Corporation (RRDX) and numbered in the 800s, forty of these cars were built in 1953 by Canadian Car & Foundry (CC&F). These cars had a capacity of 107 passengers in typical commuter seating. The more than a dozen cars acquired by Railroad Development Corporation (RDC) had upper windows that would open, and were all originally built for commuter service provided by Canadian Pacific.

In 2016, RDC acquired a smaller fleet of former Pennsylvania Railroad P70 coaches from the Austin Steam Train Association in Texas. The designation of P70 means that the car is a coach passenger car with a 70-foot long passenger compartment. The cars were 80 feet long, with 70 feet used for passengers and the rest for the end vestibules. The numbers acquired were cars #1646, #1658, #1684, #1699, #1726, and #1731.

These cars were the first of the Pennsylvania Railroad's 80-foot all-steel coaches. More than 1000 of these coaches were built for the railroad, some by the railroad's own Altoona Shops, and others by several car builders between 1907 and 1929. Until 1926, the cars were built with 88 seats, then after that with 80 seats. Multiple rebuildings over the year changed groups of the cars, making some Class P70R when air conditioning was added.

The cars acquired by Railroad Development were rebuilt after World War II into what was called a P70fbR class coach. The cars kept their old-style clerestory roofs, had their toilets relocated to one end of the car, and had the electrical and AC control cabinets moved to the other end. The new design had seating for 72 passengers using walkover seats. Many of these cars had round roofs installed later to reduce leaks. Since the purchase, the cars have gone through the car shops of the Iowa Interstate, with many of the signs of age being repaired.

The railroad has two other cars of significance, the *Hawkeye* and the *Abraham Lincoln*. Car #100, *Hawkeye*, was built as buffet-coach #1702 for the St. Louis-San Francisco Railway. It went through a number of changes, becoming car #1924 before being rebuilt into a business car. As a business car, it carried multiple numbers and names for the railroad, such as #6, *Oklahoma*, #4, and #3. The car later became Ontario Northland *Moosonee*, then a private car with the name *Texas*, then Midsouth *Prospector*, and finally Kansas City Southern #1887 *Arthur Stilwell*.

The car *Abraham Lincoln* started as Union Pacific diner #4812, built by American Car & Foundry in 1949. The car became Amtrak #8096 in October 1972, was retired in October 1981 and sold to a private individual, and then became Kansas City Southern #40 *Laredo*. It came to the Iowa Interstate in 2008.

Iowa Interstate Route Guides

Note that every station and bridge location is identified by a milepost location, shown as a number in the left-hand column of the route guides. Railroads identify locations along their routes by mileposts, much like highways do. The mileposts date back from the construction of the railroad, and the distance is measured from various places on various lines. There are signs every mile along the railroad that identify this distance.

Iowa Interstate Railroad: History Through the Miles

IAIS 714 on Bureau Switcher returning north. Photo by Barton Jennings.

Blue Island Subdivision
Blue Island (Illinois) to Silvis (Illinois)

The Blue Island Subdivision of the Iowa Interstate runs from Blue Island Yard near Chicago, to Silvis, Illinois. This unique subdivision is actually controlled by three different companies. From Blue Island to Joliet, the tracks are owned by Metra, the Chicago commuter railroad. West of Joliet to just west of Utica, Illinois, the tracks are the New Rock Subdivision of CSX. Iowa Interstate operates over this part of the route using trackage rights. West of Milepost 95 at Utica, the former Rock Island route is subleased to Bureau, and then west of there is owned by the Iowa Interstate. CSX operates over the Metra line into Chicago to Robbins where they enter their own line again. Chicago Rail Link also operates over much of the Metra route to connect to various lines they operate, and to serve several shippers.

Metra – Commuter Rail Division of the Regional Transportation Authority

This is part of the Rock Island District, the Metra commuter line from Joliet to the Chicago LaSalle Street station. What became Metra first became involved with this line in 1976 when the Regional Transportation Authority began to fund Rock Island commuter service. This support of the commuter service continued until the 1980 bankruptcy. In that year, the Chicago & North Western Railway (C&NW) began operating the Rock Island District commuter service. However, during Spring 1981, the C&NW stopped service on the line and the RTA helped create the Northeast Illinois Regional Commuter Railroad Corporation to acquire the line and to operate the commuter service. In December 1982, what became known as Metra bought the route for $35 million and commuter service began under the new organization's name.

13.8 119TH STREET – This grade crossing is at the north end of Burr Oak Yard. According to the *Rock Island Employees' Magazine*, during the early 1900s Burr Oak Yard "handled the distribution of eastbound tonnage for Chicago proper and the east via Chicago territory gateway, except eastbound connecting line merchandise, which is handled at Chicago station; Burr Oak yards being the junction between Illinois and Chicago Terminal Divisions." Burr Oak also reportedly handled westbound carload and merchandise movements for the Illinois Division. Rock Island statements indicated that the main tonnage at the time was local grain and stock shipments to Chicago firms, especially the Chicago stockyards.

IAIS 506 on BICB at Burr Oak Yard. Photo by Barton Jennings.

15.5 IOWA INTERSTATE BLUE ISLAND – This is the switch into the Blue Island Yard. "BI" is the IAIS code for Blue Island.

To the north of the two Metra stations in Blue Island is the former Rock Island Burr Oak Yard, often known as Blue Island Yard. The Iowa Interstate uses this yard and maintains its intermodal facilities here. The former CRI&P Blue Island/Burr Oak railyard was the site of a series of riots starting on June 29, 1894. Nearby, Pullman workers were already on strike when the president of the American Railway Union, Eugene Debs, gave a speech in support of the striking workers. Soon, Rock Island Railroad buildings were burning and a locomotive was knocked off the tracks, blocking the movement of all trains on the line. On July 2nd, President Grover Cleveland responded by sending federal troops to Illinois to maintain the peace and to ensure the safe delivery of the mail.

Blue Island Yard is also the location of the 1987 scrapping of Richard Jensen's Grand Trunk Western (GTW) 4-6-2 #5629. Jensen had purchased #5629 from the Grand Trunk Western in 1959 as part of a plan to operate steam-powered excursion trains across the Midwest. In 1987, GTW #5629 was stored in Blue Island yard. CRI&P sold the yard to Metra, who had plans to redesign the yard for their commuter train operations. Metra told Jensen to move the locomotive, but reportedly refused to help in making the short move to one of the Iowa Interstate tracks. A further complication came about when Metra would not allow people on the property to inspect GTW #5629. Finally, Metra gave permission to the Illinois Railway Museum to move the locomotive, but they didn't have title to it, so the result was Metra getting court permission to scrap the steamer. So, by July of 1987, the GTW Pacific was cut into scrap.

In 1926, the Indiana Harbor Belt built a new hump yard nearby to the southeast to handle growing business in the area. This Blue Island Yard had a 44-track classification yard and a large facility for loading and servicing ice-cooled refrigerator cars. For the rail history buff, this yard was the departure point for many of New York Central's eastbound road freights. The former B&O Chicago Terminal's Barr Yard is also in that area, located just north of the IHB yard.

15.7 BLUE ISLAND – This area was called Blue Island by early explorers because the ridge, created as a glacial moraine, looked like an island in a sea of prairie grass. The first settler arrived in 1835 from Charlotte, Vermont. Norman Rexford established the Blue Island House Inn here in 1836. While Blue Island incorporated in 1843, the first post office located here opened in 1850 as Worth. In October 1852, the Chicago & Rock Island Rail Road Company (later CRI&P), originally the Rock Island & LaSalle Rail Road Company (chartered to build between the two towns), arrived and named their station here Blue Island. In 1860, the post office changed its name to Blue Island, and the Village of Blue Island was incorporated during the fall of 1872.

Current Train Operations

Public funding of commuter trains on this line began in 1976 when the Regional Transportation Authority agreed to subsidize service on the line. The agreement lasted until the Chicago, Rock Island & Pacific Railroad went bankrupt in 1980. In that year, the Chicago & North Western Railway began operating the Rock Island District. This agreement lasted until Spring 1981 when the C&NW ended service and Metra (Northeast Illinois Regional Commuter Railroad Corporation) took over providing the service. To maintain service, Metra bought the former Rock Island line from La Salle station to just west of Joliet for $35 million in December 1982.

Today, the former Rock Island line through Blue Island is owned and operated by Chicago Metra. The Rock Island District Line splits at Gresham, northeast of Blue Island. The mainline heads straight to Blue Island while the Suburban Branch loops west to serve a number of communities before rejoining the main at Blue Island. The Metra station on the former Rock Island tracks is known as the Vermont Street station. This station is one of the oldest in the Metra network, having been built in 1868. To the east of the CRI&P tracks is the Metra Electric Blue Island station, the western terminus of the Blue Island branch of the Metra Electric line.

Through freight trains on the line are operated by CSX and Iowa Interstate Railroad on a trackage rights agreement. In addition, Chicago Rail Link has rights to operate local freight service on the whole district, and it also uses the line between Gresham Wye and Blue Island to connect with the Iowa Interstate and Indiana Harbor Belt Railroads. The Chicago Rail Link is one of the important connections on the east end of the Iowa Interstate. It connects to the eastern railroads and handles many of the ethanol trains

Blue Island Subdivision

heading to those railroads. The Indiana Harbor Belt handles many of the individual freight cars interchanged with eastern railroads, blocking them in their Blue Island Yard.

Where all of the tracks come together just west of the Metra station is a junction known as Western Avenue Junction (Milepost 15.9).

15.9 LITTLE CALUMET RIVER BRIDGE – The railroad uses two bridges, standing side-by-side, to cross the Cal-Sag Channel, a part of the Calumet River network. To the south is a large two-track Warren through truss span, while to the north the bridge is a single-track Warren through truss bridge. The longest span is 400 feet long. There are crossovers on each end of the bridges to connect the Gresham mainline and the Suburban Branch.

The Cal-Sag Channel, short for "Calumet-Saganashkee Channel," is a navigation canal between the Little Calumet River and the Chicago Sanitary and Ship Canal. The canal is a bit more than fifteen miles long and was built between 1911 and 1922. The Cal-Sag Channel is used by barges to serve local industries and as a conduit for wastewater from southern Cook County, including the Chicago-area Deep Tunnel Project, into the Illinois Waterway. It is also used by pleasure crafts in the summer time.

16.3 BLUE ISLAND JUNCTION BRIDGE – Blue Island Junction is actually just to the north and is where a number of railroads come together to use a common right-of-way to the southeast. The former CRI&P line crosses the tracks of CSX, Canadian National, and Indiana Harbor Belt. Just to the east of here the Metra mainline reduces to two tracks.

17.2 ROBBINS – Robbins is a Metra station and the location of the switch to the Baltimore & Ohio Chicago Terminal Railroad (reporting mark BOCT) at Blue Island Junction to the north. CSX uses this track to eventually reach their Barr Yard base of operations. A small yard and series of warehouses, once the Evans freight car manufacturing facility, are visible to the north. The IAIS uses this facility as a transload terminal.

Robbins was incorporated in 1917. During the years 1930-1933, Robbins was home to the first airport that was owned and operated by African-Americans in the United States. This airport included the only flight school at the time where African-Americans could be trained as pilots. Reportedly, this facility served as a model for the Tuskegee Airmen Program during World War II. Robbins is the home town of Mr. T (Lawrence Tero) and Nichelle Nichols (Lieutenant Uhura of *Star Trek*).

18.4 MIDLOTHIAN – Just west of where the railroad passes under Interstate 294, the Tri-State Tollway, is the Metra station of Midlothian. As with most stations on this route, the main station or shelter is on the south track, designed to serve passengers waiting for their morning trains into town. In the evening, passengers generally head directly to their cars or connecting buses, so little shelter is needed on the outbound north track.

The name Midlothian comes from an ancient borough in Scotland. Midlothian served as a milk stop for area farmers until about 1900. At that time, the Midlothian Country Club and Golf Course became popular with a number of Chicago industrialists and the Rock Island Railroad built a passenger depot and installed a spur track to serve the expanding passenger demand. By 1915, land developers began developing residential areas at Midlothian. On March 17, 1927, the community was incorporated as the Village of Midlothian, taking its name from the golf course around which the community had grown and prospered.

The first editor of the local newspaper was Kevin McGann, who later served as aide-de-camp to General Dwight Eisenhower during World War II and worked with Eisenhower on his two books.

20.4 OAK FOREST – The Oak Forest area was originally called Cooper's Grove Stand of Timber, taking the name from the first resident of Bremen Township, who reportedly settled here about 1830. The Cooper's Grove post office opened in the 1840s, and later changed its name to New Bremen in 1848.

The earliest reference to the community as "Oak Forest" is in an 1893 Chicago, Rock Island & Pacific Railway timetable. The original Oak Forest train station was primarily a milk and farm stop used by area farmers. This changed in 1894 when the DuPont family purchased property on the south side of the tracks where they built what they claimed was the world's largest gunpowder magazine and factory. The entire complex blew up in 1906. Following the explosion, the area became more residential and Oak Forest was incorporated as a village in 1947, and then incorporated as the City of Oak Forest in 1971.

Just west of the overpass over Cicero Avenue is the Oak Forest Metra station, one of the busiest on the line. The new modern station here was opened on December 20, 2013. Notice the short spur to the south at the east end of the station platform. It was once the Infirmary Spur, but today it is often used to store track equipment working in the area. Not far west of the station there is a spur track off of the north track.

23.5 TINLEY PARK – The first settlers in this area were the John Fulton family from New York, arriving in 1835. Soon the community of English Settlement developed here, taking the name of Yorktown a few years later. The general language of the community changed in the 1840s as large numbers of Germans arrived, many coming via the port of Bremen, leading to the community's next name: New Bremen.

In 1850 and 1851, the Chicago & Rock Island Rail Road Company bought a right-of-way from Chicago to Joliet, passing through this area. The community of New Bremen became official in 1853 when Dr. Samuel Rush Haven filed a plat for the village alongside the railroad. On June 27, 1892, the village changed its name again and was incorporated as Tinley Park. The incorporation took place at the train depot, and the name change honored Samuel Tinley, Sr., the longtime Rock Island Railroad station master.

    The railroad has a set of crossovers just east of Tinley Park known as CP 66th Court, located at Milepost 23.3. To the south is the new Tinley Park train station, built in 2003 after the original station burned. The Tinley Park Metra station is designed to look like a European castle of the Late Middle Ages. The station was honored by the American Institute of Architects as one of the 150 Great Places of Illinois. Most of the parking at the station uses land that until recently was used by local businesses, such as lumber yards and grain elevators. Next to the station is a small steamer, a Porter 0-4-0 fireless used by Swift & Company as their #2, today numbered 1892 to note the date of Tinley Park's incorporation. The locomotive was built for Swift in Chicago in April 1931 as construction number 7202.

    Across the street from the station was once the Bremen Cash Store, later Vogt's Department Store, once the center of the town. Today, little of this original business district still stands. Nearby is the Vogt Visual Arts Center, located in the house of the first Tinley Park Mayor, Henry Vogt.

    To the west of the station area at milepost 24.2 was once a spur to the south that served the Tinley Park State Hospital.

25.1 TINLEY PARK – 80TH AVENUE – This station is one of the newer Metra stations, originally built in the middle of a corn field before suburbia closed around it. This part of the Chicago area is one of the fastest growing, and the 80th Avenue Station is reportedly the fourth busiest station in the entire Metra system. A Metra stop first opened here in 1970, but the modern station and much of the parking was built around 2010. There are more than 2100 parking spots at this station alone. The station was built with a mix of brick and concrete with a large decorative arch facing the parking lots to the south. The 5400-square foot building features a restaurant and a 50-foot tall clock tower. Built on a high fill, this is one of the more landscaped and decorative stations on Metra.

To the south of the parking lots is the Tinley Park – Park Division Freedom Park. The park features a former Rock Island Railroad caboose. This is former CRIP caboose 17869, which was acquired by the Regional Transportation Authority in 1980 after the Rock Island shutdown. Renumbered 2002, the caboose was used on work trains.

25.8 COUNTY LINE – This county line, located about halfway between the 80th Street station and where the railroad passes under Interstate 80, is between Cook and Will Counties. Cook County is to the east while Will County is to the west.

Cook County is the second most populous county (5.25 million) in the United States after Los Angeles County. Almost 45% of all Illinois residents live in Cook County. There are more than 130 incorporated municipalities in Cook County, the largest of which is the county seat, Chicago. Cook County was created on January 15, 1831, out of Putnam County. It was the 54th county established in Illinois and was named after Daniel Cook, one of the earliest and youngest statesmen in Illinois history. Daniel Cook had a short but busy political career. In 1817, he was sent to London to accompany John Quincy Adams, Secretary of State under James Monroe, back to the States. In 1821, Cook married Julia Catherine Edwards, the daughter of Ninian Edwards, governor of the Illinois Territory. Cook also served as the second U.S. Representative from Illinois and as the first Attorney General of the State of Illinois.

While Cook County has the historic population, **Will County** is one of the fastest growing counties in the United States. Will County was formed on January 12, 1836, and was named after Dr. Conrad Will, a politician and businessman involved in salt production in southern Illinois. Dr. Will was a member of the first Illinois Constitutional Convention and a member of the Illinois Legislature until his death in 1835.

27.5 HICKORY CREEK – The Hickory Creek station is another one of the newer Metra stations built to serve the growing communities. It was built in 1993. To the north the railroad has a spur into the Ozinga Illinois RMC cement plant. A bit to the west is a track into the Schilling lumber complex to the south.

29.6 MOKENA – To the east of the Mokena station is a series of tracks once used to serve area manufacturers. Just to the west of the station is a set of crossovers known as CP Mokena.

During the early 1830s, a number of families settled along the banks of Hickory Creek, a tributary of the Des Plaines River. In 1838, the post office of Chelsea was established for the community. However, in 1852, the Rock Island Railroad built its line just north of Chelsea and Allen Denny platted a new community along the railroad. The new community of Mokena soon became the market center for a large farming area. Mokena finally incorporated in 1880. Reportedly, the Mokena name is derived from Algonquian for "turtle," chosen because of the many streams and ponds in the area.

33.4 WABASH BRIDGE – Overhead is the former Wabash, St. Louis & Pacific Railway Chicago to St. Louis line. Today, this line is owned by Norfolk Southern and used by Metra as their SouthWest Service line to Manhattan.

The bridge is a single 150-foot long Baltimore through truss span, built in 1917. The Baltimore truss is a type of Pratt truss, with additional bracing in the lower section of the truss to prevent buckling. It was a popular design in the railroad industry.

34.0 NEW LENOX – This is another relatively new Metra station, built before the area was urbanized. Parking lots just keep getting added to the complex to handle the growth in the area.

Blue Island Subdivision

New Lenox has a similar background to many other area communities. It started as a small farming community alongside Hickory Creek known as VanHorne Point. With the arrival of the railroad in the early 1850s, the area saw a spurt in growth. Will County was reorganized in 1852 and New Lenox Township was established. Reportedly the name came from Lenox, New York, the original home of the first supervisor of the Rock Island Railroad in the area.

At about the same time, George Gaylord, a merchant and grain dealer from Lockport, laid out plans for a community here. Originally, he named it Tracey after the superintendent of the Rock Island Railroad. Later, Mr. Tracey requested that the name be changed and Rock Island supervisor John Van Duser named the community after the Township – New Lenox. Authors of the Federal Writers' Project *Guide to 1930's Illinois*, published in 1939, described New Lenox as a "community of small farms, poultry yards, and kitchen gardens."

An effort by community leaders in 1945 led to a vote to officially organize the community, conducted during the spring of 1946. With that, the Village of New Lenox was finally incorporated on October 4, 1946. The community stayed rural for several more decades. However, with the arrival of Interstate 80 and the growth around Chicago, today's New Lenox is a heavily populated suburban community.

The railroad will pass under Interstate 80 about a mile west of the station. Just to the south of the tracks here is US-30, the Lincoln Highway.

35.5 **CP 35.5** – This set of crossovers is directly below Interstate 80. Immediately to the south is U.S. Highway 30, the Lincoln Highway. The Lincoln Highway was one of the first transcontinental roadways designed for cars. Built from Times Square in New York City, to Lincoln Park in San Francisco, the planning started in 1912 and the roadway was formally dedicated on October 31, 1913. The Lincoln Highway, often known as "The Main Street Across America," was the first national memorial to President Abraham Lincoln. Its success attracted interest in other roadways, helping to create a boom in road construction.

38.9 EJ&E CROSSING – Today, this line is owned by Canadian National. It is the east-west line between Joliet and the steel mills around Gary, Indiana. EJ&E/CN trains crossing the diamond southward are heading east. Just north of here is the large EJ&E (Elgin, Joliet and Eastern Railway) Joliet Yard. There is a seldom-used interchange track in the northeast quadrant of the crossing.

39.2 MC TOWER – MC Tower was named for the Michigan Central and was located at the former crossing of the MC and the Rock Island.

39.5 CP MILLER STREET – West of here is Metra's Joliet Yard, used to store and service Metra trains overnight. This crossover allows trains to go in or out of the east end of the yard and reach either main track.

39.9 CP RICHARDS STREET – The railroad goes to a single mainline at the west end of Joliet Yard at a location known as Richards Street.

40.0 METRA JOLIET – This new Metra station complex allows service to Joliet without blocking the north-south train activity at UD Tower – the Joliet diamond.

40.1 UD TOWER – UD Tower is an interlocking tower once used to protect the former crossing of the Rock Island main line with the former Alton and ATSF main lines. Today, Metra controls UD tower, and thus the crossing of the Metra line with today's BNSF and Union Pacific lines. This Metra control meant that in the past it was not uncommon to see hot intermodal trains from both directions waiting for Metra-Rock Island trains to cross. There are plans to preserve the tower and turn it into a railroad museum.

A connecting track in the southeast quadrant of the interlocking is heavily used by Metra trains between the north-south line and Joliet Yard to the east.

40.2 JOLIET – Like many of the towns and cities in the Chicago area, the history of Joliet includes several name changes and battles over its incorporation. The local European history started in 1833 when Charles Reed settled on the west shore of the Des Plaines River. The next year, Reed gained neighbors across the river when James B. Campbell, treasurer of the canal commissioners, laid out the village of "Juliet", named after his daughter. Juliet was incorporated as a village by 1837, and taxes went up almost immediately. Juliet residents soon petitioned the state to rescind their incorporation to end Juliet's ability to tax. A name change took place in 1845 when the community's name went from "Juliet" to "Joliet," believed chosen for the French-Canadian explorer Louis Jolliet, who in 1673, along with Father Jacques Marquette, explored this area. The city was again incorporated in 1852.

With the crossing of railroads, Joliet became a railroad center. The Rock Island reached Joliet in October of 1852, thus the city's reincorporation that year. For many years, Joliet was the dividing point between Subdivision 1 of the Illinois Division (Chicago to Joliet) and Subdivision 2 (Joliet to Rock Island). The EJ&E, Santa Fe, Chicago & Alton, Milwaukee Road, Illinois Terminal, and Michigan Central also reached Joliet.

The most impressive railroad structure at Joliet is the Union Station. The Blackhawk Chapter of the National Railway Historical Society (NRHS) has a great website about Joliet, and a few details are included here.

Before 1900, every railroad in Joliet had their own station and yard facilities, creating chaos in the community. At the insistence of the city, the tracks in downtown Joliet were realigned and elevated from 1908-1910. As part of the realignment, the three major railroads in town combined their passenger facilities at the new Union Station. The station, opened in October of 1912, was designed by the prolific Chicago architect Jarvis Hunt, whose work includes the Kansas City (MO) Union Station, the Union Pacific Railroad headquarters building in Omaha (NE), and the Great Lakes Naval Station in North Chicago (IL). As built, there were passenger platforms with canopies between the first and second tracks on both the east and south sides of the station. The platforms were reached by underground walkways. The station handled passenger, express and mail business, but each railroad still had their own facilities in Joliet for freight and less-than-carload (LCL) shipments.

Joliet Union Station was built at the crossing of the Atchison, Topeka & Santa Fe (now BNSF) Chicago to Fort Madison line; the Chicago & Alton (now Union Pacific) Chicago to St. Louis line; and the Chicago, Rock Island & Pacific (now Metra) Chicago to Rock Island line. The four tracks on the east side were used by the C&A and the AT&SF, while the four tracks on the south side were used by the CRI&P and the Michigan Central. The MC was a tenant in the station from 1912 until 1925 when it discontinued passenger service to Joliet. The MC's "Joliet cutoff" from East Gary, Indiana, connected with the Rock Island about one mile east of the station. The Michigan Central line was abandoned in the early 1970s. Today, east of Joliet, the right-of-way is a biking and hiking path called the Old Plank Road Trail.

After years of neglect and decay, the station building was restored between 1989-1991. Today, the City of Joliet owns two-thirds of the facility and Metra owns the other third. Tracks 1 and 2 on the east side belong to BNSF while tracks 3 and 4 are used by Union Pacific and Canadian National. Metra's Heritage Corridor trains and all Amtrak trains traditionally used tracks 3 and 4. The track to the south is owned by Metra and used by CSX and Iowa Interstate for freight service.

With the construction of the new Metra and Amtrak stations on the east side of UD Tower, Joliet Union Station no longer hosts passenger trains as of September 26, 2014.

Multiple plans for the station have come and gone, and as of 2016, the money for the project has been spent and few things have been completed.

CSX - New Rock Subdivision

When the Rock Island Railroad went bankrupt, the railroad was liquidated, and the rail route became a part of the railroad's successor corporation, Chicago Pacific Corporation (CPC), a diversified holding company. To preserve rail service over the line, in August 1980, CSX entered into a fifty-year lease agreement with the trustee of the bankrupt Rock Island Railroad to operate this line from Joliet west to Bureau, Illinois. CPC was acquired by the Maytag Corporation in 1989. Maytag then sold the railroad between Joliet and Council Bluffs, with the line west of Bureau going to Heartland Rail Corporation/Iowa Interstate. Between Bureau and Joliet, the line was sold to International Mining Corporation (IMC), which now controls the lease to CSX.

Effective February 3, 2006, the Surface Transportation Board approved the Iowa Interstate "to sublease from CSX Transportation, Inc. (CSXT), and operate a line of railroad totaling approximately 31.9 miles. The rail line, presently leased and operated by CSXT extends from milepost BIF 95, in Utica, IL, to milepost BIF 126.9, in Henry, IL."

This leaves Metra in charge from Chicago to Joliet, CSX in charge from Joliet to Utica, and Iowa Interstate in charge west of Utica. However, Iowa Interstate has trackage rights across all of the route.

40.7 BRIDGE 407 – This bridge, a Warren through truss with a vertical lift, crosses the Des Plaines River. Also known as the Joliet Lift Bridge, the current bridge was built in 1932 by the American Bridge Company and installed by the Ketler-Elliot Erection Company of Chicago, Illinois. When built, the bridge carried two tracks; today only one still exists. An interesting design feature of this bridge is that the lift machinery is incorporated into the two towers instead of being placed directly on the lift span. This was the same design as the Rock Island bridge at DeValls Bluff, Arkansas.

The bridge is 552 feet long, with the lift span being 302 feet. The east approach span is 100 feet long while the west approach span is 150 feet long. The bridge was built as a part of navigational improvements on the Des Plaines River. It replaced a five-span through truss bridge built in 1900. Today, this lift bridge is owned and operated by CSX as part of their New Rock Subdivision, as is the track west of here to milepost 95. East of here the track is owned and dispatched by Metra. You know that someone is about to cross the bridge when you hear on the radio that they can "jump the bridge."

The Des Plaines River starts in Wisconsin, flows south into Illinois and around the west side of Chicago, and eventually merges with the Kankakee River northwest of Kankakee to create the Illinois River. The river, less than 140 miles long, has a long history of being used for transportation. Early French explorers Marquette and Joliet (1673) found the river already being used for trade, as a route between the Great Lakes and the Mississippi River. The name Des Plaines is believed to refer to the American sycamore or the red maple, trees which lined the river. It is believed that the name was given because the trees resembled the European plane tree.

The Des Plaines River is a part of the Illinois Waterway, a commercial river route from the Mississippi River, up the Illinois River and then the Des Plaines River to the Chicago Sanitary and Ship Canal (CSSC) at Lockport Lock and Dam. The route then continues up the CSSC and the Chicago River to Lake Michigan. A second route is the Calumet-Sag Channel (CSC), which splits from the CSSC near Lemont, Illinois. The CSC eventually also connects to Lake Michigan using the Little Calumet and Calumet Rivers.

This area also saw the Illinois & Michigan Canal, designated as a National Heritage Corridor in 1984. The I&M Canal was built to connect Lake Michigan with the Mississippi River and was built 1836-1848 between Chicago and

Blue Island Subdivision

LaSalle. Funded by a Federal land grant, the canal was heavily impacted by the construction of the Rock Island Railroad, but lasted until the end of the century. The history of the canal states that it was the only major American canal to pay off its construction debts and make a profit. As boats got larger, the canal became useless and was eventually replaced by today's Illinois Waterway.

41.1 CENTER STREET – At one time, there were a number of industries here, including Stockdale Midwest Corporation, Blockson Chemical Company, the E.F. Schundler Company, and American Steel & Wire Company. Today, little exists of these industries. CSX timetables show Scrap Services at Milepost 41.3.

The Illinois Terminal once followed the Rock Island from here west to Ottawa and La Salle, having a grade immediately to the south of the CRI&P tracks. This line was built as the Chicago, Ottawa & Peoria Railway (CO&P), an electric interurban railway operating between Joliet and Princeton. It was one of the longest interurban lines in Illinois. Construction on the railroad started on the west end, being built from Ladd through Peru and LaSalle to Ottawa in 1904. The line reached here on December 16, 1911. Near here, the route turned east across the Des Plaines River using the road bridge. Once across the river, the railroad turned northward to connect with the Chicago & Joliet Electric for access on into Chicago. The CO&P became the Illinois Terminal's Illinois Valley Division in 1923. At first the railroad was modernized, but the Depression cut into the line's traffic, and the Rock Island's mainline diverted most of what was left. The electric line could not hold on and service ended on May 14, 1934.

Just west of here the railroad again passes under Interstate 80. Just west of I-80 is a lock and dam. Known as the Brandon Road Lock and Dam, creating the Brandon Road Pool, it is used to improve navigation on the Des Plaines River. The lock and dam was opened in 1933 and modified in 1985. The lock is 110 feet wide and 600 feet long, capable of holding as many as eight barges (35 feet wide by 195 feet long) and one line boat, the standard on the Illinois Waterway. This dam raised the level of the water so there was no longer a need for the old I&M Canal. The old canal is now the Illinois and Michigan Canal Trail.

42.7 ROCKDALE – This area was named Mount Jolliet by French-Canadian explorer Louis Jolliet and Father Jacques Marquette in 1673. They camped here for several days. The hill was made up entirely of clay. The spot was mined by early settlers and is now a depression. With the ground leveled, it was soon settled and became known as the town of Rockdale.

The area once was heavy with manufacturing. Little business still exists but the small support yard and office is still used by CSX and locomotives are often parked here. The railroad has a one-mile long "West Pass" to the north and a much longer "East Pass" to the south. At the west end of the yard the EJ&E, later the Joliet Junction Railroad, used to cross over the Rock Island. This line also served the industries located along the Illinois & Michigan Canal to the south. Today, this railroad is abandoned and the grade is used as the Joliet Junction Trail.

43.5 ROCKDALE XO – This is a crossover between the two former mainlines, with the south track mainly being used for switching and storage. To the west is an industrial track that heads south to serve the large Johns Manville facility. The line once crossed the I&M Canal to serve the Caterpillar assembly plant and other industries. Next is a spur to the south that serves the Ecolab facility. At the west switch of the East Pass is the Amaco Spur, a track that serves a large industrial park to the south with shippers such as Canal Terminal, Road River Rail Tank Properties, and Flint Hills Resources. All of this industry explains why CSX acquired this part of the line.

For trains heading west, they exit the Rockdale Yard Limits at Milepost 46.4 and enter DTC Block "Mino,"

Blue Island Subdivision

named for nearby Minooka, Illinois. DTC (direct traffic control) is a method of authorizing train movement over a stretch of track. With a DTC system, the railroad dispatcher gives track authority directly to the train crew via radio. For the system, the railroad is broken down into formal blocks and crews are given authorization to enter and pass through each block. At Milepost 47.4, the tracks will pass under Interstate 55, which connects the Chicago area with St. Louis.

48.0 DUPAGE RIVER BRIDGE – The railroad bridge consists of four deck plate girder spans, each 54'-6" long. Note that the bridge was built for two tracks while only one exists today, in this case the north track.

The DuPage River is about 30 miles long. It is created when the West Branch of the DuPage River merges with the East Branch of the DuPage River between Naperville and Bolingbrook. The West Branch starts up in Schaumburg, Illinois, while the East Branch begins in Bloomingdale, Illinois. The combined waterways flow south before entering the Des Plaines River.

The 1882 History of DuPage County, Illinois appears to be the first written text to explain the name of the DuPage River. This history states that the river was named for a Mr. Du Page, a Frenchman who had settled on the river prior to 1800. Some reports state that he ran a trading post near the mouth of the river. Nearby DuPage County was apparently named for the same early settler.

50.8 COUNTY LINE – This is the county line between Will County (to the east) and Grundy County (to the west). The county line is at the east side of Minooka and the first train entered Grundy County here in 1852. **Grundy County** was created out of a part of LaSalle County and was established on February 17, 1841. Its county seat is Morris. The latest census resulted in the center of Illinois population being located in Grundy County. The county's population is about 50,000, or less than one percent of nearby Cook County.

The name Grundy is actually not that rare, there are four counties in the United States with that name. The county was named for Felix Grundy, who was a U.S. Congressman and U.S. Senator from Tennessee. Grundy also served as the 13th Attorney General of the United States under President Martin Van Buren beginning in July 1838. Grundy was a mentor to future President James K. Polk. Polk later purchased Grundy's home called "Grundy Place" and changed the name to "Polk Place."

51.1 MINOOKA – Minooka was and still is the highest point in Illinois on the Rock Island Railroad route at an elevation of 601.6 feet. This is the top of a long 0.3% grade from both east and west. Because of the hill, early railroad workers called this location "Summit." As part of the line's improvements, the tracks were lowered in the 1920s, leaving them about fifteen feet below street level. Before that, the passenger station was just east of the Wabino/Waben Avenue grade crossing.

Until the arrival of the railroad, the site of Minooka was a grass-covered prairie hill overlooking the Illinois River valley. The first white settlers arrived in 1833. The Village of Dresden, located to the south of Minooka, was begun by one of the first settlers and thrived along the I & M Canal. However, with the construction of the railroad, traffic moved north to the Rock Island and Dresden failed.

Minooka was the result of the railroad. Ransom Gardner, a railroad surveyor, purchased 500 acres in the northeast corner of Grundy County and plotted Minooka. George Comerford, an Irish immigrant, also played an early role in the community. Like Gardner, Comerford worked as a railroad surveyor and was involved in the actual construction of the Chicago & Rock Island. With the construction of the railroad, Comerford became the first agent at the Minooka Depot. Comerford also helped to establish the Minooka post office in 1853 and served as its postmaster for nine years.

Reportedly, Minooka was given its name by Dolly Smith, who was the wife of Ransom Gardner's real estate agent in town, Leander Smith. She spoke the Potawatomi language and called the town Minooka. It has been said that the meaning of the word is "high point," "place of contentment," "good Earth" or "place of the maples." The town was incorporated on March 27, 1869.

51.4 HBD – This is a talking hot box detector designed to inspect passing trains.

At Milepost 51.6, the Elgin, Joliet & Eastern Railroad (EJ&E) passes overhead. This line serves an industrial area to the south, including the former Relco locomotive shop facility. In 1888, the EJ&E built this branch line, which ran from Gardner to their mainline at Plainfield. The railroad was originally used to carry coal and freight from the coal mines south of the Illinois River to the steel mills in the Joliet and Chicago area.

Just west of the overpass, CSX serves a United States Cold Storage facility to the south. Temperatures in this USDA and FDA certified facility range from -20°F to +45°F. The 12.1 million cubic foot facility has 58 truck and 4 rail doors.

52.9 EAST MINOOKA SIDING – This is a new siding on the railroad, located to the south of the mainline on the grade of the original second track. Train crews use their radios to align the switch and to confirm the direction the turnout will take them.

55.3 WEST MINOOKA SIDING – The new siding at Minooka has its west switch just east of Tabler Road.

56.7 EAST MORRIS – Historically, East Morris served as an interchange location between CSX and the EJ&E near the USI Quantum Chemical complex. Track profiles from the 1980s call this area the Aux Sable Industrial Complex. Modern CSX employee timetables show this to be Equistar.

The tracks serve a number of chemical plants and a large A&R Logistics transload and warehouse facility to the south (compass east).

Trains heading west enter DTC Block "Rocket" at Milepost 56.8.

60.5 MORRIS SIDING – This is the east switch to the Morris siding to the south, with the west switch at Milepost 61.6. Sponge Cushion is the name given to the switch off of the siding here by CSX. The spur heads south to the Sponge Cushion factory. The company manufactures premium carpet cushion for industrial and home use.

The spur to the south was once the Morris Terminal Railway. The Morris Terminal Railway was incorporated on February 10, 1905, to build four miles of track between Morris and the I&M Canal. It went south, had a diamond with the Chicago, Ottawa & Peoria, crossed the I&M Canal and turned west. Between the south bank of the canal and the Illinois River, the line once served a number of industries. By 1912, the railroad was controlled by the Rock Island and was purchased by the CRI&P on July 1, 1914. It was consolidated into the larger railroad on January 1, 1948. Little of the line still exists. One exception is a through truss bridge over the I&M Canal, now used as a walking trail, next to the Calhoun Street bridge.

61.8 MORRIS – Welcome to the county seat of Grundy County and the home of about 14,000 people, the largest community in Grundy County. The old Rock Island station and freight house, both built of brick, still stand at Morris. The passenger station, built in 1907, is used by the Chamber of Commerce. The freight house, built about the same time, is used by a local business.

In 1834, the very first log cabin was built in Morris. Eight years later, the Village of Morris was established on April 12, 1842, when the plat of Morris was acknowledged by various officials, including Isaac N. Morris, for whom the town was named. Later, there was an attempt to change the name to Xenia. However, there was an argument about how to spell the name so the change did not happen. The I&M Canal gave Morris a boost when it opened through the village in 1848. This led to the organization of Morris Township and then the incorporation of Morris on August 15, 1850. The railroad arrived here in January 1853.

Morris is the home of what is called the "Morris System," an electronic telephone switching system. The world's first electronic switching system was installed at Morris in early 1960. The system used electronic tone ringers which used up to eight different tones rather than the traditional bell ringer. Morris is also known for hosting the annual Grundy County Fair and Grundy County Corn Fest.

The I&M Canal has been mentioned, so here are a few details. Construction began in 1836, and the 96-mile length took twelve years to complete. Beginning in Chicago and ending in LaSalle, it was the first link between the Great Lakes and the Mississippi River. The canal resulted in faster transportation at a lower cost. Immediately, grain prices tripled in value as this became the primary mode of transportation for farmers. However, the railroad soon replaced the canal and the last boat passed through in 1914.

During the early 1900s, a number of grain elevators and processors were located at Morris. Just north of the tracks once stood a large Quaker Oats mill and warehouse, also known as the Morris Oatmeal Company.

Besides the I&M Canal and the Rock Island Railroad, Morris also was served by two electric interurban railroads. The Chicago, Ottawa & Peoria Railway came to Morris in 1910 and a line was installed in 1913 down Liberty Street. Eventually highways brought an end to the interurban and operations ceased in 1934. The old Morris depot, built in 1911, can still be seen on the southeast corner of Benton and Liberty Street, two blocks south of the Rock Island depot.

The Fox & Illinois Union Railway, another interurban, headed northward out of Morris. The original plan for the railroad was to link the Fox and Illinois Rivers. However, the line only succeeded in connecting Yorkville, on the Aurora, Elgin & Fox River Electric Railway, and Morris, on the Chicago & Illinois Valley Railway (formerly the Illinois Valley Division of the Illinois Traction Company). The line was built in 1911 by McGuire-Cummings and seems to have been inspired by the Illinois Traction System. On February 3, 1931, passenger service ended. Freight service continued to operate under the ownership of the five grain elevators on the line. On February 20, 1938, total abandonment was authorized, and the final run was made on October 21, 1938.

63.4 STOCKDALE CROSSOVERS – Stockdale was the name of a set of crossovers when the railroad still had two main tracks in the early 1970s. It was named for the station to the west.

West of here at Milepost 64.8 is the start of the DTC Block "Seneca" for westbound trains. The old grade of the Chicago, Ottawa & Peoria Railway can be seen curving away to the south.

65.3 STOCKDALE – This is a spur into Masterblend International and its Tyler Enterprises Division fertilizer facility, located to the south.

The original Stockdale was at Milepost 65.5. No community ever existed at Stockdale, however there was a station and a large set of stockyards here, located to the south. The stockyards were here to support the Chicago stockyards. According to the *History of Grundy County*, published in 1914, Stockdale was where "immense consignments of cattle and sheep from western shippers are unloaded and kept until sufficiently recovered from the hardship of the long trip across country, and restored to their original weight by careful feeding and watering. From Stockdale these consignments, when in proper condition, are forwarded to the Chicago stock yards."

71.3 EAST SWITCH SENECA YARD – To the south is a two-track yard, as well as a wye track, all located on the east side of Seneca. This is the former junction with the Kankakee & Seneca Railroad Company, a railroad that was jointly owned by the Cleveland, Cincinnati, Chicago & St. Louis Railway Company (CCC&STL) and the Chicago, Rock Island & Pacific. With this being the end of the line and the end of CCC&STL operations, the railroad had a five-stall roundhouse in the middle of the wye.

The railroad was incorporated on March 7, 1881, with the goal of building eastward to Kankakee, which it did by early 1882, completing a 42-mile railroad. The purpose of the line was to provide a bypass around Chicago but the business never developed to the levels planned. Because of this, the line was officially abandoned on February 24, 1933.

A month later, on March 27, 1933, the New York Central turned its share of the line over to the CRI&P and the line was soon torn out. All that is left of the line, known as the ETI Spur, are several miles of track to the south that serves industries on either side of the Illinois River, and an impressive three-span Pratt through truss railroad bridge over the Illinois River east of Seneca. The bridge still exists to serve H. B. Fuller, a manufacturer of industrial adhesives, coatings, and sealants. This plant was once a DuPont explosives plant, later operated by ETI. Other customers on the line include Biewer Lumber, Renewable Energy Group (biofuels producer), Martin Resources (fertilizers and agricultural chemicals), and Growmark's river elevator.

To cross the Illinois River, the line has a large bridge consisting of (from north to south) a through truss span, a lift truss, a through truss, and two deck plate girder spans. The bridge was originally a wooden deck truss that was replaced by a steel truss bridge in 1910. This bridge was somewhat famous because it was damaged by a train derailment and partial collapse on August 18, 1916. The train was a westbound CCC&STL freight pulled by Alco 4-6-0 steam locomotive #6221. The first four freight cars behind the locomotive's tender hit the water. It was rebuilt again with the Illinois Waterway project in the 1930s.

During World War II, Seneca was the site of the Chicago Bridge & Iron Company shipyard, building 157 Navy warships called LST's or Landing Ship Tanks. Today, this site is operated by the Seneca Regional Port District and served from the former K&S line. The importance of the railroad, and CSX which serves it, can be found in the name of part of the facility: Seneca I-80 Railport.

71.6 COUNTY LINE – This is the county line between Grundy County (to the east) and LaSalle County (to the west). **LaSalle County**, named for French explorer, René-Robert Cavelier, Sieur de La Salle, was formed on January 15, 1831, out of parts of Tazewell and Putnam Counties. La Salle traveled the Mississippi River upriver from the Gulf of Mexico, claimed the land for France, and named it Louisiana. The county seat is the largest city in the county, Ottawa.

72.1 SENECA – Seneca is the railroad name for this location. Even though the railroad called the station here Seneca in 1854, the community was incorporated on February 16, 1865, as the Village of Crotty, named after its founder, Jeremiah Crotty. Crotty was an Irish immigrant who contracted to build eleven miles of the Illinois & Michigan Canal, which bisects Seneca. This created an issue as the official name was Crotty while most locals called it Seneca. It wasn't until 1957 that the town's name changed to Seneca with a new incorporation.

In 1680, Father Gabriel de la Ribourde, a French missionary, explored this area with the La Salle party from Quebec. The group was ambushed by a band of Kickapoo Indians and the Father was killed. It is believed that he was killed near the current St. Patrick's Catholic Church, where a cross remembers the priest who is described as Illinois' first martyr to the Catholic faith.

The former wooden CRI&P depot, built in 1912 to replace a station that burned mysteriously on the night of November 30, 1911, still stands near Main Street. The de-

Blue Island Subdivision

pot has been rebuilt with plans for a museum and meeting rooms.

The Illinois Traction Company depot and transformer station was at the corner of Armour and East Streets, just north of the I&M Canal.

72.6 EAST SENECA – Seneca Siding is the normal location of meets between the Iowa Interstate CBBI and BICB trains. The mainline is to the north and the siding is to the south. This switch is a spring switch which directs westbound trains down the north track.

This is also the location of the sign for DTC Block "Sand" for westbound trains.

74.3 WEST SENECA – Each end of Seneca Siding has a spring switch to allow trains to pass without the crew needing to line switches.

Just east of here at Milepost 74.2 is the westbound sign for DTC Block "Marseilles."

74.8 HBD – This is a talking hot box detector. Just east of the hot box detector and the grade crossing with East 2659th Road, also known as Phosphate Road, is a spur track that heads south to serve PCS Phosphate, which is located on the Illinois River and has its own barge facility. The phosphate products produced here are generally used in making animal feeds.

75.9 EAST MARSEILLES – Look for the crossover between the mainline and the several tracks to the south. This small yard is used to serve customers east of Marseilles, including PCS Phosphate (ex-National Phosphate), Glen Gery Brick, Independence Tube Corporation (ex-Pittsburgh Des Moines Steel), and Inframetals. The CSX employee timetable also shows the PCS switch at this location.

77.0 MARSEILLES – This area was known as "The Grand Rapids" and the "Rapids of Maninumba" when Lovell Kimball arrived here in 1833. This location was at the upper end of three miles of rapids, a spot likely to be important with a canal. Knowing that the Illinois & Michigan Canal Bill had passed and that there would be a lock at this location, Kimball hired a surveyor to lay out a town. Kimball called the town Marseilles after the town in France. He chose the name because he thought that Marseilles was a major European industrial center like what he hoped his town would be. The town was officially platted on June 3, 1835. Changes in the town's design took place twenty years later when the railroad arrived and began to replace the canal.

While Kimball's dream wasn't fully realized, the Marseilles area soon became heavily industrialized. The canal started the boom, but when the railroad arrived in February 1853 and built a wooden depot and freight house just east of Main Street, Chicago was less than a day's travel away. In 1911, the Marseilles Hydro Station opened to power the Chicago, Ottawa & Peoria Railway, later the Illinois Traction. In 1922, Howe & Davidson opened the largest factory building between Chicago and St. Louis here, an eight-story paper pulp mill. About that time, Terry Simmons, editor of the *Marseilles Plaindealer*, wrote that, "No city between Joliet and Moline ships as many tons of manufactured goods on the Rock Island Road as does Marseilles. In fact, Marseilles ships out a larger tonnage of manufactured goods than any city of equal size in Illinois."

The industrial image of Marseilles still exists due to the number of companies operating in the area. To the east of town are Glen Gery Brick, Agrium, Infra Metals, Independence Tube, and PCS Phosphate. To the west of town is SABIC Innovative Plastics and the Garvey International Ottawa Terminal barge dock and storage facility.

The former Rock Island station, built in 1917 using brick and stucco, still stands on the north side of the tracks at Marseilles. This station replaced the original wooden depot, built in 1867. It came about when citizens in the city won a 40-year battle with the railroad and a U.S. circuit court ordered a new station be built at a cost not to exceed

$20,000. The new station was designed and built by T. S. Peak, a Chicago builder, and used the American Craftsman architectural style. The station opened on August 6, 1917, and was dedicated on August 16th. The old station was moved to Young Street in town and converted to a house. The railroad's freight house once stood just to the southeast.

The 1917 station was in operation until 1974 and was sold to a private business owner in 1984. It was used as a restaurant 1984-1988, and then converted into a medical clinic in 1993. The depot was added to the U.S. National Register of Historic Places on November 7, 1995.

The second railroad in town – the Illinois Traction – had their station at the corner of Main and Broadway. Located alongside the Northern Illinois Public Service head race on the Illinois River, the station also included freight and waiting rooms.

The CSX DTC Block "Ottawa" sign for westbound trains is at Milepost 77.0.

78.0 WEST MARSEILLES – West Marseilles is at Glen Road, west of downtown Marseilles. The grandly named Marseilles Land & Water Power Company once existed to the south. This area was once full of tracks and industries.

79.3 EAST END GE SIDING – To the south is a long siding used to switch several local industries. A spur track also heads south to the SABIC Innovative Plastics facility. On October 21, 2008, SABIC completed a purchase of GE Plastics from General Electric, creating SABIC Innovative Plastics. The company focuses on the global growth of thermoplastics and engineering plastics.

80.8 ADM OTTAWA TERMINAL – This is another facility on the Illinois River to the south, located at river mile marker 243. Besides grain, the facility also handles bulk and break bulk materials, steel, grain and grain by-products. This is the old Material Service facility.

Just west of here at Milepost 80.9 is a set of crossovers between the mainline and the side track to the south. This is about the middle of a ten-mile-long tangent piece of railroad, one of the longest on the route. It stretches from Milepost 74 to Milepost 84.

81.7 WEST END GE SIDING – This is the west end of the switching siding to the south. Just west of here at Milepost 82.2 is the Minigrip-Zip Pack switch where a spur track to the north serves several shippers. Just further west at Milepost 82.5 is a switch to the south known by CSX as Maintenance of Way. It is a short spur track generally used to store track equipment.

83.0 EAST END OTTAWA RAIL CAR SWITCH – To the south, this siding is used to serve the Ottawa Railcar facility, a company that performs maintenance and repair work on railroad freight cars.

In *CRI&P Employee Timetable #1*, dated March 18, 1979, the Subdivision 2 timetable for the Illinois Division showed a station of Brickton at Milepost 83.1. This area has become dominated by small businesses. A private collector reportedly still keeps several railroad passenger cars stored here.

83.8 WEST END OTTAWA RAIL CAR SWITCH – The west switch is also the location of the Ottawa Yard Limits.

83.9 FOX RIVER BRIDGE – There are three Fox Rivers in Illinois, but the other two are in southern Illinois and flow into the Little Wabash and Wabash Rivers. This Fox River is about 200 miles long and starts west of Milwaukee and flows southward into the Illinois River at Ottawa, about a mile south of here.

This former Rock Island bridge is made up of several deck plate girder spans for a total of 450 feet long. It was built in 1899. To the south can be seen the abandoned deck plate girder bridge of the Illinois Traction System. There are plans to use this bridge as part of a pedestrian trail.

84.5 OTTAWA – Ottawa is an Indian name derived from the Algonquin word "adawe" which meant "to trade." The term was common among many area tribes and was assigned to the Ottawa Indians, who were considered the great traders and barterers of the Great Lakes Region.

Ottawa was first settled in 1823, platted in 1829 by the I&M Canal Commission, and grew into a small community by 1837. Its location at the junction of the Fox and Illinois Rivers, especially after the completion of the I&M Canal, made it a center for trade. The Chicago & Rock Island arrived here in February of 1853 and Ottawa was incorporated later the same year. Ottawa was also made the county seat of LaSalle County, showing its importance to the area. Its importance is also demonstrated by Ottawa being selected as the site of the first of the Lincoln-Douglas debates of 1858.

Ottawa is known for several other things too. On February 8, 1910, William Dickson Boyce, then a resident of Ottawa, incorporated the Boy Scouts of America. Also, Ottawa has historically been a major sand and glass center due to numerous silica sand deposits. Ottawa sand continues to be extracted from several quarries in the area, and is recognized in glass-making and abrasives for its uniform granularity and characteristics.

During the mid-1800s, Ottawa was the home of the portable telegraph key called the Caton Pocket relay. The key was manufactured by the Caton Telegraph Instrument Shop, founded by Illinois Supreme Court Judge John Dean Caton in 1849. Using his political connections, Caton was able to get laws passed that supported the development of the telegraph industry in Illinois, creating a demand for his products. Judge Caton also founded a business that built new telegraph lines across the Midwest, and is credited with doing some of the initial research on wood types for poles. Eventually the company was acquired by Western Union. According to the "Key and Telegraph" column for the quarterly journal of the Antique Wireless Association, this factory in Ottawa was the second largest of those owned by

Western Union, which was at that time an industry giant. In 1872, the business was sold to the Western Electric Manufacturing company and the shop equipment and employees were moved to Chicago.

A less happy story started in 1922 when the Radium Dial Company (RDC) moved from Peru, Illinois, to a former high school building in Ottawa. The company actually started as a division of the Standard Chemical Company and was based in the Marshall Field Annex building in Chicago. The company moved to Peru in 1920 so that it was closer to Westclox, their major customer, and then to Ottawa. The company employed hundreds of young women who painted watch dials using a paint called "Luna" for watch maker Westclox. The workers, almost all women, became known as "Radium Girls." The women, who had been told the paint was harmless, ingested deadly amounts of radium after being instructed to lick their paintbrushes to sharpen them. Many of the women became ill and died. RDC went out of business in 1936, two years after the company's president, Joseph Kelly Sr., left to start a competing company, Luminous Processes Inc., a few blocks away. Many claim that Kelly made the change to avoid a lawsuit brought against RDC and that the creation of Luminous Processes saved much of his wealth and business. When RDC closed, many of the workers switched over to the new business.

Luminous Processes continued to operate during the Depression, and with the economy, young women continued to work there. The company was able to grow during World War II when Albert Einstein and President Roosevelt met with the firm and awarded it additional contracts, including the production of polonium for possible use in atomic bombs. With the end of the war, studies about the health hazards began, but the firm didn't close until 1978. Meanwhile, there were reports that the community was becoming more contaminated and mysterious deaths continued. The original Radium Dial Company building was torn down in 1968 after having been used as a meat locker. Reportedly the family that ran the meat locker had all but one member die of cancer. Parts of the building were collected as souvenirs, moving the radioactive contamination throughout the town. The U.S. Environmental Protection Agency has spent years cleaning up the town since 1986.

Railroads

Ottawa, being a transportation center, also has a number of railroad structures of interest. The first train from Chicago arrived at Ottawa on February 14, 1853, reportedly at the original wooden station built at the time. It was replaced with a brick station in 1888. Today, alongside the CSX/IAIS tracks is the third Rock Island passenger station, built of brick in 1910. This large station is known for its round two-story track-side tower, and is of the same design as Rock Island stations in Iowa City and Council Bluffs, Iowa. Across the tracks was the location of the Rock Island freight house. In the 1960s and 1970s, this was the location of the TOFC (intermodal) ramp.

The former Chicago, Burlington & Quincy (CB&Q) station, built of brick in 1913, is located at the corner of Walnut & Madison Streets, south of the Rock Island and near the downtown area. This structure was built to replace the original wood-frame depot. A wood-frame freight house once stood nearby. Both were torn down. Today, the brick station is used as the headquarters of the Illinois Railway, formerly Illinois RailNet.

The interurban railway, the Chicago, Ottawa & Peoria, ran east-west within a block of the CB&Q station. Northern Illinois Light & Traction had a generating facility, car barn, offices and other facilities at the corner of LaSalle and Mill Streets.

84.9 IR CROSSING – This rail line was built from Montgomery, near Aurora, Illinois, southwest to here and then south to Streator. It was organized as the Ottawa, Oswego & Fox River Valley RR (OO&FRV) and incorporated on August 22, 1852, with plans greater than what was built. It wasn't until 1866 that surveys actually took place and the company was reorganized in May, 1866.

In 1869, the General Assembly of Illinois formally authorized the cities of Ottawa and Aurora, and the counties of Kane and Kendall, to sell bonds to pay for stock in the railroad. Construction soon began northward from Streator and the railroad finally opened to Montgomery on January 15, 1871. On August 20, 1870, the CB&Q gained control of the railroad, allowing the railroad to extend ten miles further on May 1, 1871, from Aurora (Geneva Switch) to Geneva. The OO&FRV became the property of the CB&Q on June 1, 1899.

Operated as the Streator Branch for decades, the line hauled grain, coal, livestock and sand to customers in the Chicago area. However, by the 1990s, much of the freight was gone and the line saw only the occasional local freight train. On December 12, 1997, the line was sold to Illinois RailNet, an operator of shortline railroads. On May 1, 2005, the railroad was sold to Illinois Railway (IR), becoming their Ottawa Branch. In recent years, business on the line has increased as fracking (frac) sand movements have become a regular part of the railroad. The IR parks its locomotives just north of the diamond.

86.0 EAST SWITCH OTTAWA YARD – This is the east end of Ottawa Yard. There is a long siding here, almost 7000 feet long. The yard basically has one purpose - sand! With the increased use of frac sand in the early 2010s, the yard was often packed with cars. To the south is a large sand plant, also switched by Illinois Railway. A track profile from 1985 shows many sand companies here, including Griffith Sand, American Silica (several plants), and Ottawa Sand.

In this area, the Rock Island had a spur track southward to the large National Plate Glass factory, where Pilkington North America is now located. Pilkington North America manufactures glass and glazing products for the automotive industry (70% of sales) and architectural markets. Today, this line serves the large U.S. Silica sand facility to the south.

Blue Island Subdivision

To the north is another spur that serves Cimco Recycling Ottawa. This facility handles bulk shipments of non-ferrous metals, scrap iron and steel, corrugated cardboard, office paper and industrial thermoplastics.

87.2 WEST SWITCH OTTAWA YARD – This area is also known as the CSX New Rock Yard. After CSX turned over the railroad west of Utica to the Iowa Interstate, this became essentially the west end of CSX operations. This leaves them most of the major freight customers on the line and freight trains are based out of this yard.

For westbound trains, the sign for DTC Block "Utica" is at Milepost 88.0, the west end of the Ottawa Yard Limits.

89.0 ARZNER – Arzner is about a half mile west of the abandoned overhead road bridge. To the north are the barren spoils of former coal strip mines. To the south along the Illinois River is Buffalo Rock State Park, developed as part of the mine restoration project. This area is said to have served the French as an early military, trading and missionary post. Through the years, Buffalo Rock was used by a religious sect as a place for holding camp meetings, and still later was used as a site for a tuberculosis sanatorium. The Crane Company of Chicago purchased Buffalo Rock in 1912 and for a period of about 16 years maintained a sanatorium for sick employees and a summer vacation ground for thousands of employees and their families.

There was once a connection with the Illinois Terminal to the south. The remains of the grade can still be seen as a curving tree line across the pasture. The grade of the retired siding to the north is also visible in places.

Further west, the railroad runs along a series of bluffs.

92.8 EAST END UTICA SIDING – The east switch is the location of the DTC Block sign for "LaSalle." The mainline is surrounded by tracks at Utica, built to serve the silica sand industry here. The plant to the north is owned by Unimin Corporation, the world's largest producer of low-iron nepheline syenite used in glass, ceramic, paint and plastics, the largest producer of quartz proppants for oil and natural gas stimulation and recovery, and the world's leading producer of high purity quartz, a highly specialized product used in the fabrication of integrated circuits, solar photovoltaic cells and high intensity lighting.

94.0 WEST END UTICA SIDING – This switch is just west of Division Street in North Utica, Illinois. To the south is PQ Corporation, which describes itself as "a leading worldwide producer of specialty inorganic performance chemicals and catalysts." The company started as a Philadelphia family soap and candle business in 1831. The company expanded into sodium silicate in 1861 to replace rosin in soap formulations. Today, according to their website, PQ is the world's largest producer of soluble silicates.

94.3 UTICA – Utica, or more technically North Utica, is the site of an Unimin Corporation silica sand mine facility, the last customer served by CSX. For years, the presence of clay, sand and hydraulic limestone has attracted industry. Brick making also became an important early industry of North Utica. Records show that American Silica, Philadelphia Quartz, and Illinois Hydraulic Cement all once had facilities here.

Originally, Utica grew up alongside the Illinois River, near the site of the Indian village Kaskaskia. However, after the construction of the Illinois and Michigan Canal to the north, the community moved to what was called North Utica, and then was incorporated in 1852 with the arrival of the railroad construction crews. However, the name Utica is used for almost everything but official government documents.

Today, the LaSalle County Historical Museum is housed in the former I&M Canal Warehouse in Utica. Unfortunately, the former CRI&P brick station was falling apart by 2006.

Blue Island Subdivision

Iowa Interstate Railroad

Effective February 3, 2006, the Surface Transportation Board approved the Iowa Interstate "to sublease from CSX Transportation, Inc. (CSXT), and operate a line of railroad totaling approximately 31.9 miles. The rail line, presently leased and operated by CSXT extends from milepost BIF 95, in Utica, IL, to milepost BIF 126.9, in Henry, IL."

From here west to Bureau, the Iowa Interstate operates and maintains the railroad, although CSX has the primary lease on tracks owned by International Mining Corporation. West of Bureau, full ownership of the railroad is by the Iowa Interstate. Because of this, the Iowa Interstate's Blue Island Subdivision is shown as being from Milepost 95.0 to Silvis at Milepost 171.9 in their employee timetable.

95.0 END CSX/BEGIN IAIS – As stated, this is where the 2006 agreement turned the tracks west of here over to the Iowa Interstate Railroad.

96.0 PECUMSAUGAN CREEK BRIDGE – According to old Rock Island documents, the railroad bridge is 103 feet long, consisting of two through-plate girder spans. Note that the former north track is now the mainline while the south track was removed. The creek starts on the highlands about ten miles north of here, flows under the railroad and turns west into the old Illinois and Michigan Canal. It follows the canal for about a mile before flowing through Split Rock Lake into the Illinois River.

To the north is the Illinois Pecumsaugan Creek – Blackball Mines Nature Preserve. The area is noted by its mix of dolomite cliffs, dolomite prairie, and upland and flood plain forests. The preserve may be best known for its large abandoned limestone mine, home of at least five species of bats. The mine was created to obtain limestone to make cement. Remains of the old kilns still remain from the company which operated here about 1870-1900, until the Portland cement process began to dominate the industry.

96.6 SPLIT ROCK TUNNEL – The original Chicago & Rock Island route included a tunnel here, one of five on the entire system (the other four tunnels on the railroad were between St. Louis and Kansas City). This tunnel, built in 1854, is the oldest railroad tunnel in Illinois. The Rock Island later on built a second parallel line just to the south making the line double tracked. Eventually, the northern line through the tunnel was abandoned and the tunnel is no longer used.

The grade of the Chicago, Ottawa & Peoria Railway interurban route, which has been to the south of the Rock Island, crosses over to the north side on top of the tunnel.

97.7 INTERSTATE 39 – Look up to see this highway. I-39 is a relatively short interstate highway, running about 325 miles northward from Normal, Illinois, to Rib Mountain, Wisconsin. It was designed to replace US Highway 51, which in the early 1980s was one of the busiest two-lane highways in the United States.

East of the Interstate, the CRI&P once served the tipple of the La Salle County Carbon Coal Company Rockville Shaft. The coal complex was on the hillside to the north. There was also a long tramway across the CRI&P tracks and the I&M Canal to reach the waste dumps.

98.2 LITTLE VERMILLON RIVER BRIDGE – This bridge consists of three deck plate girder spans, two that are 51 feet long and one that is 54 feet long. The current mainline uses the north side of the bridge. There are actually two rivers with the name Little Vermillon; one that flows into the Wabash River, and this one that flows into the Illinois River. This Little Vermillon River starts near Mendota (IL) and flows south about 35 miles. It enters the Illinois River just to the south of the bridge, basically opposite of where the Vermillon River enters on the other side of the Illinois River.

On the east bank of the Little Vermillon River was the German American Portland Cement Works, served by a number of tracks off of the Rock Island mainline. Today, this is the Illinois Cement plant and it has no rail service.

98.3 ILLINOIS CENTRAL RAILROAD OVERHEAD –

The Iowa Interstate passes under a very historical railroad at this location, with claims of several "firsts" in its history. In 1850, the Illinois General Assembly, after years of supporting canals, was working on plans for a series of railroads to crisscross the state. The first of these was to run from the northwest corner of the state near Galena to the southernmost part of the state near Cairo. To support the construction, President Millard Fillmore signed a bill providing a land grant the same year, making it the first land grant railroad constructed.

Construction on the line began at Freeport in 1851, and it worked southward until it reached Cairo in 1856. When completed, it became the Illinois Central, the longest railroad in the world. Construction continued, and the line eventually stretched on west to the Mississippi River. La Salle was at the middle of the 252-mile-long line and thus served as an important station. The IC station, yard, coaling tower and stone engine house were just to the north.

Even though this was the original charter line of the Illinois Central, it was also one of the first to see major traffic losses. Known by many as "The Gruber Line," the last through train operated over the line on December 21, 1985, and abandonment of the line between Freeport and Heyworth (south of Bloomington) began in 1986. The overhead bridge and a few miles of track south of the Illinois River were preserved, designed to serve the Lone Star Cement plant at Oglesby. Today, the few miles of track and bridge are owned and operated by Buzzi Unicem, created with the merger of Lone Star Industries (Dyckerhoff) and RC Cement (Buzzi Unicem SpA) in 2004. The operation uses parts of the former IC La Salle yard at the north end of the bridge, and a connection is made with the Iowa Interstate just to the west.

The overhead bridge is regionally famous, being called the "mile long bridge" even though it is really about half that length. The first bridge, which crossed the Chicago, Rock Island & Pacific Railroad, the I&M Canal, the Illinois River, and eventually a CB&Q line, was built between 1852 and 1855. The bridge was originally built with 17 cast and wrought iron Howe deck truss spans, with a deck girder approach on either end. The piers were made up of ashlar sandstone. Construction of the bridge was delayed many times due to labor strikes, battles between Irish Catholic immigrants and native-born Americans, and several cholera epidemics.

As trains got heavier, the bridge needed repairs and strengthening, and in 1893 the spans were replaced with pin-connected, steel Pratt deck trusses. In 1920, the deck plate girder span over Rockwell Road, once the route of the Chicago, Ottawa & Peoria Interurban (to the immediate north of the IAIS), was rebuilt by the American Bridge Company. With the Illinois Waterway project in 1932, two deck trusses were replaced with a single Parker through truss span (built by McClintic Marshall Corporation of Pottstown, Pennsylvania) to provide a wider navigational channel. The next rebuild project was when the south approach was rebuilt in 1933 (some sources say 1920). While some repairs and modernizations continue, parts of the bridge still date back to its original construction. Most notable are the original sandstone piers, especially the swing pier near the south end of the bridge.

The area north of the Iowa Interstate and just west of the IC bridge was once the location of the LaSalle Shaft of the La Salle County Carbon Coal Company. The Illinois Central had a number of tracks into the tipple. The IC passenger station was just to the north between Main and 2nd Streets.

98.9 LaSALLE – LaSalle was named in honor of the early French explorer, Robert de LaSalle. LaSalle was once an important point on the Illinois River as this was as far as the river was navigable. Upstream from here were a series of portages in which boats had to be carried around rapids. During the 1830s, the Illinois and Michigan Canal was built to eliminate these portages and to connect the Illinois River with Lake Michigan. LaSalle was the southwestern terminus of the canal with Chicago the northeastern. LaSalle was the location of locks 14 and 15 on the canal. Basins (harbors) were located here for the canal boats and the steamboats that came up the river from as far away as New Orleans. LaSalle hosted a number of warehouses, boat building docks, and hotels to support the trade. With the plans for the canal, LaSalle was platted in the 1830s, but wasn't incorporated until 1852. At the time LaSalle was larger than Chicago, but access to eastern railroads and Lake Michigan soon helped Chicago outgrow LaSalle.

The Chicago & Rock Island Rail Road arrived at LaSalle during late March, 1853, and the Illinois Central was building through the area at the same time. The combination of transportation and raw materials soon led to two major industrial developments. Zinc was the first, and the Matthiessen & Hegeler Zinc Company completed a zinc smelter here by May 1860. In 1866, a zinc rolling mill was added in order to produce sheet zinc. With the local availability of zinc and the ability to process it, LaSalle and nearby Peru took the joint nickname of "Zinc City." In 1910, M&H was one of the largest zinc companies in the world. The company became known for having some of the highest wages and shortest work hours in the region, allowing production to continue even while other area industries experienced labor strikes. However, a combination of financial problems and foreign competition eventually forced M&H to end zinc smelting in 1961 and sulfuric acid manufacturing 1968. In July of 1978, the company closed its operation.

Due to their importance in the community, the Matthiessen and Hegeler families were leaders in the community. They brought a number of industries to the LaSalle area, including the LaSalle Machine and Tool Company, Western Clock Company (Westclox), and the Open Court Publishing

Company (whose mission was "establishing ethics and religion upon a scientific basis," making LaSalle "Buddhism's Gateway to the West"). Frederick William Matthiessen was mayor of LaSalle 1886-1895, and he provided money to help build the sewer system, the electric light plant, the LaSalle-Peru High School, the Hygienic Institute to combat epidemics, and various roads and bridges. Matthiessen also hired about fifty workers to develop his property as a 176-acre private park known as Deer Park. It included trails, bridges, stairways and check dams in a long, narrow canyon with a small stream, and was open to the public for a small fee. When Matthiessen died in 1918, the property was donated to the state and opened as a public park. In 1943, the park was renamed Matthiessen State Park, and has since grown to almost 2000 acres of land.

Coal was the second product that developed in the area thanks to access to the canal and railroads. The first coal shaft was built by the LaSalle Coal Mining Company and opened in 1856. Many other small mines opened during the mid-1800s, and they slowly merged into several large operations by the 1880s. Reports indicate that there were at least six coal shafts in the area by 1884, with the deepest one 452 feet deep. The Financial Panic of 1893 led to layoffs and lower wages, and 1894 saw the "Bituminous Coal Miners' Strike." In May of that year 40 sheriff's deputies faced 2000 striking miners in a two-day gun battle, with the law officers retreating with many wounded. A second battle in July between the strikers and a posse of 60 well-armed men was intended to protect the properties of the mining companies and the nearby communities.

A third industry boomed in the LaSalle-Peru area from the 1930s until the 1950s - drinking and gambling. These activities actually dated to the Prohibition era, but grew even more after alcohol was legal again. Much of this activity centered on the Kelly & Cawley liquor and gambling house on First Street, surrounded by dozens of clubs and a reported 60 to 80 saloons. All of this activity earned LaSalle the nickname of "Little Reno." This activity ended with a

1953 federal raid on Kelly & Cawley and the accompanying presence of dozens of federal agents.

Today, the history of LaSalle is told in two locations. The first is the La Salle Canal Boat *Volunteer* and the adjacent Museum and Visitors Center, located at the I&M Canal's Lock 14 basin at First and Joliet Streets. The *Volunteer* is a replica canal boat that provides history lessons during a one-hour ride. Numerous reenactors also work the areas around the historic part of town. The Hegeler-Carus Mansion is a restored home from the zinc era with tours available. A unique feature of the building is the underground tunnel that connected the house to the M&H Zinc foundry. It brought steam to the mansion for heat, and later for the clothes dryer.

The Railroads

For the Iowa Interstate, LaSalle is the switch to the interchange track with the Buzzi Unicem operations on the former **Illinois Central** line, located in downtown LaSalle. The shops, yard, and passenger station were on the east side of town along the Little Vermillon River.

The former **Rock Island** Peru-LaSalle brick and stone station still stands on the north side of the tracks at the west end of LaSalle at Milepost 99.1. The station is two stories, being built into the hillside. This leaves the front only one story. The First Street (main) entrance is at the second-floor level. During the liquor and gambling era, the station was in the center of the activity, bringing a great deal of passenger business to the railroad. For almost thirty years, the station was a lawn mower and small engine repair shop. It was sold in 2015 with future plans unclear. Sanborn insurance maps show that the CRI&P once had a freight house on the north side of the tracks just east of Bucklin Street, a block east of the station.

Since the historic station is within the limits of the I&M Canal National Heritage Corridor, the National Park Service has a report about the station included in their Historic

American Engineering Record. It states that "Throughout the late-nineteenth century LaSalle-Peru was served by three railroads: the Rock Island, the Illinois Central, and the Chicago, Burlington & Quincy. The latter carrier maintained a passenger depot in Peru, with LaSalle being the location of depots of the Rock Island and the Illinois Central. About 1900, the Rock Island Railroad replaced its old passenger depot with a new brick and stone building. Situated at the base of a steeply sloping hillside, the depot was used by residents of LaSalle and Peru. (Local residents referred to the steeply sloping road that led down to the station as 'Rock Island Hill')."

The Times newspaper of Ottawa, Illinois, had an interesting story about the Rock Island Railroad and LaSalle in their February 5, 2015, issue. The article stated that when the railroad was surveyed through LaSalle in 1853, the railroad followed the foot of the bluffs along the river. However, LaSalle was located on the bluffs above the river. A citizen's group led an effort to force the railroad to change its route and build across the higher ground, and even threatened violence. Reportedly, the city council passed an ordinance providing for a $10 fine to be levied on any "healthy male over the age of 21 and under that of 50 who should refuse to obey the call" to use forcible means against the railroad builders. Apparently, the matter even reached the Illinois legislature where an amendment to the charter was passed allowing the railroad to build along the Illinois River. Railroad operations reached LaSalle in late May, 1853. Over the years, the Rock Island combined the Peru passenger station with the La Salle station.

To the south is the former **Chicago, Burlington & Quincy** line that used to run between Zearing (IL) and Streator, now abandoned from LaSalle to Streater. The line once crossed the Illinois River just downstream of the Illinois Central, and actually passed under the south spans of the IC bridge. Today the line is operated by the Illinois Railway and they often park a locomotive just south of the

CRI&P station at the end of the tracks. The Iowa Interstate crosses this line on the west side of Peru.

A 1912 Sanborn map shows that the CB&Q had a passenger station with an attached freight and baggage room to the west of Creve Coeur Street, on the north side of their mainline. This area is today a storage yard often stacked full of pallets and other materials. On the south side of the CB&Q tracks were two warehouses. The one on the west side of Creve Coeur Street was labeled as the Schlitz Brewing Company Depot while the one on the east side of the street was labeled as the Pabst Brewing Company Depot.

The same map shows that the **Chicago, Ottawa & Peoria Railroad** and The Citizens Lighting Company had their power house and gas plant on the bank of the Illinois River, a few blocks further south. The car barns for the CO&P were shown to be on the north side of 3rd Street, between Chartres Street and Peru Street, then LaSalle Street, which was the boundary between LaSalle and Peru. The barns were about where the empty lot is between the current Precision Car Wash and Subway Sandwich restaurant.

The McGraw Electric Railway Manual of 1905 had a report on the **Illinois Valley Railway Company**, described as the successor to the Illinois Valley Traction Company, which was in turn the successor to the City Electric Railway. It was in operations from LaSalle to Ladd (11.9 miles), in the city of LaSalle (3.8 miles), Marseilles to Utica (16.72 miles) and Utica to LaSalle (4.24 miles of recently completed track). The report also stated that "on May 1, 1903, the Illinois Valley Traction Co. took over the Ottawa, Marseilles & Morris River Ry." The railroad in total was described as having 36.6 miles of track, built to a gauge of 4' 8-1/2" using 60-pound rail. The cars were described as being "St. Louis cars" and included 14 closed and 3 open motor cars, and 3 trailer cars.

To complete the story, the company started with the incorporation of the Illinois Valley Traction Company in 1902. In 1904, it was acquired by Illinois Valley Railway Company, which was acquired in 1909 by Western Railways & Light Company as subsidiary Chicago Ottawa & Peoria

Railway Company. In 1913, the operation became a subsidiary of Illinois Traction Company, and then a part of the Illinois Power & Light Company in 1924.

The line from Marseilles to Spring Valley and then north to Ladd were built in 1902. The line to Ladd was abandoned in 1924 while the Marseilles-Spring Valley line was discontinued in 1934. Eastward, the line from Marseilles to Seneca was built in 1906, Seneca to Morris in 1909, and Morris to Joliet in 1912. Heading west, the line was extended from Spring Valley to Depue in 1906. The entire line was discontinued in 1934. Two branches, Depue-Princeton and Ottawa-Streator, were abandoned a few years earlier in 1929.

99.8   PERU – The east end of Peru has almost always been a busy place. In 1916, the CRI&P had a coal chute on the north side of the track at Milepost 99.5. Further north were several tracks serving the Carbon Coal Company's Union Shaft. To the south was a huge Peru Plow & Wheel Company factory. Peru Plow Company started in the mid-1800s here. In 1874, the company took a major step forward when it hired William Bettendorf (born in Mendota, Illinois, in 1857) as a machinist's apprentice. In 1878, Bettendorf invented the first power lift sulky plow, allowing farmers to raise and lower the plow from their seat. Bettendorf moved on to several other companies over the next few years before returning to Peru as a supervisor at the Peru Plow Company. He soon invented the Bettendorf metal wheel and established a shop to manufacture the wheel at Peru Plow. Soon this business was a major part of the company and the name of the company was changed to Peru Plow & Wheel Company. To gain more capacity, Bettendorf later moved his wheel business elsewhere, eventually building his own factory at Bettendorf, Iowa. Peru Plow reportedly lasted until 1941.

To the south today are the facilities of ADM (Archer Daniels Midland) and CGB (Consolidated Grain & Barge). ADM's LaSalle Terminal is located on the Illinois River at mile marker 223 and is served by the Illinois Railway. ADM operates its own fleet of barges through ARTCO (American River Transportation Company), and is one of the largest owners of railcars, so their equipment gets a lot of use here. A competitor, CGB, operates their own grain terminal and facility just to the west.

The Rock Island Railroad had a depot in Peru located just east of the IL-251 bridge over the Illinois River. A freight depot was a block further east, surrounded by a number of small industries, including W. H. Maze Company Lumber Yard, Illinois Zinc Company Mine No. 8, and Chamberlin Metal Weather Stripping Company. The CB&Q depot was to the south at about Milepost 100.5. It was on the north side of their mainline at the east end of their small downtown yard.

Peru's first settler, John Hays, arrived in 1830. Hays operated a ferry across the Illinois River for the next decade, creating a small settlement. The first commercial steamboat, *Traveler*, reached Peru in 1831. When the township was established, Section Sixteen was set aside to support and fund a school. As the population grew, the need for a school became obvious and in 1834, the school commissioners laid out and sold the southwest quarter of Section Sixteen as the community of Peru, using a name believed to be the Incan word for "wealth." A post office opened at Peru in 1836, served by a regular boat route from Peoria. Peru was organized as a borough in 1838, and was officially incorporated as a city on March 13, 1851.

The Illinois River helped Peru with freight and passenger business using its port. However, the I&M Canal made LaSalle the dominant community in the area. The arrival of the C&RI in April 1853, and later the Illinois Valley & Northern Railroad in 1888, allowed industry to boom here. The area's coal and zinc deposits helped make Peru a zinc manufacturing center in its early history. Originally zinc ore was brought down from Galena, Illinois, by way of the Mississippi and Illinois rivers. Peru was the cheapest location within reach of these rich ores with sufficient coal for processing. This business attracted other manufacturers, including companies like Maze Lumber, Maze Nails, Peru Plow and Wheel Works, Huse and Loomis Ice Co, and Brunner Foundry. In 1884, the United Clock Company formed in Peru. Although soon a failure, Frederick William Matthiessen reorganized the company as the Western Clock Company, making it one of the largest companies in the industry, manufacturing more than 1 million alarm clocks per year by 1905. The firm soon trademarked the name Westclox. They also created some new business strategies to keep workers as World War I started, providing life insurance, a limited work week, a safety committee, and a number of other employee benefits. These companies attracted workers, and a June 1916 Sanborn map stated that there were 7000 residents of Peru (today there are about 10,000).

At its peak, the company made almost 2 million clocks and watches annually and employed more than 4000. The factory closed in 1980. Even with this, Peru is still the home of at least three very old companies. These include American Nickeloid (1898); W. H. Maze Company, America's last nail maker (dealing in lumber and nails since 1848); and Carus Chemical Company (1915), the largest manufacturer of potassium permanganate in the world.

101.0 ILLINOIS RAILWAY CROSSING – This at-grade crossing is with the Illinois Railway at their Milepost 27.8. For BNSF, this was their LaSalle Subdivision. The line dates back to 1887 when the Illinois Valley & Northern Railroad Company was incorporated on May 25th to build from Walnut (IL) sixty miles southeast to Streator (IL). The project actually started a year earlier when the Star Coal Company constructed a track from the CB&Q at Streator, heading northwest to near the village of Ripley. The railroad was leased to the CB&Q on January 2, 1888, the line was completed on June 1st of that year, and then sold to the CB&Q on June 1, 1899. The route passed through Zearing on the Chicago-Galesburg mainline, and through LaSalle on its way to Streator. The track north of Zearing was abandoned by 1954 and south of LaSalle by 1980.

Blue Island Subdivision

For the Illinois Railway, this is their LaSalle Branch which connects LaSalle with the BNSF mainline at Zearing, Illinois, about twenty miles northwest. The 18-mile-long line from LaSalle to the BNSF mainline at Zearing was sold to the Illinois RailNet in 2004, which later became the Illinois Railway. The Illinois Railway, a subsidiary of OmniTRAX, commenced operations on May 1, 2005, after purchasing the Illinois RailNet from owner North American RailNet. The Illinois Railway operates four separate ex-BNSF lines in Northern Illinois.

OmniTRAX also operates the Peru Industrial Railroad, three miles of track at the Peru Industrial Park north of town alongside I-80. OmniTRAX acquired the railroad in February 2015 from the City of Peru.

102.7 COUNTY LINE – LaSalle County is to the east while Bureau County is to the west. **Bureau County** was organized out of Putnam County in 1837 with its county seat at Princeton. It was named for Michel or Pierre de Beuro, French Creoles, who ran a trading post from 1776 until 1790 near where Big Bureau Creek empties into the Illinois River. The county's population is less than 40,000.

The southern part of Bureau County includes part of the Military Tract. In May 1812, an act of Congress was passed which set aside bounty lands as payment to volunteer soldiers who participated in the War of 1812. The bounty land in Illinois was located in the western part of the state between the Illinois and Mississippi Rivers. Of the 5.4 million acres included in the tract, approximately 3.5 million acres was deemed fit for cultivation and was set aside for military bounties. The tract was surveyed in 1815-1816 and opened to settlement. At the time, the land was a mix of forest and wild prairie. Today, major parts of the county are planted in corn or soybeans.

104.2 SPRING CREEK BRIDGE – The railroad crosses the creek on a two-panel deck plate girder bridge. Spring Creek forms southwest of Mendota and flows south, becoming part of the route used by the CB&Q to Zearing. Just south of here it flows into the Illinois River.

104.3 SPRING VALLEY – Spring Valley was founded in 1884 by Henry J. Miller, one of the first settlers of this area, and his son-in-law, Charles J. Devlin. They acquired 5000 acres of mineral rights and bought 500 acres on which to build a town, all with plans to develop the coal fields alongside Spring Creek. For financial help, they worked with E. N. Saunders of St. Paul, Minnesota, a director of the Chicago & North Western Railroad. They also brought in a number of experienced coal capitalists, including William L. Scott of Erie, Pennsylvania, a United States Senator during the administration of President Grover Cleveland.

Two companies were formed as a part of this plan – the Spring Valley Coal Company and the Spring Valley Townsite Company. Spring Valley, nicknamed "The Magic City," was designed to be a large city, and its St. Paul Street became one of the widest streets in Illinois. Reportedly more than $2.5 million was spent in less than four years to build the town.

According to a 1926 Sanborn map, the Rock Island passenger and freight station was on the north side of the tracks just west of the Spalding Street grade crossing, now an overpass. The Chicago & North Western line had a switch with the Rock Island just east of the bridge, and their depot stood less than 100 yards up the line. The C&NW also had a six-stall roundhouse and yard at Spring Valley, located just north of today's U.S. Highway 6.

The CRI&P arrived here in late summer 1853, passing right on through the area. It wasn't until the coal mining began that the railroad paid any attention. However, starting in 1884, the Northern Illinois Railroad was built to Spring Valley from Belvidere, down through De Kalb and Earlville. On June 9, 1888, the Chicago & North Western acquired the company, entering Spring Valley from the north adjacent to the former CB&Q line to Zearing. With the C&NW basically backing the mines, the Rock Island received little of the coal. However, the C&NW served Spring Valley Coal

Mine #1 (just north of the C&NW-CRI&P switch), Mine #4 (north of the roundhouse), Mine #2 (north of Mine #4), and Mine #3 (on a branchline at the northwest corner of Spring Valley at a place called Location).

Mine #1 was sunk in 1884, becoming the first active mine of those owned by the Spring Valley Coal Company. It eventually closed in 1923 and was dismantled in 1927 when the company folded. Mines #2 and #4 were actually joint mines. Mine #2 was sunk in 1885 and Mine #4 was sunk in 1887, connecting with the older mine and being used as an escape shaft. This plan was a good one as both mines were destroyed in January 1909 by fire. They were not rebuilt. Mine #3 was unique as it survived after the Spring Valley Coal Company. The mine was sunk in the spring of the year 1885. It closed in 1927 when the coal company closed, but it was reopened in 1935 by a group of local citizens. It stayed open until 1947, providing some local work and income.

Spring Valley was for many years a mining company town, bringing with it the issues such places faced. For example, many miners complained that their paychecks didn't even cover the cost of living at Spring Valley. In 1896, a national miners strike found its way to Spring Valley, with even local merchants participating. Reports indicate that the company store was looted and many local businesses were driven away by the coal company and strikers. However, in 1913, there were still 2500 miners working in the Spring Valley Coal Company's mines.

Large scale coal mining ended in Spring Valley by 1927, and traffic over the C&NW became limited to grains and local business. The line hung on, with the north end abandoned in the early 1940s, and the track between Troy Grove and Spring Valley gone by the mid-1970s. Today, the line remains in service between DeKalb and the large Unimin sand facility at Troy Grove, operated by Union Pacific.

As for Spring Valley, today it is mainly a residential community with a major Walmart Distribution Center on the north side near Interstate 80. It should be noted that during the mining era, the Spring Valley area was almost treeless. Today, it is surrounded by woods and farms.

107.8 MARQUETTE – On top of the hillside to the north is Echo Bluff Park, a reminder of what was once the community of Marquette, and before that, Loceyville. Loceyville started in the late 1870s when G. H. Locey opened an underground shaft coal mine here, reportedly with a depth of 300 feet to reach a 3-foot coal seam. To support the mine, Locey created Loceyville, building houses, stores, a school, and even a tavern. By 1884, the mine and machinery was described as "old and worn" but the coal as "good quality." A report stated that to "make this a mine of the first class it will be necessary to enlarge the shaft from top to bottom, build new engine and boiler rooms and put in new machinery. The mine is under the management of Edward Lewis." While improvements were made, by 1887 the mine was in the hands of a receiver.

In 1890, the mine was reported as being owned by the Chicago, Wilmington & Vermilion Coal Company, with a number of improvements underway. An 1895 mine report stated that, "The Marquette Coal Company has purchased the mine formerly run by the C. W. & V. Coal Company, at Loceyville, Bureau county. They have changed the name of the town to Marquette; have the mine in first-class condition, and are now busy grading for railroad tracks on top, and no doubt expect to mine coal extensively in the near future." Reports indicate that the community peaked with a population of about 2000 at this time.

The company was reorganized as the Marquette Third Vein Coal Company in 1901, with some reports showing some control by the Spring Valley Coal Company. The mine burned in December 1905, but the "shaft has been resunk and retimbered, a new tower erected and coal hoisting was again resumed in October, 1906." However, the mine was closed by 1914 and a fire of "suspicious" nature destroyed most of the buildings.

Blue Island Subdivision

When the mine closed, jobs went away and the town almost disappeared. The village government was voted out of existence in 1916, but the local school continued to operate until the 1950s. Today, this brick schoolhouse is the only remaining structure. When the school closed, the Girl Scouts of American were given free use of the land, and restored much of the vegetation with the help of the Illinois Valley Garden Club. The land then passed into the hands of Hall Township, which maintains the park.

108.6 NEW YORK CENTRAL BRIDGE 188.0 – Look for the abandoned two-span through plate girder bridge overhead. Built in 1907 by the American Bridge Company of New York, it totals 120 feet long. A 1973 Rock Island track profile shows this bridge to be Penn Central, but it has a very interesting earlier history, finally being abandoned in 1980. The New York Central knew this location as Howe, located at NYC Milepost 188.3. The railroad had a large yard here, a depot named Howe, and a connection with the Depue & Northern Railroad Company. A direct interchange was made with the Rock Island by a track south of the bridge at what was known as DePue Junction.

This line was part of what many called the Kankakee Belt Route, which extended from South Bend, Indiana, through Kankakee, Illinois, and westward to Zearing, Illinois. A major part of this construction was by the Indiana, Illinois & Iowa Railroad (the "3 I Line"), which built from Momence, Illinois, to Streator, Illinois, in 1881. The idea for the line was to transport corn and other grains to eastern markets, but to also reach new interchange points outside of Chicago.

In 1899, the next step in the plan took place when the Streator & Clinton Railroad began construction toward the Illinois River near DePue. *The New York Times* reported that funding for the project came from the Indiana, Illinois & Iowa Railroad, and that by 1900 the "3 I" was in charge of the project and railroad. With that, the Indiana, Illinois & Iowa Railroad built a line from DePue northward to a junction with the CB&Q at Ladd, and then eastward to a junction with the C&NW at Churchill, Illinois. The railroad eventually gained trackage rights over the CB&Q to reach the mainline at Zearing.

The bridge across the Illinois River became the challenge in completing the line. It was designed and built by the Wisconsin Bridge and Iron Company, which used the bridge in their advertising. The bridge featured a turn span to allow river navigation, and the company stated that it was built for the Streator & Clinton Railway Company. The *Annual Report of the Chief of Engineers United States Army* (1899) reported on the bridge. It stated that "Bridge of the Streator and Clinton Railroad Company across Illinois River near Marquette, Ill. – Plans and map of location were submitted July 24, 1899; approved by the Secretary of War August 11, 1899."

The Indiana, Illinois & Iowa Railroad was merged into the Chicago, Indiana & Southern Railroad (CI&S) in 1906, which became part of the New York Central Railroad (NYC) in 1914. The line gained another interchange when the Chicago, Milwaukee & St. Paul Railroad (Milwaukee Road) built into Ladd from Mendota about 1900. It then gained trackage rights over the NYC between Ladd and Granville (several miles southeast of Hennepin) where it built its own line east to Oglesby, Illinois.

The reason for the interest in Ladd by the Chicago, Milwaukee & St. Paul Railroad was coal. A subsidiary, the St. Paul Coal Company, provided coal to the company and they built and operated several mines in the area. The railroad had a major roundhouse and yard there, and reports state that as many as two dozen trains daily operated out of the terminal during its peak years, and it remained a major terminal into the early 1960s.

The NYC line prospered for a number of years, but the completion of the Illinois Waterway made water rates lower to the east, and much of the corn and grain moved to water for the journey. One source states that thanks to the waterway improvements, water movements to Chicago and then rail on east had "a total shipping cost of 53.625 cents for corn and 54.125 cents for corn products" while the Kankakee Belt Line had rates of "72 cents for corn and 72.5 cents for corn products."

The NYC became a part of Penn Central in 1968, and then Conrail in 1976. With Conrail abandoning and selling lines, a decision was made to get rid of the track west of Granville. The Milwaukee Road took over the Ladd to Granville line. This left the Milwaukee Road as the last user of the S&C's Illinois River bridge. The Milwaukee Road's own failure in 1980 ended this service, but the line between Granville and Moronts (near Hennepin) was saved to serve the Hennepin Power Plant. The bridge over the Illinois River was almost immediately removed. In 1999, NS gained control of many of the Conrail lines, including what became known as the Kankakee Branch and Granville Industrial Lead.

109.1 EAST DEPUE – This location was identified as a 4900-foot siding in CSX timetables from the 1980s. A small yard also once existed to the south and this was the east switch. In the early to mid-1900s, a siding and interchange track existed to the north, now just a short spur track in the brush. Early maps of DePue show several centers of development and population, probably leading this area to be known as East DePue.

109.6 DEPUE – DePue was originally known as Newport Steamboat Landing when it was a river town full of warehouses to support Illinois River traffic. In 1853, Benjamin Newell laid out lots and streets along the river here and called the place Trenton. However, there was already a Trenton in Illinois so the post office took the name of Selby. However, mail delivery problems caused the community to be renamed Sherman by 1865. During February 1867, the community decided to rename itself DePue, but it wasn't until June 1869 that it became official. Despite the official spelling of DePue, the town's shield spelled it Depue until 1908.

New Jersey Zinc once had a major processing facility at DePue, known about 1905 as Mineral Point Zinc Company. Today, it is a Superfund site. According to the U.S. EPA, "the primary zinc smelting facility on the site began operations in 1903 on 175 acres of farmland, but expanded to more than 860 acres over the years as additional plants were added. The original plant produced slab zinc, used in the automobile and appliances industries, and sulfuric acid. Zinc dust was also produced and used as an additive to produce corrosive-resistant paints. The plant was bought by New Jersey Zinc in 1938, but it wasn't until 1955 that the use of the Mineral Point Zinc name ended and the plant was known as New Jersey Zinc Company. In 1967, in response to the increase in the demand for phosphate fertilizer, DePue/New Jersey Zinc constructed a diammonium phosphate (DAP) fertilizer plant. Mobil Chemical leased the DAP and sulfuric acid plants from New Jersey Zinc in 1972 and later purchased the plant in 1975. Due to economics, Mobil ceased manufacturing operations at the plant in August 1987 and the plants were demolished in April 1991."

The zinc plant seemed to have also caused the creation of a new railroad – the Depue & Northern Railroad Company. A report in the July 23, 1904, issue of *Railway World* stated: "DEPUE AND NORTHERN RAILROAD. A railroad from DePue to Seatonville, Ill., is contemplated by the Depue and Northern Railroad Company, which has been incorporated in Illinois to build between the two places in Bureau County. Capital is fixed at $25,000, and the incorporators are William B. Mcllwaine, of Lakeside; Houston C. Adock, of Western Springs; John P. Wilson Jr., William R. Dickinson, and Edwin L. Johnson, of Chicago. Headquarters will be established in Chicago." Later ICC records show that the zinc company owned the Depue & Northern.

Records of the Interstate Commerce Commission state that the railroad built 0.72 miles of track in 1905-1906 between Howe (on the NYC) through DePue and to the zinc plant at Nassau. It added to the railroad corridor through DePue, as this was the northernmost track (located north of Marquette Street), next to the CRI&P, then the Illinois Traction interurban line, then a CRI&P rail yard, and then an interchange track of the New York Central. A 1916 map of DePue shows six tracks at Depot Street, and more than a dozen just to the east.

Apparently, the railroad played a number of games with their rates to get interchange traffic and to benefit the zinc company. The July 6, 1912, issue of *The Black Diamond* has as its lead article a detailed story about the role the Depue & Northern played in an ICC rate case involving a coal movement to the Mineral Point Zinc Company at Nassau. It seems that a number of railroads, including the New York Central, Rock Island, and others, had coal rates to DePue and rates to DePue for moves to points beyond the location. Nassau was considered to be in DePue by most people, so that rate was used. However, when the 20,000 tons arrived, the coal company was charged the higher rate, forcing the coal company to take a loss on the move. The ICC ruled that the lower rate should apply, and that the "Commission hints very broadly that this establishes a relation between the Mineral Point Zinc Company, the Depue & Northern Railroad, and the Rock Island Railroad, which the Commission may find it necessary to look into in future." This series of rulings may have ended the benefits of the railroad as it was not listed in ICC or Illinois Railroad & Warehouse Commission reports much longer.

The old CRI&P wooden depot once stood just west of Depot Street (Milepost 109.9), on the north side of the tracks, in DePue. It was removed in early 2017. Just east of Depot Street is the Selby Township Library, located in the former Chicago, Ottawa & Peoria Railway (Illinois Traction) station, originally built in 1906. The interurban's tracks were to the north of the station.

Former Illinois Traction interurban station, now Selby Township Library at DePue. Photo by Barton Jennings.

110.3 WEST DEPUE – This was the west switch to the DePue Yard. The Mineral Point Zinc Company facility at Nassau was east of East Street and on the north side of the tracks.

113.5 EAST BUREAU – Early CSX timetables show the east switch for a 6104-foot siding, located to the south, at Milepost 112.9. Current IAIS timetables also show this location, but has the official station of East Bureau at Milepost 113.5 – look for the station sign. The west switch is at Milepost 114.1, just east of the wye switch. This siding is often used to spot cars for westbound pickup.

To the south is Spring Lake, a part of the Illinois River. The Lake Depue State Fish and Wildlife Area includes the lake

114.0 BUREAU – The Rock Island reached Bureau Junction on September 12, 1853. Although its official name is Bureau Junction, the village is more commonly called Bureau, and Bureau is the main name used by phone companies, the Federal Board on Geographic Names, and the United States Post Office. The name came from the same source as the county, from Michel or Pierre de Beuro and their trading post on the Illinois River.

In the June 6, 1872, edition of the *Henry Republican*, it was stated that "Bureau Junction has the significance of being the midway station between Chicago and Rock Island, and nothing more nor less than being a railroad town, relating solely to the interests of the C. R. I. & P. R. R. (Chicago, Rock Island and Pacific Rail Road). Here is where railroad men live; here is where trains come and go, conductors stop, trains are dispatched, cars and locomotives repaired, passengers get their 'inner man' replenished, and where there is cessation of locomotive snorts neither day, night or Sundays. Look which way you will and you see endless tracks side by side, and a sea of cars everywhere. The houses are occupied by railroad men and their families. The school is filled with scholars thereof, and its railroad business forever and aye."

This subject was continued in the September 13, 1877, issue of the *Henry Republican*. An article stated that "the staid little 'City of Side Tracks' remains in status quo. It is always lively when trains are passing and this is about every hour in the day and night. It's a railroad town, having the advantage of other places, being a railroad town and nothing else. Here is a round house with a dozen locomotives ready for use, and where exchanges are hourly made. And it might be said to be the 'seat of government' of the C. R. I & P. R. R., so much business of the line seemingly centers at this point."

Coming into Bureau from the east, the line to Peoria switches off the mainline at Milepost 114.1, crosses Nebraska Street, and goes straight ahead. Westbound trains on the mainline curve hard to the right. A third track at the west end of Bureau (Milepost 114.7) creates a large wye here. The Peoria line was built by the Peoria & Bureau Valley Railroad Company, chartered on February 12, 1853, to "locate, construct and finally complete a railroad from the City of Peoria, in Peoria County, to the Valley of the Bureau in Bureau County." The line was leased in perpetuity to the Chicago & Rock Island Rail Road Company on April 4, 1854, and finally sold to the CRI&P on November 17,

1950. The line was built from Bureau Junction to Peoria, a total of 47 miles, by November 7, 1854. For details on this line, check out the route guide for the Peoria Subdivision on page 241.

During the days of passenger service, the main line was double track on a 40-mph curve. The junction switch for the Peoria main track was just east of the depot along with a crossover. Bureau was open 24/7 as the operator ran the CTC machine that controlled the tracks from west of Bureau to near Peru. All trains to Peoria received orders at Bureau. To serve this line, Branch Yard was located on the south side of the Peoria main between the depot and wye switch. The former CRI&P wood station still stands at Bureau Junction, just inside the east wye switch. Parts of the old station platforms still exist on each side of the station. On today's Chicago to Omaha mainline, there is 550 feet of brick and concrete platform. On the Peoria side, there is still 300 feet of brick platform.

Maps from 1892 show the Bureau House Hotel just west of the station, and an office, a five-stall roundhouse, and a repair shop further west, all inside the wye. South of the depot, the town had two blocks of business and houses, and three blocks to the north. Except for the depot, none of the rail structures remain, although some of the foundations can still be found in the brush.

Former CRI&P station at Bureau, Illinois. Photo by Barton Jennings.

Blue Island Subdivision

Just west of the west wye switch at Bureau Junction is the grade crossing with Illinois Highway 29, and then switches to two tracks (one to the north and one to the south) which serve as a local yard. These tracks are known as the North Conveyor (4400 feet long) and the South Conveyor (3770 feet long). The Iowa Interstate generally bases a train and crew here that makes a daily roundtrip to Peoria, known as the Bureau Switcher. This yard stretches west to near Milepost 115.6, where the south track ends and the railroad goes to two tracks. There are a set of crossovers here that allow trains to move in and out of the siding to the north.

115.6 BUREAU – This is the milepost used by the Iowa Interstate for the siding to the west of Bureau (BU); it is at the crossovers between the two tracks.

The Hennepin Canal is immediately to the south. The canal was built to connect the Illinois and Mississippi Rivers, but funding didn't become available until 1890 and the canal wasn't completed until 1907, reducing the distance from Chicago to Rock Island by 419 miles. However, by the time it was finished, the cost of shipping by rail had decreased (and was faster) and barge sizes and freight loads had increased making the Hennepin nearly obsolete. However, it did achieve some fame. It was the first American canal built of concrete without cut stone facings, and some construction techniques were used on later, larger canals such as the Panama Canal. Because of this, the canal is listed on the National Register of Historic Places.

The canal was built with 33 locks (32 remain), and 14 of them used the unique Marshall gates, which raised and lowered horizontally. By the 1930s, the canal was primarily used for recreational traffic, and it closed to boat traffic in 1951. Today, the canal is basically a recreational area and a popular walking trail, with "93.5 miles of bike trail, 172 miles of hiking and cross-country skiing trail, 90.9 miles of snowmobile trail, 73.6 miles of equestrian trail, and 95 miles open for canoeing." For those interested in the construction, five of the locks have been restored to working condition, and six of the nine aqueducts remain.

116.3 EAST BUREAU CREEK BRIDGE – East Bureau Creek flows in from the north (it used to pass under the Hennepin Canal) then turns to the southeast to flow into Big Bureau Creek, which then flows south and into the Illinois River. To the south, the Hennepin Canal once used an aqueduct to cross the creek.

116.5 UNDER INTERSTATE 180 – Look up to see one of the least used Interstate highways in the country – it sees only 2000 to 4000 vehicles daily. Stretching from I-80 east of Princeton, south to Hennepin, Illinois, it is just more than 13 miles long. Completed in 1969, it was built to provide access to a new Jones & Laughlin steel plant built at Hennepin in 1965. The steel plant has opened and closed over the years, reducing the need for the highway.

116.7 WEST BUREAU SWITCH – This is the west switch for the siding to the north side of the mainline. The Iowa Interstate has built a new office on a low hillside to the south.

119.1 HENNEPIN CANAL BRIDGE – This bridge consists of two deck plate girder spans, each 48½ feet long. Just to the north are the remains of concrete Lock #6.

119.3 BUREAU CREEK BRIDGE – This bridge consists of four 51-foot long and two 48½-foot long deck plate girder spans. Here the railroad is using the south track alignment. The old bridge for the north track still exists, but is deckless.

Bureau Creek is the stream on which Michel and Pierre de Beuro had their trading post, located at the mouth where it flowed into the Illinois River. The creek starts about ten miles north of Mendota and flows southwest to near Princeton. Here it turns south and then east to the Illinois River. It is about 75 miles in total length.

Blue Island Subdivision

122.4 TISKILWA – Tiskilwa was established in 1834 and is today a small town of about 800. The former CRI&P brick depot still stands here. The railroad once had two main tracks through town, plus a short siding to the north and a long spur track to the south. On the south side of the tracks were stockyards, the W. H. Mettler grain elevator, and the lumber yard of H. E. Curtis and Company. Today, only a single mainline plus a short spur to the north exists. Just west of the spur switch, the railroad crosses a small bridge at Milepost 122.6.

Downtown on Main Street, the former United Methodist Church is now the home of the Tiskilwa Historical Society. They publish a newsletter regularly on their website about the history of the community. It carriers the name *The Wapsipinicon*, "from the Potawatomi name for the creek that flows into Tiskilwa from numerous springs in the hills to the west, eventually joining Big Bureau Creek east of town."

Tiskilwa is known for two festivals. The first is their Strawberry and Artisan Festival, generally held on the second Saturday in June. The festival also includes a town-wide garage sale. The second is Pow Wow Days, held the first weekend in August. Pow Wow Days is a three-day event that includes a Native American pow wow, a parade, and a number of other events.

For baseball fans, Tiskilwa is the birthplace of Warren Giles, onetime general manager of the Cincinnati Reds and then president of the National League (1957-69).

125.0 WEST BUREAU CREEK BRIDGE – This bridge is more than 200 feet long and consists of four 51-foot deck plate girder spans. West Bureau Creek flows to the southeast and eventually merges with the east branch, and then flows south to the Illinois River.

Several hundred feet to the north is the Hennepin Canal with preserved Lock #13. The railroad soon has a grade crossing with County Road 1700 E. The railroad will be right next to the canal and Bridge #7, an abandoned Pratt through truss bridge over the Hennepin Canal. This bridge was once used by the county road.

125.9 LOCK #14 – Look for the railroad grade crossing with County Road 1280N. To the north is Hennepin Lock #14 and Bridge #8. The Pratt through truss span was once used by County Road 1280 N. There are three more locks over the next mile. The railroad and the canal stay close to each other through this area.

126.9 LOCK #17 – Immediately to the north is Lock #17 and Bridge #9, a Pratt through truss that once carried County Road 1550 E.

127.6 WEST BUREAU CREEK BRIDGE – This bridge, consisting of two 60-foot deck plate girder spans, crosses another part of West Bureau Creek. Just to the north the Hennepin Canal also crosses the creek on Aqueduct #3. Lock #18 is not much further west.

The number of locks through this area show the steady westbound climb that both the canal and the railroad is experiencing. For the railroad, it is a steady grade of 0.3%, not much for a railroad but something that does require locks for a waterway.

128.7 WYANET – Look for the Wyanet Road overpass, which also crosses the Hennepin Canal. Hennepin Canal Lock #19 and Bridge #10, a Warren pony truss bridge, are close to the north. The canal turns north here while the Iowa Interstate curves to the west and follows Pond Creek, moving them apart for the first time since Bureau.

The Rock Island never went through Wyanet, but instead passed south of the community. Nevertheless, the Rock Island once had a depot here, located on the south side of the tracks and the east side of the road. Maps show that there was also a grain elevator here.

The first settlement here was reportedly in 1821 by an Indian trader named Bulbona. He called the location Center. A sawmill and a flour mill opened in the mid-1830s on Pond Creek, immediately south of today's Iowa Interstate tracks, and the community began calling itself Pond Creek. The name was changed again to Kingston when the CRI&P built through here in 1853, named for Henry and Mary King who donated land for the station.

Reportedly, Wyanet for many years was one of the best grain markets in this part of the state with the first carload of grain being shipped in 1854 by William Moffatt. Soon, a warehouse was erected in 1855 and the CB&Q, which passes through the center of Wyanet, added a rail car to be used as a depot. The Village of Wyanet was laid out in 1856 by the CB&Q, and in 1857 a permanent depot was built by the CB&Q, the same year that the town was incorporated.

129.7 WYANET CROSSING – This Wyanet is where the IAIS passes under the BNSF Chicago-Omaha mainline. Some maps from the late 1800s and early 1900s show this to be a "railroad junction" but there was never a connecting track. However, for a number of years, it was a passenger connection.

At one time, there was a three-story joint depot at this location, located in the western quadrant. The lowest level served the Rock Island, the middle level of the depot contained ten sleeping quarters and a dining room for guests, and the upper level served the CB&Q and provided sleeping quarters for the agent. An elevator was available for handling mail, kitchen goods and other bulky items. Records seem to show the first operator here arrived in 1867. Edward John Engel arrived at Wyanet in 1878 to become the operator/agent of the Rock Island – CB&Q Junction. Engel had unique experience that made him suitable for the job – he had previously worked for both railroads. As part of the agreement, his mother, Jacobina, handled the lodging.

Complicating the work at the Wyanet crossing was that it had two names. On the CB&Q, it was known as the Rock Island Crossing, and on the Rock Island it was the CB&Q

Crossing. The agreement for the station ended when it burned on February 4, 1910. The CB&Q moved their work to the station on King Street in downtown Wyanet, while the Rock Island moved theirs to the Pond Creek, later Wyanet, station.

While no connecting track ever existed here, there are plans to add a connecting track at Wyanet so that Amtrak trains for the Quad Cities can use today's BNSF line to get out of Chicago but use the IAIS to access Moline, Illinois.

134.2 UNION PACIFIC BRIDGE OVERHEAD – Iowa Interstate passes under Union Pacific, the former C&NW line between Peoria and the mainline at Nelson. Union Pacific acquired this line when it bought the railroad in April, 1995. When it was acquired, the line stretched from Nelson (Illinois) almost to St. Louis (Missouri). In reality, the line went south to DeCamp (Illinois) and got on the Litchfield & Madison (the C&NW had acquired the L&M in 1958) to Madison (Illinois) and the St. Louis area. UP soon negotiated rights over the Chicago & Illinois Midland from Barr to Springfield to get on their former Alton route. The line from Barr to Girard was abandoned in 1999. A new connector was built at Girard so trains from the Alton route could access the coal mine at Monterey. South of there, the line was sold to Norfolk Southern all the way to DeCamp. South of there it was mostly abandoned in 2000.

136.5 SHEFFIELD – The Chicago & Rock Island arrived at Sheffield in early October, 1853. Sheffield was founded by Joseph E. Sheffield and Henry Farnam in 1852. Both Sheffield and Farnam were involved with building the railroad and the town site was intended as a coaling station for trains. According to Farnam, he and Sheffield flipped a coin to see for whom the town would be named. Today, a monument to Joseph E. Sheffield, and the Rock Island Railroad, stands in Sheffield's town square. The frame CRI&P station also serves as a reminder of the rail line's history.

Blue Island Subdivision

In 1932, Sheffield had a number of tracks. The depot was just west of Main Street and there were three tracks to the north and three to the south. South of the station were the B. S. Williams Grain & Coal and the Framers Grain Company. Parts of the round Farmers elevator still stands. To the west were stockyards and the Wood, Howard & Company lumber yard. Less than a mile west of Sheffield was the Sheffield Shale Products Company, located just to the east of U.S. Highway 34 where it turns south.

Heading west, the track becomes straight and the next significant curve is in 26 miles, located west of Geneseo.

141.9 MINERAL – The depot at Mineral was once on the south side of the tracks just east of the Central Street grade crossing. Across the tracks to the north were stockyards and a grain elevator.

Coal was discovered near here in 1834 by John Green Reed, reportedly one of the first discoveries in the county. Soon, a number of small mines opened up south of here and a community of 300 developed with the name Mineral. In 1850, Mineral was officially organized, and then later platted by William Riley. The part of town north of the tracks became known as Riley's addition due to his work. William Riley had other impacts upon the community as he was the first postmaster of the village, the first agent for the railroad, and he built and donated the first school at Mineral. The population of Mineral peaked in the 1940s and started to drop as the coal mines closed. Today, Mineral is a small farming community with a post office and a few businesses.

143.0 COUNTY LINE – This is the line between Bureau County (to the east) and **Henry County** (to the west). Henry County was formed on January 13, 1825, from part of the existing Fulton County. It was named for Patrick Henry, the American Revolution spokesman who made the challenge "give me liberty, or give me death." With its county seat at Cambridge, the county's population is about 50,000. Most of the county is farmland, a profession celebrated each year at the Antique Engine & Tractor Association show in September.

143.2 EAST SWITCH PATRIOT RENEWABLE FUELS – This is the east switch for the Patriot Renewable Fuels ethanol plant which produces 125 million gallons of ethanol annually. The plant and supporting rail yard are to the north. The Iowa Interstate employee timetable includes the warning that, "Remote control locomotives are in use at Patriot Renewable Fuels."

This facility opened in 2008, and purchased and processed more than 200 million bushels of corn from area farmers in its first five years of production and created 550 million gallons of ethanol. On June 1, 2015, it was announced that CHS Inc. was buying this facility, the second ethanol plant that CHS purchased. Their first was the former Illinois River Energy plant at Rochelle, Illinois, which they bought in June 2014.

CHS is one of those companies that few have ever heard of, but it is a Fortune 100 company. It is a global agribusiness founded in 1929 and is "owned by farmers, ranchers and cooperatives across the United States" and "supplies energy, crop nutrients, grain marketing services, animal feed, food and food ingredients, along with business solutions including insurance, financial and risk management services. The company operates petroleum refineries/pipelines and manufactures, markets and distributes Cenex® brand refined fuels, lubricants, propane and renewable energy products," according to their website.

145.0 WEST SWITCH PATRIOT RENEWABLE FUELS – The yard at the plant has six tracks, with the track next to the mainline being 9000 feet long. The lead into the plant is on the west end and thus is switched from this west end. According to the company, the private rail yard is the largest on the IAIS track system with storage capacity for approximately 500 cars of corn, distillers grains and ethanol. The plant uses their own locomotive for switching.

The Iowa Interstate occasionally operates unit trains of ethanol out of this facility. When they do, they use "AN" for Annawan as the train code.

145.6 ANNAWAN – The first settler arrived near Annawan in 1846 and their first efforts were to drain the local swamps so the land could be farmed. Mud Creek and the Green River were used to help drain the land, making land available. The Rock Island was building through this area in 1853, and land owners Charles Atkinson and James Grant plotted the Village of Annawan on some of the higher lands alongside the railroad. Some reports stated that the name came from a Winnebago Indian Chief.

Efforts continued into the early 1900s to drain the land for farms. Today, a number of drainage canals lace the area making farming possible. Annawan serves the local farming communities, hosting a post office, several stores, a farm co-op, and a farm supply store. Its population was 878 in the 2010 census. An issue with the legal status of Annawan exists, as the community claims to be a village while the Secretary of State states that it is an incorporated town, not a village.

In the 1960s, the railroad had a spur track off the south mainline and a short siding off the north track, both just west of State Street. Only a mainline passes through today. Just north of town is Interstate 80 and then the Hennepin Canal.

146.5 MUD CREEK BRIDGE – Mud Creek drains much of the area west of Annawan. Note the unused second grade to the north, demonstrating that the Rock Island mainline was two tracks through here. The small pony truss bridge on the local road to the north was built in 1899.

148.9 INTERSTATE 80 – The railroad passes under Interstate 80 for the fourth time since Blue Island.

151.5 ATKINSON – Atkinson is named for Charles Atkinson, an eastern capitalist who arrived here in 1843 and began buying land. Just as he did at Annawan, Charles Atkinson platted a town on the new railroad. Atkinson advertised the community (and others) across Europe and brought a number of new immigrants from Belgium and Holland to settle here during the 1860s. In 1867, Atkinson was incorporated. Much of the community's history can be found at the Atkinson Museum.

In the 1960s, there were two main tracks, a siding to the north, and several industry tracks. Today, the railroad has a 9500-foot passing siding to the north and a spur track to the south into Atkinson Grain & Fertilizer. Atkinson also has a post office and several stores serving the almost 1000 residents.

154.6 SPRING CREEK BRIDGE – This deck plate girder bridge includes four spans, all less than 35 feet long. Throughout this area the railroad is climbing over low ridges and dropping back down into a number of creek and marsh bottoms. The grade in each direction from here is 0.4% to 0.5%. Spring Creek flows to the north, under the Hennepin Canal, and into Green River.

159.1 GENESEO – The railroad built to Geneseo by Christmas Day, 1853. Look for the old wooden Rock Island depot to the south, now expanded and used by a local insurance company, at the Oakwood Avenue grade crossing. The Rock Island once had a freight house across the tracks to the north. Today's railroad is only a shadow of what was once here – two main tracks, several sidings, and a number of industry tracks. Companies such as Sommers & Bollen (coal and grain), Guild & Sons Elevator, The Red Mill (feed mill), Standard Oil Company of Indiana, Geneseo Canning Company, a lumber shed, and a grocery warehouse once existed here and used the railroad. Today, at the east end of town, the railroad serves the River Valley Cooperative's Agronomy and Energy facility. River Valley Cooperative dates back to 1906 when a group of local farmers started pooling their grain together. The Co-op now operates more than twenty facilities across eastern Iowa and western Illinois.

Geneseo is also home to the famous gun manufacturing company, Springfield Armory, Inc., which is located on Main Street. It was founded in 1974 by the Reese family. Also in Geneseo is Armalite, owned by Strategic Armory Corps of Phoenix, Arizona, but all manufacturing is still conducted in Geneseo.

The gun manufacturing in Geneseo is unusual based upon how the community was founded. In 1827, members of a Congregationalist church in Geneseo, New York, started planning a new community in the "Old Northwest" – Illinois. In May 1836, a delegation (the "New York Committee" or "New York Group") visited the area and surveyed the property. Soon, members of seven families departed New York to create a "church in the wilderness," naming the community after the city in New York where they started. The trip took much of the year as the group was not prepared for country without roads or the harsh winter weather.

After building a few crude cabins, the first act of the new settlers was reportedly to create a temperance society and then start construction on the original First Congregationalist Church. Its first communion was held on April 18, 1838, with those in attendance having to fight a large hail storm which broke out almost all of the windows in town. Next came the creation of the Geneseo Seminary, which closed in 1857 due to considerable debt.

The arrival of the railroad reportedly helped the community's situation. The editor of the *Rock Islander* reported that there were "one hundred new buildings erected in Geneseo" in 1854 alone and "seventy [more] built in the present year [1855]." This boom allowed Geneseo to become a town in 1855 and a city in 1865. This is the era that gives Geneseo its nickname of "Victorian Geneseo" as the new wealth was often spent on large and impressive homes.

Most remain and are featured during the annual Christmas Walk.

Geneseo's population today is about 7000, making it big enough for a planned Amtrak stop on the proposed Chicago-Quad Cities train. Heading west, the railroad continues to pass through miles of farmland.

163.5 HENNEPIN CANAL – The Rock Island Railroad and the Hennepin Canal come back together here, with the canal still to the north. Look for the two concrete locks #25 and #26.

167.8 GREEN RIVER – Look for the grade crossing with Green River Road. The small community to the south is called Green River after the river to the north. This station was listed in the 1967 *Rock Island List of Stations*. Green River is the location of the westbound distant signal for the Colona crossing. For rail enthusiasts, the signal has an interesting history. It is the old eastbound Rock Island tri-light signal, rotated 180 degrees to signal westbound trains.

168.9 INTERSTATE 80 – The railroad again passes under I-80, this time in the middle of a marshy, wooded area.

169.3 GREEN RIVER BRIDGE – The Green River has closely followed the Rock Island Railroad to the north. When Henry County was drained, the Green River was straightened and channelized as a part of the work. The river flows a few miles further south and west before entering the Rock River south of Carbon Cliff.

The bridge, from east to west, includes a 150-foot lattice through truss span, and then five deck plate girder spans of 36'-8" each. The truss was built in 1900 and the bridge is a total of 340 feet long. The Iowa Interstate uses the former south track's alignment over the bridge.

169.5 HENNEPIN CANAL BRIDGE – Look to the north to see Lock #28.

Blue Island Subdivision

169.6 COLONA – The BNSF Barstow Subdivision, which runs 96 miles between Galesburg (IL) and Savanna (IL), crosses the Iowa Interstate at Colona. The crossing used a diamond until November 22, 2003, when a BNSF freight derailed on it. A switch was installed near the old diamond to allow the IAIS access to their mainline east to Chicago, requiring the railroad to use BNSF tracks between East Moline and Colona. It wasn't until July 7, 2004, that the second switch was installed and the Iowa Interstate could again use its own tracks heading east out of the Quad Cities.

Colona is a community created by the merger of the City of Green Rock and the Village of Colona in 1997, reportedly the first communities in Illinois to merge by popular vote. According to the Henry County Tourism Bureau, Colona was named after its founding family, Eric and Natasha Colona, and their children Abdul and Elaine.

Colona is located where the Green River and Hennepin Canal flow into the Rock River. The Hennepin Canal, also known as the Illinois & Mississippi Canal, was first proposed in 1834 as a waterway between the Mississippi River at Rock Island and the Illinois River near Hennepin. Congress authorized preliminary surveys on the project in 1871, construction began in 1892, and the first boat went through in 1907. The canal was never much of a success since it was built to older standards, and by the 1930s, was used primarily for recreational traffic. The canal was open to boat traffic until 1951 at no cost. Today, the canal is a water and hiking recreational facility and is listed on the National Register of Historic Places.

170.8 ROCK RIVER BRIDGE – The Iowa Interstate crosses the Rock River on a bridge consisting of 21 deck plate girder spans. The Iowa Interstate uses the north track, and eight of the western spans on the south track have been removed. The bridge is a total of 1350 feet long.

The Rock River, approximately 300 miles long, starts in Fond du Lac County, Wisconsin, and wanders along the Wisconsin-Illinois border before entering the Mississippi

River in the Quad Cities area, just a few miles downstream from here. Sources say that the Sauk and Fox Indians called the river "Sinnissippi," meaning "rocky waters."

In this area, the Rock River serves as the county line between Henry County (to the east) and Rock Island County (to the west). **Rock Island County** was established by an act of the Illinois Legislature on February 9, 1831. The county was formed out of parts of Jo Davies county and named for an island located in the Mississippi River. Almost immediately, the arrival of new settlers threatened a war with the several area tribes, such as the Sauk and Fox people. The resulting small battles and political maneuvers basically prevented the county from being organized until 1833. George Davenport, for whom Davenport, Iowa, is named, was elected as one of the three first county commissioners. The City of Rock Island is the county seat.

171.8 CARBON CLIFF – Carbon Cliff is the east switch to the IAIS Silvis Yard, located just west of North 1st Avenue. An old Rock Island tri-light style signal still stands at Carbon Cliff and acts as a distant signal for eastbounds approaching Colona. The signal is constantly lit yellow.

Carbon Cliff formed not long after the Chicago & Rock Island Railroad reached here in 1854. Soon it was a coal mining community with a number of mines on the nearby hillsides. In particular, the mines on the bluffs to the west were some of the first and led to the community's name. Besides coal, the area also produced clay for the Argillo Works fire brick and farm-drain tile business. With the growth, Carbon Cliff was incorporated on December 8, 1906. However, by the 1930s, both industries were gone and today the community has less than 2000 residents.

While the east switch to the Silvis Yard siding is at Milepost 171.9, there is also a crossover between the mainline and siding at Milepost 172.6.

173.7 SILVIS – The town here was originally known as Pleasant Valley, but was renamed when the Village of Silvis was incorporated in 1906. The name Silvis comes from Richard Shippen Silvis, an early settler, and his Silvis Mining Company. Silvis is the home of Hero Street, USA. Hero Street was named in honor of eight soldiers of Mexican-American descent, all of whom who lived on Hero Street (renamed from the original Second Street), who gave their lives fighting in World War II. This street, consisting of roughly twenty-five homes, has sent over one hundred residents into the military since World War II.

Silvis is a famous name in Rock Island Railroad circles. The community of Silvis was incorporated as the railroad built its general line shop here, a shop that was regarded as the largest locomotive-repair shop in the world. A freight yard (known as Kelly Yard), railcar repair facility, and a massive 80-pocket chute coaling tower finished out the more than 800-acre terminal. Over the years, the railcar shops were known for rebuilding hundreds of boxcars into cabooses (more than 180 cabooses converted from a 1915 era Class B-2 type boxcar between 1938 and 1944) while the locomotive shops were a railfan favorite for the variety of steam, and then diesel power, that could be found in its vicinity. In 1949, the railroad had improved the freight yard by adding a small hump and retarder yard, converting the old classification yard into a receiving yard.

On March 31, 1980, the Chicago, Rock Island & Pacific operated its last train. In 1981, Chrome Crankshaft purchased the Silvis shops and used it to rebuild locomotives for the resale market. In June 1990, the properties and facilities of Chrome Locomotive were sold to National Railway Equipment (NRE). Today, NRE has developed the site into a fully modern locomotive and component rebuilding facility. The 82½-acre facility has more than 275,000 square feet under roof and approximately 8 miles of yard and running track. Look for the large fleet of locomotives awaiting sale, rebuilding, or scrapping. The NRE spur joins the IAIS near the west siding switch.

The former CRIP Silvis shops are surrounded by railroad tracks. The Iowa Interstate passes by on the south side while BNSF is on the north. Both can interchange locos and/or cars to the shop. When the railroad was acquired, only the old eastbound mainline and a long siding remained for IAIS to use. In an attempt to gain more room for switching, the railroad built a new yard, engine shop, and office building here in 2010, using "SI" as the station code. This allowed the railroad to move most work away from its yard in downtown Rock Island. The new Silvis Yard includes seven yard tracks, varying from 4600 feet long to 6300 feet long. They often hold cars awaiting pickup by various through trains, and are used to switch trains that start or end at Silvis.

IAIS 719 at Silvis, Illinois. Photo by Barton Jennings.

In downtown Silvis at the corner of 1st Avenue and 11th Street is a small park with restored Rock Island caboose #17882, originally built in 1930 and rebuilt in 1950, on display. The park is officially named Railway Park and includes a gazebo shelter. Unfortunately, the railroad cannot be viewed from the park.

Iowa City Subdivision
Silvis (Illinois) to South Amana (Iowa)

The Iowa City Subdivision of the Iowa Interstate stretches from Silvis to South Amana, officially Mileposts 173.4 to 259.2. The route is much of the former Mississippi & Missouri and was built by 1865. The line became part of the core Rock Island system over time, providing a connection to the Union Pacific mainline at Omaha as well as providing the shortest connection to the Nebraska, Kansas, and Colorado parts of the Rock system. In the Iowa Interstate era, three major changes have occurred with this part of the route.

From east to west, the first is the construction of the new yard at Silvis to replace the much smaller Rock Island Yard. Next, the connection between the IAIS mainline and the CIC line (former Milwaukee line, now Cedar Rapids & Iowa City) near Homestead was built. Named Yocum Connection, the connection is now the major interchange point between the two railroads, eliminating the challenging reverse moves up the hill track in Iowa City. Finally, a large shops and yard complex was built at South Amana to replace much of the work once conducted at Iowa City and Council Buffs..

Traffic across the Iowa City Subdivision features the two main trains – BICB (Blue Island to Council Bluffs) and CBBI (Council Bluffs to Blue Island). The IAIS also operates at least one daily freight to and from Smith-Dows Yard outside Cedar Rapids. Several switcher assignments are also found at Iowa City and South Amana.

173.4 SILVIS – This is the dividing line between the Blue Island and Iowa City Subdivisions.

174.3 ILLINOIS HIGHWAY 84 – Known locally as 19th Street, this is the west switch to the Silvis Yard.

175.1 EAST MOLINE – The Rock Island once had a depot on the north side of the tracks and just west of the 9th Street grade crossing. There was also a freight house on the north side of the tracks a block to the north for the Chicago, Milwaukee, St. Paul & Pacific.

East Moline started as several failed attempts to create a planned community. In 1890, Bailey Davenport (son of George Davenport) died, leaving several hundred acres of land available for development. Included in this land was Port Byron Junction, earlier known as Rock Island Junction, consisting of a depot surrounded by frog ponds located near Ninth Street and Fourteenth Avenue in the present city of East Moline. In 1895, a land syndicate was formed under the name East Moline Company, later renamed the East Moline Land Company, to develop a town here. However, it was a financial disaster.

In 1900, Deere & Company established its first large factory in East Moline when the Union Malleable Iron Company began operations with several hundred employees. The next year saw the Root and VanDervoort Engineering Company begin manufacturing gas engines in East Moline. Within a few years, manufacturers of automobiles, agricultural equipment, scales, and other products located in the city. In February 1903, East Moline was incorporated as a village, and as a city in April 1907. To the north of the tracks can be seen the John Deere Harvester Works, one of the early industries that still exists. The John Deere Harvester Works is the largest employer in East Moline and manufactures combines and associated headers. This is Deere's largest harvester assembly plant in the world, and tours are available.

The single track mainline between 7th Street (Milepost 175.4) in East Moline and 44th Street Rock Island Yard (Milepost 180.4) is used by all railroads in town and is known as the "BNSF Industrial Track." BNSF owns and maintains the single track line while the IAIS dispatches it.

To the north there are several views of the Mississippi River, the border between Illinois and Iowa, backed up by Lock & Dam No. 15. The shoreline is lined with marinas, parks, and a few homes and businesses.

Iowa City Subdivision

177.3 EAST SWITCH MOLINE SIDING – Located west of 41st Street, this siding is to the south on the old Rock Island mainline, saved when the mainlines were consolidated in the early 1990s. The siding is often used by BNSF and IAIS to interchange unit grain and ethanol trains.

177.6 34TH STREET – To the north is the new Quad Cities campus of Western Illinois University, built on the site of the old John Deere Tech Center.

To the south is the Midland Davis Corporation scrap yard. As the company states, "our 15-acre Moline property houses our original scrap yard and processing facility for metals, paper, wood and Moline curbside pickup materials." The company started in 1892 when Louis Livingston partnered with his brother Ike to enter the scrap industry. In 1908, he acquired this scrap yard in East Moline and named it Midland Iron & Steel. The company is known for all of the rail cranes that exist throughout the facility.

If you look at the west side of the property, you can see a building that looks to be part of a railroad roundhouse. In 1912, Sanborn showed that the building was being used by the Deere & Company Natick Lumber Yard as a large lumber shed. This entire area was covered with tracks and lumber storage sheds. Before John Deere acquired the property, this was the Natick Yard of the Chicago & Rock Island. The old lumber shed was once a brick roundhouse, a building that once curved more than 270 degrees around the central turntable. Documents show that the roundhouse and related shop facilities were moved to Silvis in 1906 when that facility opened.

178.5 WEST SWITCH MOLINE SIDING – The west switch is just east of 23rd Street in Moline.

178.8 INTERSTATE 74 – The railroad passes under the east end of the I-74 Mississippi River bridge. Until June 21, 2016, a depot stood a block north of here on River Drive. This station had been built for the Davenport, Rock Island

& Northwestern Railroad in 1901, and also served the Milwaukee Road. It later was used as the home of the Quad Cities Chamber of Commerce, then abandoned. With the building in the way of the new I-74 Mississippi River bridge, there was an effort by preservationists to save and move the building, but insufficient funds and time led to its destruction beginning on June 16, with the building coming down on June 21, 2016.

DRI&NW station in Moline, Illinois. Photo by Barton Jennings.

178.9 MOLINE – In Moline, the Rock Island once had a station just east of the 13th Street grade crossing, just opposite of where the John Deere Pavilion stands today. The Pavilion is a combination museum and new product display. It features restored equipment as well as equipment right off of the production line. It also features a large John Deere company store with everything from clothes to toys. Where the Pavilion stands today was once a John Deere foundry. This location is where the community is planning to build their new Amtrak station as part of a hotel development project.

Moline is sometimes known as "John Deere Town." In 1843, a factory town was platted under the working name of "Rock Island Mills." However, the name was not popular and the name Moline ("City of Mills," from the French moulin) was chosen. The town of Moline was incorporated on April 21, 1848, and soon became an upper crust resi-

Iowa City Subdivision

dential community for managers and well-paid and skilled factory workers. An article in the *Moline Workman* in 1854 noted that a "much duller town could not be scared up this side of Sleepy Hollow." About the same time, the town's future was made certain when John Deere, the inventor of the self-scouring steel plow, relocated his steel plow company from Grand Detour, Illinois, to Moline. The corporate headquarters of Deere & Company is still located in Moline.

Moline is one of the "Quad Cities," a name used to refer to the Davenport (IA) and Rock Island (IL) general area. Despite the fact that the Quad Cities area is "the largest metropolitan area between Chicago, Omaha, Minneapolis, St. Louis, and Kansas City," the area remains relatively unheard of except for John Deere. Before World War I, the area was called the Tri-Cities, encompassing the cities of Davenport, Rock Island, and Moline. However, with the growth of East Moline, the region became known as the Quad Cities during the 1930s. In 1948, Alcoa opened a plant in Bettendorf and there was talk of changing the name to the Quint Cities. However, like some football conferences today, the name and the count don't always agree.

179.7 WILLIAMS WHITE & COMPANY MACHINE SHOP NO. 3 – Note the traditional manufacturing building to the north. The building has long been a landmark in the Moline area. The firm started as two companies in 1854 – Williams, Heald & Company and Moline Iron Works, both in Moline, Illinois. The founders stated that Moline was chosen because it was on the Mississippi River near the "great rapids" providing tremendous water power. The company renamed itself Williams & White in 1867 and formally incorporated in 1871 as Williams, White & Company. The company began manufacturing steam engines for mills in 1875, the "Bull-Dozer" in 1880, and coaling stations for steam locomotives in 1885. Today, the company manufacturers hydraulic presses of all sizes.

Further to the north are several John Deere assembly facilities. This includes the John Deere Seeding Group which makes planters.

180.4 44TH STREET – This 44th Street is in Rock Island and represents the western end of the BNSF Industrial Track that is shared by the Iowa Interstate. This is also the east end of the former CRI&P Rock Island Yard. This yard has mostly been replaced by the new yard at Silvis, but some local work is still based here and cars are often stored here until needed. In addition, interchange work with BNSF and Canadian Pacific take place here.

Just west of here was the "Have a Happy Day" bridge, a local photo prop with its slogan and smiling faces. However, the bridge was replaced with a solid wall due to the failure of several major components in December 2016. Further to the west, the Rock Island Yard is located just north of the Rock Island passenger station. The yard once included a roundhouse.

IAIS 152 switching at Rock Island yard. Photo by Barton Jennings.

181.1 ROCK ISLAND – Located at 3031 5th Avenue is the former Rock Island passenger station, built in the Renaissance Revival style. This building was erected in 1901 by the Rock Island Railroad to serve as the third Rock Island passenger depot. Charles S. Frost of Frost & Granger, Architects, of

Chicago, designed the station. Frost was the most prolific railroad-station architect in the country, and was responsible for about 200 large and small stations for Chicago & North Western, Milwaukee Road, Great Northern, and Rock Island railroads. The depot was constructed by Rock Island building contractor John Volk at a cost of about $75,000.

The original depot had a smoking room and men's toilet on the west side (behind the fireplace), and a retiring room and women's toilet on the east end. The ticket office was in front of the bay window. The general waiting room was in the center of the building and offered a direct view of the trains. A platform canopy protected those waiting outside for trains from the weather.

The last scheduled passenger train left this station on May 31, 1978, and the depot was closed in April of 1980. At the request of the City of Rock Island, the deteriorating depot was listed on the National Register of Historic Places in 1982. Efforts to revive the classic structure failed until 1994, when the City of Rock Island purchased the property from the Iowa Interstate Railroad. The City restored the exterior in 1996, and replaced the 80-foot tall clock tower. The adjacent freight house, built to the same style, was demolished in 1997 with its bricks and tiles salvaged and used as necessary for replacements on the depot renovation. In 1999, the station was sold and is now used as a brunch and banquet facility.

Rock Island to Des Moines was Subdivision 4 of the Rock Island's Illinois Division. The Iowa Interstate's Quad City yard was located in Rock Island at milepost 181.3 when the railroad was formed. The yard consisted of several tracks sandwiched between the IAIS mainline to the south and BNSF tracks to the north. Most of the yard's use was moved east to the new Silvis Yard when it was built, but the railroad still has "RI" assigned to the yard.

The Rock Island location has long been considered an important strategic location. In the 1830s, the U.S. Army began to secure the area and found that the area was the location of a large Sauk village, headed up by the great Sauk warrior Black Hawk. In the Mississippi River near the eastern shore was a large island known as Rock Island. This island made a perfect location for a military encampment and fortification, and soon a community began to grow up near the river.

With the growth of the area, the original city plat was filed on July 10, 1835, and named Stephenson. In 1841, the town was renamed Rock Island. The Chicago & Rock Island built into Rock Island by February 22, 1854, and the community boomed with access to eastern markets and the trade on the Mississippi River. Some of the first businesses included agriculture, lumber, railroad supplies, and heavy manufacturing of farming and mill equipment.

Rock Island is one of the "Quad Cities," joining Moline (IL), East Moline (IL), and Davenport (IA). The population of Rock Island is about 40,000 of the almost 400,000 of the metropolitan area. It is the county seat of Rock Island County and is home of the Rock Island Arsenal, the largest government-owned weapons manufacturing arsenal in the United States. The Arsenal is also the largest source of employment in town.

181.3 TERMINAL JUNCTION – Also known as BN Crossing, the former CRI&P mainline turns northward to cross the Government Bridge at the west end of the Rock Island yard. The IAIS Milan Branch turns to the southwest. The Burlington Northern once crossed the Rock Island on a diamond here, but today uses the Iowa Interstate tracks to the junction.

The Milan Branch heads south. BNSF, CP, and IAIS use this trackage until BNSF and Canadian Pacific swing west to cross the Mississippi River via the Crescent Bridge, although CP also uses the Government Bridge. The IAIS continues south to serve a number of industries, passing the old Milan depot at 4th Street and 4th Avenue in Milan. The Milan Branch splits at the depot. The line to the east used to pass through the coal mines at Coal Valley and eventually went all the way to Peoria, but the track was cut back in

Iowa City Subdivision

the 1950s. The track to the west is the former Rock Island Southern trackage that extended to Monmouth. More information about this line can be found on page 269.

181.6 SYLVAN SLOUGH BRIDGE – This bridge crosses a part of the Mississippi River to reach Arsenal Island, once known as Rock Island. It is known as the Sylvan Slough Bridge as this area was once more marsh, but Lock & Dam No. 15 has raised the level of the Mississippi River in this area and increased the water flow through this channel. The bridge was built in 1924 by the Fort Pitt Bridge Works as a series of through plate girder spans measuring a total of 705 feet long. This bridge once supported two tracks. Today, the north track has been removed. The western-most span has recently been replaced by a modern deck span.

Not far off the west end of this bridge is a spur track into the Rock Island Arsenal. A bit further west, the railroad goes to two tracks before the Government Bridge. The west end of this two-track segment ends at Milepost 182.6.

182.0 MISSISSIPPI RIVER BRIDGE – The Mississippi River separates Rock Island County in Illinois, and Scott County in Iowa. The Mississippi River flows just over 2,300 miles south from its source in Minnesota to the Gulf of Mexico. A major navigable waterway, it has played a key role in the history of the United States. The name means "Father of Waters" (from the Algonquian *misi sipi* or "big water").

Rock Island County was established by an act of the Illinois Legislature entitled "An act to establish Rock Island County," approved on February 9, 1831. The county was formed out of Jo Davies County and named for an island located in the Mississippi River. Almost immediately, the arrival of new settlers threatened a war with the several area tribes, such as the Sauk and Fox people. The resulting small battles and political maneuvers basically prevented the county from being organized until 1833. George Davenport, for whom Davenport, Iowa, is named, was elected as one of the three first county commissioners. The city of Rock Island is the county seat.

Scott County was surveyed in 1837, and the county was established by the Wisconsin territorial legislature in that same year. (At the time, what is now Iowa was part of the Wisconsin Territory.) It was named for General Winfield Scott, the presiding officer at the signing of the peace treaty ending the Black Hawk War. Scott, known as "Old Fuss and Feathers" and later the "Grand Old Man of the Army," served on active duty as a general longer than any other man in American history, and as the Commanding General of the United States Army for twenty years, again, longer than any other holder of the office. During his forty-seven-year career, he commanded forces in the War of 1812, the Black Hawk War (1832), the Second Seminole War (1835-1842), the Mexican-American War (1846-1848), and, briefly, the American Civil War. Scott is famous for conceiving the Union strategy known as the Anaconda Plan that would be used to defeat the Confederacy.

Government Bridge

The Mississippi River Bridge, otherwise known as the Government Bridge, is a 3150-foot long double-deck, through-truss structure owned and maintained by the Army Corps of Engineers as a link between Davenport (Iowa) on the west, Arsenal Island (in the middle of the river), and Rock Island (Illinois) on the east. This bridge has a great deal of historic heritage. This is near the location where railroad and water transportation had its greatest battle and set the stage for a national railroad network. As the U.S. Corps of Engineers has stated, "Direct transport of goods to and from the East by land rather than by water to St. Louis or New Orleans appeared to be a threat to the steamboat industry. Because of the steamboat monopoly on transportation of goods, prices were high. When the first bridge across the Mississippi was built at Rock Island, Steamboat Packet companies definitely felt their livelihood threatened."

A website established by the Army Corps of Engineers gives a good history of the Rock Island area, including the Government Bridge. This website provided much of the information that follows.

The first train crossed the Mississippi River Bridge at Davenport on April 14, 1856. On May 6 of the same year, the steamboat *Effie Afton* was making a trip north to Minneapolis-St. Paul. Passing under the bridge, the boat hit one of the pilings, proceeded a little ways further, stopped, and then the boat was carried by the current back down river, crashing into the bridge. A fire ignited the *Effie Afton,* destroying the boat and parts of the bridge. The ship's owner sued the railroad and bridge company in an effort to have the bridge removed, but Abraham Lincoln successfully defended the railroad all the way to the Supreme Court.

Over the next decade, a combination of bridge strikes by boats and damage by ice caused a need for a new bridge. During the study, the government proposed the bridge be moved to its present site. Major G. K. Warren of the St. Paul Office of Engineers was placed in a supervisory position overseeing the construction of the new Rock Island Bridge in 1869. He made numerous design changes to provide both better rail alignment and an improved route for steamboats. Warren designed the bridge with the railroad on the upper level and the wagonway on the lower level. Warren's drawspan was 366 feet long and operated on a pivot. That pivot is still in operation today, though the rest of the bridge has been redesigned. Because of funding problems, Warren designed the bridge as a single track operation although the piers were designed and built for double track. The 1546-foot long bridge was completed under the direction of Colonel John N. Macomb and opened to traffic in November of 1872. The total construction cost was $999,261.

By 1888, with a mule-drawn streetcar using part of the bridge, heavier railroad cars and engines, and the need for double track for the railroad, the bridge was quickly becoming outdated. In March 1895, Congress authorized construction to replace the 1872 bridge. Construction took place span by span to keep rail traffic moving. The updated bridge finally opened on December 1, 1896. Except for the limestone piers being covered with a layer of concrete in the 1920s, the bridge has remained essentially the same since this rebuild. Joint ownership was held by the Rock Island Railroad and the government for 84 years. In 1980, the railroad went out of business and the ownership of the bridge and all its features were deferred to the government.

Speaking of trolleys on this bridge, trolley service continued between Davenport (IA) and Rock Island (IL) until 1940, when the bridge line was discontinued. This was the last trolley line in the area as all other trolley lines in the Quad Cities had been discontinued in 1936.

Under the east end of the bridge is the lock for Lock & Dam No. 15, with the dam located just downstream. The bridge's turnspan is used to clear many of the lineboats pushing barges up and down the river. Opened on March 7, 1934, the dam is built with 11 gates and is a total of 1203 feet long. The gates are hollow metal tubes that can be lowered into the water to block the river flow. This is reported to be the largest dam in the world made exclusively from roller gates. These roller gates were new technology in the late 1920s. In fact, the U.S. Army reportedly stole the technology from Germany after WWI.

The Railroads

The west end of the bridge passes over the Canadian Pacific mainline to Kansas City. These tracks have a somewhat confusing history. Many people think of these tracks as being former Milwaukee Road. That is somewhat true. In reality, these tracks were part of the Milwaukee Road's Kansas City Cutoff. However, the Milwaukee Road originally used the tracks of other railroads from Clinton (IA) to Davenport and on south to Muscatine (IA).

Beginning just south of this bridge, the Milwaukee Road used CRI&P tracks south from Davenport to Mus-

Iowa City Subdivision

catine (IA). These trackage rights were made available in return for the Rock Island using the Milwaukee Road tracks between Albert Lea (MN) and the Minnesota Twin Cities. Northward toward Clinton, the Milwaukee Road used the Davenport, Rock Island & North Western Railway, jointly owned by the Burlington and the Milwaukee Road.

The Davenport, Rock Island & North Western Railway (DRI&NW) started in 1884 as the Davenport & Rock Island Railway Bridge Company. In 1895, it became the Davenport & Rock Island Bridge Railway and Terminal Company, and the DRI&NW in 1898. The railway operated from Clinton to Davenport, and then across its own bridge (known as the Crescent Railroad Bridge) to East Moline. In March 1901, the owners of the DRI&NW leased all of their property to the CB&Q and the Chicago, Milwaukee & St. Paul for an estimated profit of over one million dollars. The railroad was split in 1995 with BN getting the bridge and the Illinois trackage, and Soo Line (it had bought the Milwaukee Road in 1985) getting the track in Iowa. The I&M Rail Link acquired this line on April 5, 1997, which became the Iowa, Chicago & Eastern Railroad on July 31, 2002. In 2008, the line was sold back to Canadian Pacific, which owned the Soo Line.

Also near the west end of the bridge at one time was the Clinton, Davenport & Muscatine Railway, an electric interurban line. The company dates back to the Iowa Illinois Railway, which in 1904 built a 35-mile long interurban electric railway from Clinton to Davenport. In 1912, the Davenport & Muscatine Railway built an interurban electric railway from Davenport to Muscatine. That same year, United Light & Railways bought both interurbans, but operated them independently until merging them in 1926. With business declining and nearby steam roads providing freight competition, the line to Muscatine was abandoned in 1938. Two years later the Davenport-Clinton line was abandoned except for the 14 miles from Davenport to LeClaire. This section was acquired by the Davenport, Rock Island & North Western.

183.2 DAVENPORT – Davenport was named for Colonel George Davenport. The town was established in 1839 and incorporated on February 5, 1851. Davenport is the county seat of Scott County.

Davenport, Iowa, was part of the Louisiana Purchase. During the War of 1812, the British military, along with the Sauk and Fox Indian tribes, fought against the Americans near Davenport in 1814. In August, Major Zachary Taylor, later President, fought a battle east of what is now Credit Island Park, in Davenport. After the war, the U.S. Army established Fort Armstrong on the northwestern tip of Arsenal Island. It was assigned the responsibility of monitoring fur trade traffic in the area and keeping the peace between local Native American tribes. Colonel George Davenport arrived in 1816, working as a supplier for the garrison. Davenport later participated in founding several area communities (including Muscatine and Rock Island) and served on the first county commission for Rock County, Illinois.

In May, 1854, the first rail for a railroad in Iowa was laid in Davenport at the highwater mark. The first locomotive on Iowa soil was set up at Davenport a few weeks afterward, and was christened *Antoine Le Claire*. Antoine Le Claire, the son of a French-Canadian father and a mother from the Potawatomie tribe, was an important leader in early Davenport and is considered to be one of its principal founders. Le Claire worked as a U.S. Army interpreter and was able to explore the area, claiming land in the Davenport area. He also was involved with the first railroad in Iowa, thus the name of the locomotive.

The line between the west end of Government Bridge and Western Avenue was raised by the railroad in 1902 to eliminate the many grade crossings. The mainline was built to hold two mainline tracks, with the north track still used today. To cross the many streets, the bridges were built as deck plate girder spans. However, two were upgraded in 1928 as Warren through truss spans – 3rd Street and 4th Street – to add clearance for larger trucks on the streets.

Iowa City Subdivision

The Rock Island had a passenger station between Harrison and Main Streets on the north side of the Davenport City Hall. It is gone and the space is used as a parking lot. The Davenport Union Station (used by CMStP&P, DRI&NW, and CB&Q and today listed on the National Register of Historic Places) has been restored and is used as a welcome center. The two-story brick station was built in 1924 and is located along the Mississippi River south of the Government Bridge at 102 S. Harrison Street. It replaced three separate stations that were located over the several blocks to the east. Next door is the former Union Station mail and express building, also built of brick in 1924. Today, it is used as an office building.

Several freight houses also still stand in Davenport. The Milwaukee Road brick freight house, built in 1917, located a block west of the Union Station, is listed on the National Register of Historic Places. The building has a two-story office building on the eastern end and is used by the local farmer's market. The Rock Island freight house is located at 505 Iowa Street, several blocks north of the IAIS tracks at the west end of Government Bridge. Today, this brick building is used as lofts and still maintains its "Rock Island Lines" lettering above the west entrance. The open area to the east of the building was once full of tracks used for local freight service. The Rock Island development in this area started in the 1880s when a rail yard was built east of Iowa Street. In 1887, the railroad added a locomotive roundhouse and a freight car repair shop. The shops and yard were removed by 1910 and the area was instead used to serve local warehouses and factories.

Former Rock Island freighthouse in Davenport, Iowa. Photo by Barton Jennings.

183.7 MISSOURI DIVISION JUNCTION – This is the junction between the east-west line between Chicago and Omaha, and the River Route Bypass line to Kansas City and the southwest. Today, the line acts as an interchange track to the Canadian Pacific.

Trains heading west must face a 1.0% grade for the next several miles as the railroad curves its way out of the Mississippi River valley and through Davenport.

186.2 FARNAM – Farnam is basically a part of Davenport. The railroad location was named for Henry Farnam, one-time Chief Engineer, board member, and president of the Mississippi & Missouri Railroad. Farnam's engineering career got its start when he studied mathematics on his own during his teens. In 1820, he gained employment on the Erie Canal. There, he studied surveying and engineering under Benjamin Wright, one of America's most famous civil engineers at the time. After learning the craft, Farnam was employed as a surveyor on the Erie Canal and as a construction superintendent on the New Haven & Northampton Canal, also known as the Farmington Canal. He was later instrumental in building the railroad that replaced the canal in 1848. In 1850, Henry Farnam moved to Illinois where he partnered with Joseph E. Sheffield to build the Chicago, Rock Island & Pacific Railroad, serving as its chief engineer. In 1854 he became that railroad's president, an office he held until his retirement in 1863.

Just east of Farnam the railroad serves Phoenix Closures, delivering carloads of plastic pellets. Phoenix Closures makes injection-molded closures – yes, lids for items like peanut butter jars.

Until 1899, Farnam was the west end of double track out of Chicago.

186.3 BRAMMER – Brammer, and Farnam, are in an industrial area just west of Central Park Avenue, in the western part of Davenport. Brammer was the location of the Brammer Manufacturing Company, now Brammer Company LLC. Brammer manufactures wood kitchen cabinets and counter tops.

186.6 DUCK CREEK BRIDGE – The railroad crosses Duck Creek, and the Duck Creek Parkway Trail, using the southernmost of two 63-foot deck plate girder spans. Duck Creek is about twenty miles long and flows into the Mississippi River between Bettendorf and Riverdale. The parkway follows much of the creek but is less than 15 miles long, passing through multiple parks. The parkway is the oldest recreational trail in the Quad Cities and dates to the 1930s when the first section was built as a park road.

189.8 INTERSTATE 280 – The railroad bridges over I-280, which wraps around the southwest and west sides of the Quad Cities and serves as an alternative route through the metropolitan area. The railroad has just about reached the top of the grade here at an elevation of 760 feet. Heading west, the railroad passes through a number of large farms and slowly drops to the Cedar River at Moscow, following the route of Mud Creek.

Just west of here was once the station of Turnout, located at Milepost 190.0. Documents from 1910 show that this was a day and night telegraph station and that the Telegraph Call was "AU." However, no agent was listed for the station.

194.1 WALCOTT – There is a 6520-foot siding to the north of the mainline on the east side of town between mileposts 193.0 and 194.2. After 1899, the second track was extended west. When the railroad reverted back to a single main track, the south track was kept and the north track abandoned. This siding uses some of the old north main track. There is also a short industry track downtown that serves Central Petroleum Company and River Valley Co-op, a grain elevator and fertilizer storage facility.

Until the railroad arrived, this part of Iowa was an almost endless open prairie, the home of the Kaskaskia Indians. Before European settlement began, the Kaskaskias were driven out of the area by the Mesquaki tribe, part of the Canadian Iroquois. The Mesquaki remained in the area with many obtaining land or marrying with Europeans. The tribe is known as the "only Indian Tribe to purchase land in Iowa" when they established the Mesquaki Indian Settlement on July 13, 1857. The Meskwaki Nation also owns the Meskwaki Bingo Casino Hotel in Tama, west of Cedar Rapids, Iowa.

The City of Walcott, today with a population of about 1600, was originally platted in 1854 by the railroad. Within a year, the railroad was providing service to the community and its population began to grow. Also in 1855, William Walcott donated $500 for the construction of a school building, with the requirement that the town be named after him. Walcott, being a director of the Chicago & Rock Island Railroad, had a great deal of influence and got his way.

Iowa City Subdivision

In 1857, the railroad sponsored a land sale around Walcott (spelled Wolcott on some documents from the time) with prices as low as 75 cents an acre. At first, the land was bought by Scotch-Irish who were working on the railroad, and farms began to develop south and west of the town. In the early 1870s, a major change in the population occurred as large numbers of Germans moved to the area, most from northern Germany. With the population growth, Walcott was incorporated in July, 1894.

Germans continued to settle in the area, and by 1910, nearly nine-tenths of the farmland in Scott County was owned by German immigrants or their descendants. The farms were on rich soils, and with good transportation to the markets, several local banks held large volumes of cash. In fact, in 1911, Walcott was declared the richest town in the USA in consideration of the bank deposits for its population, according to Dunn & Co. in the *Bankers' Journal of New York*. While not quite as rich today, Walcott is home of the world's largest truckstop, Iowa 80 Truckstop, to the north on Interstate 80.

195.3 COUNTY LINE – This county line is between Scott County to the east and Muscatine County to the west. The county line can be seen at an old farm field road just west of Walcott. **Muscatine County** was named for the Muscatine Island in the Mississippi River. The word Muscatine is believed to be a version of a Fox word for flat place or prairie. Muscatine County was formed on December 7, 1836, and the county seat is Muscatine, located on the Mississippi River southwest of the Quad Cities.

199.2 STOCKTON – Stockton is not a big place, with a population of about 200. It has a post office, several blocks of houses, and a small grain elevator on the southeast side of town. The street to the south of the tracks is Depot Street while Railroad Street is to the north. There are no tracks here today except for the Iowa Interstate mainline.

Stockton is another Iowa town created by the railroad as it built through the area. The town was established in 1855, the same year that a post office opened. It was incorporated in 1902. Some sources report that the area had other names earlier, names such as Farnham, Fulton and Prairie Mills. The railroad seemed to have had a say in the naming, but the source is not clear. The railroad built a number of stock pens here and Stockton was once a major cattle and hog shipping point. Because of this, there have been suggestions that the town's name came from the stock raised and shipped here.

Stockton was once a railroad junction town. A Rock Island line between Bennett (IA) to the north, and Blue Grass (IA) and on into Davenport to the south, once crossed the original mainline. The Davenport, Iowa & Dakota Rail Road Company (DI&D) was incorporated on May 29, 1882, to build a railroad between Davenport and the Territory of Dakota. An 1888 amendment added "through the State of Iowa, and into and through the State of Minnesota and Territory of Dakota, to the Pacific Coast and to the British Possessions; and from Davenport, Iowa, into and through the State of Illinois to the great lakes and the Atlantic Ocean." Obviously, the company had grand plans to build rail lines across much of North America.

Within several years, the line from Davenport to Stockton and on to Sunbury was built. The line was extended another five miles to Bennett by 1890, a pace far short of the company's charter. On November 21, 1892, the DI&D was sold to the Burlington, Cedar Rapids & Northern Railway Company, later part of the Rock Island system of railroads. As the Rock Island consolidated their many parts, the duplicate lines west from Davenport were eliminated, with the CRI&P abandoning the DI&D line between Stockton and Davenport in 1925. The line northward to Bennett lasted a bit longer, but was abandoned in 1943 due to lack of business and the need for the track material elsewhere during WWII.

Iowa City Subdivision

At Stockton, little remains of the Davenport, Iowa & Dakota. The line passed through the south side of town about two blocks south of the current Iowa Interstate line through what is today Smith Drive, basically an alley between buildings. It then crossed the IAIS mainline just north of today's Daniel Schumaker Farm just west of Stockton.

200.3 MUD CREEK BRIDGE – The railroad crosses Mud Creek where the north and south forks merge. The bridge consists of three 33-foot long deck plate girder spans. The unused spans for the north main track still exist.

201.1 COUNTY LINE – The county line can be found where U.S. Highway 6 comes in from the north side of the tracks and turns west to follow the tracks into Durant. Heading west, the railroad is actually heading slightly northwest. In this area, **Scott County** wraps around the east and north side of Muscatine County, so the railroad re-enters Scott County for less than a mile.

201.4 COUNTY LINE – The county line is 14th Avenue, also known as Vail Avenue, on the east side of Durant. At this county line, the railroad exits Scott County and enters Cedar County. **Cedar County** was created on December 21, 1837, from sections of Dubuque County, and named for the Cedar River, which flows through the county. It is the only county in Iowa that shares the name of a tree. Tipton, located to the northeast of Iowa City, is the county seat.

Cedar County seems to have a history of unique violence. In the 1850s, John Brown (of Harpers Ferry fame) established a headquarters in the county while planning the raid on Harpers Ferry. Cedar County was also the focus of the Iowa Cow War of 1931. This series of protests and actual battles began in 1929 when Iowa passed a law that required all dairy and breeding cattle be tested for tuberculosis by veterinarians, and any sick cows be destroyed with the State paying an indemnity. For two years, farmers from this area unsuccessfully protested the law, claiming that the test was unreliable, caused abortions in cattle, lowered the quality of milk, and reduced a cow's milk output.

In February 1931, an estimated one thousand farmers took a train from Cedar County to Des Moines to protest the law. They also began threatening veterinarians, preventing them from conducting their tests. Iowa responded by providing legal escorts, which led to the September 21, 1931, stand-off at the Jake Lenker farm south of Tipton. Reportedly, two veterinarians and 65 officers were met by 400 farmers and violence erupted. The next day, the Iowa governor declared martial law and sent 31 Iowa National Guard units to Tipton. Eventually, the testing was done and several of the Cow War leaders were arrested, convicted, and sentenced to three years in the Iowa State Penitentiary. They were all quickly paroled and the challenge to the law ended by 1935.

Herbert Hoover, the 31st president, was born in the county in 1874. The Herbert Hoover National Historic Site at West Branch (east of Iowa City) preserves the cottage and blacksmith shop where Hoover was born. He was orphaned at age nine, and then left West Branch, never to live here again.

202.0 DURANT – Durant was founded in 1854 and incorporated on July 1, 1867. Some sources show that this location was to be named Fulton, but then initially named Brayton for its founder. According to the City of Durant's website: "In 1854, Benjamin B. Brayton, a civil engineer employed by the Rock Island Railroad, came to town to negotiate railroad business. During this time, Mr. Brayton laid out and platted the town. It was then that Mr. Thomas C. Durant, a close friend of Mr. Brayton's, announced that he would donate $800 to be used for the construction of a schoolhouse for the children of this community. To honor this contribution, Mr. Brayton named this new town 'Durant' in honor of his esteemed friend."

Dr. Thomas Clark Durant is famous in railroad history. He was an initial investor in the Mississippi & Missouri Rail

Road and made a fortune by buying land along the route. Durant was reportedly the person who hired Abraham Lincoln to defend the M&M after the Mississippi River Bridge was hit in 1856. Durant later helped found Union Pacific, which in 1862, was selected by President Lincoln to be the eastern leg of the first transcontinental railroad. He was vice-president of the Union Pacific in 1869 when it met the Central Pacific Railroad at Promontory Summit in Utah Territory.

The town of Durant used to have a simple wooden train station with an agent and semaphores for issuing train orders, located just east of the Columbus grade crossing and on the south side of the tracks. At the time, track charts showed there to be two main tracks, a siding to the north, and several industry and team tracks to the south. Today in downtown Durant, there is a short industrial spur into Microbial Genetics, a division of Pioneer Hi-Bred International. On the west side of town, there is a busy spur into the Norfolk Iron & Metal facility to the south. They have been a family-run business since 1908, starting as a hide and scrap metal company and now cutting and manufacturing carbon steel parts for a number of area manufacturing firms. The population of Durant is about 2000.

203.2 BIG ELKHORN CREEK BRIDGE – Big Elkhorn Creek forms from several small streams about ten miles north of here, flows south and enters into Mud Creek just to the south. The railroad has a bridge made up of two 44-foot long deck plate girder spans.

Twin State, Inc., formerly Twin-State Engineering and Chemical Company, is to the south. The firm was founded in March, 1958, and manufactures and markets a complete line of liquid fertilizers. The switch to serve them is just west of the Big Elkhorn Creek bridge.

204.0 TWIN STATES – There is a 5360-foot siding to the north with the switches at mileposts 203.5 and 204.5. The siding was named for the nearby Twin State facility.

205.0 COUNTY LINE – At Durant, the railroad turns back to heading slightly southwest and then crosses back into Muscatine County just west of the Wahkonsa Country Club.

207.6 WILTON – Wilton was originally known as Glendale, but was named Wilton Junction when the town was officially established in 1854 on property owned by a Mr. Stone and a Mr. Green. The name Wilton came from Wilton, Maine, the original home of an early resident, a Mr. Butterfield. The town was incorporated on February 12, 1878. Wilton German English College existed here from 1894 to 1905. The property was later turned into City Park and some of the original buildings still stand. Today, Wilton is the center of a large agricultural area and has a population of about 3000.

The Mississippi & Missouri Rail Road Company had built to Wilton by mid-September, 1855. The company also built a line southward from Wilton to Muscatine (IA) by November 20, 1855. However, after the River Route Bypass from Davenport to Muscatine was completed in 1880, this line existed on local service. The Depression and local roads ended that source of traffic and the line was abandoned in May 1934.

There was also once a short branchline from Wilton to Lime City to the north. Lime City was created in the 1880s because of the lime industry. In 1883, it was known as Lime Kiln. During the 1880s, T. Munn owned the grocery store and secured a post office which he named Munn. In 1894, the post office was renamed Lime City, but it closed about 1903 when the quarry town closed. Apparently, the railroad was abandoned about the same time.

As can be seen, Wilton was once a busy railroad town. According to the National Register of Historic Places report, there was a "quarter-round roundhouse" here, along with several related repair buildings, that were removed by 1890. There were also once two different water towers, one east (1880-1950s) and one west (1920s) of the station.

Iowa City Subdivision

The first passenger train arrived at Wilton on November 20, 1855. At the time, the station was a simple wooden shed, replaced in 1856 by a more formal depot and freight house. Being at a division point, the railroad assigned a number of train crews to the location and built servicing facilities for the cars and locomotives. By 1866, a roundhouse and turntable, a carpenter shop, and a dispatch office were all in operation at Wilton. Soon, the railroad had 100-125 employees here. By 1885, the repair shops had doubled in size and the roundhouse had nine stalls. However, the facilities were removed during the next decade.

The current station was built in 1898. The station was listed on the National Register of Historic Places in 1988. According to the application, at its peak, the brick station "was located at the east end of a triangular-shaped railroad property in the center of the town. The Wilton Branch, connecting Muscatine to the south, with Wilton, connected with the main line at that point. A large open area to the east and south of the depot featured bricked walkways, and a park-like setting."

Today, the station is owned by the Wilton Historical Society, which has placed CRI&P caboose 17087 next to the building. The caboose is actually a former Milwaukee Road car, not Rock Island.

In downtown Wilton, the Iowa Interstate serves an agricultural supplier. On the west side of town off the North Star siding, there is a spur to the north to reach JM Eagle, the world's largest plastic pipe manufacturer. Look for the piles of blue pipe.

210.0 NORTH STAR – Just west of Wilton is North Star siding, stretching from Milepost 208.5 to 210.9. North Star siding is named for the large electric-arc furnace mini-mill to the north, originally built in 1974 by North Star Steel Company. The steel company, founded in October 1965 in St. Paul, Minnesota, had just been bought by Cargill. On November 1, 2004, Gerdau Ameristeel acquired the mill.

According to the company's website, the "Wilton plant is a steel mini-mill that uses an electric arc furnace (EAF) for steelmaking and 100% recycled steel scrap to manufacture steel products. The recycled steel scrap is melted in the EAF and refined by adding alloys, carbon, and other materials. The molten steel is tapped into a preheated ladle and transferred to the tundish at the billet caster. From the tundish, the molten steel flows into molds that make square billets that are then cooled, solidified, and cut to length. The billets are stored until needed, then fed into the reheat furnace and brought to a temperature of about 2,200°F. When the correct rolling temperature is reached, the billet is passed through water-cooled roll stands where the steel is formed and shaped. The final step involves shearing the steel products into custom lengths, which are bundled together for storage. The Wilton plant produces structural steel products including flats, angles, rebar, and round-cornered squares."

210.3 SUGAR CREEK BRIDGE – The Sugar Creek area was referenced in many early reports about the area, with the valley described as fertile. In 1840, a project was started to change the route of Sugar Creek, turning it west to enter the Cedar River at Moscow. There were also plans to build a dam across the creek to obtain a fourteen-foot drop for mills. Little work was actually accomplished.

According to the *Sixth Annual Report of the Directors to the Stockholders of the Chicago Rock Island and Pacific Railway Company* for the year ending March 31, 1886, "near Moscow, Iowa, a substantial iron bridge, 127 feet in length, has been substituted for a wooden one over Sugar Creek."

211.2 MOSCOW – Moscow is a small town on the east bank of the Cedar River. While the river attracted settlers from the beginning, Moscow wasn't laid out until 1836 when Henry Webster and Dr. Charles Drury developed the community. Reportedly, the name was chosen because a number of the residents were from Moscow, Ohio. The Moscow post office opened on May 1, 1837.

Iowa City Subdivision

When founded, the Cedar River and water transportation was the center of focus. Because of this, there were plans to build a canal from here to the Mississippi River at Muscatine. The Moscow Canal, as it was known, was actually incorporated on January 12, 1839, as the Bloomington & Cedar River Canal Company. The canal was never built, and the arrival of the railroad in 1855 ended any major canal plans. However, the Cedar River was still important and brought industry to Moscow as a great deal of sand was shipped by rail and the river was used for decades by the ice industry. Moscow boomed for a few years with the railroad, but was soon surpassed by other communities in the region.

211.4 CEDAR RIVER BRIDGE – The Cedar River Bridge is an eleven-span, deck girder design. It was originally double track, but today only the northernmost track is still in place and used. The current bridge was built in 1913, with the superstructure supplied by the American Bridge Company of New York and the substructure work done by the Cedar Rapids Construction Company of Cedar Rapids, Iowa.

IAIS 705 eastbound on the Cedar River Bridge, Moscow, Iowa. Photo by Barton Jennings.

212.3 WENDLING QUARRIES SPUR – This spur is 530 feet long and is located at the small community of Hinkeyville. According to an 1865 history of the area, "A quarry of good limestone is opened by the railroad west of Cedar River." This later became the Wendling Quarries to the south.

215.9 ATALISSA – Atalissa was founded in 1856 and incorporated on March 26, 1900. It was named by Captain William Lunby, one of the town's founders. The name Atalissa came from a mining community in California that was named for a local Indian woman. The old wooden depot, heavily boarded up, still stands on the south side of the tracks next to Railroad Street, even though Depot Street is to the north. There is also a short spur track here serving the County Wide AG Service complex, generally handling fertilizers.

Just west of town, the railroad has a grade crossing with U.S. Highway 6, the Grand Army of the Republic Highway. The highway stretches from Bishop, California to Provincetown, Massachusetts. It follows the Iowa Interstate across parts of Iowa.

IAIS 705, Atalissa, Iowa. Photo by Barton Jennings.

Iowa City Subdivision

220.4 WAPSINONOC CREEK BRIDGE – This is actually the East Branch of the Wapsinonoc Creek as the West Branch is west of West Liberty. The name comes from an Indian name meaning "smooth-surfaced and meandering stream." The surrounding Township was named for the creek. The stream flows to the south and eventually enters the Cedar River.

The bridge consists of two 60-foot long deck plate girder spans. The IAIS uses the north CRI&P track alignment, and the south spans still cross the creek

221.3 WEST LIBERTY – West Liberty was originally established nearby and was known as Wapsipinoc Settlement. The first post office in the West Liberty area was established on March 24, 1838, and was known as Old Liberty. When the railroad built through the area in 1855, the town started moving to the railroad. Soon a new community was platted and the town of West Liberty was created. West Liberty was named for Liberty, Ohio, with the word "west" added since it was west of Ohio. The town was incorporated on January 1, 1868. The railroad was lined with grain elevators, lumber and coal sheds, and stockyards.

Originally, as far as railroading goes, West Liberty was notable as the junction point between the Rock Island's east-west mainline (now the IAIS main) and the Rock's former north-south Burlington, Cedar Rapids & Northern Railway mainline from Manly, Iowa, south through Cedar Rapids, West Liberty, and finally to Burlington, Iowa. At the junction sat the 1897 passenger depot, serving both lines.

The April 1, 1899, CRI&P annual report stated: "Second Track. – A Second Track has been constructed from Farnam, Iowa, to West Liberty, Iowa, a distance of 34-77/100 miles, which makes a continuous double track from Chicago, Ills., to the connection with B., C. R. & N. R.R. at West Liberty, Iowa, 221 miles." This construction was caused by the move of most Davenport to West Liberty rail traffic to this line, with traffic then split between the lines west toward Omaha and north toward Cedar Rapids.

In 1901, the line was double track all the way west to Milepost 236.8 at Iowa City, but was back to single track west of Milepost 221.3 soon after. The double track west of here was replaced by CTC signaling.

At one time, the diamond at West Liberty had interchange tracks on all corners except the southeast. A seven-stall roundhouse and turntable once stood between the diamond and interchange track in the northwest quadrant. Tracks from both mainlines reached the turntable. A five-track yard, with each track assigned a specific direction, once existed just west of the diamond.

Today, the Rock Island station and its museum is the center of Railroad Park and Heritage Park. Besides the station, there is restored Rock Island caboose #2013, one of those cabooses built from a wooden boxcar in the 1930s and 1940s. There is also a steam locomotive, a small 0-4-0ST built by Davenport Locomotive Works in 1925. Carrying construction number 2056, it was built for P. T. Clifford & Sons of Valparaiso, Indiana, and was moved to West Liberty in June 2014. A number of small buildings such as a barn, a one-room schoolhouse, and a tourist cabin are also preserved in the park.

IAIS 513 eastbound at West Liberty, Iowa. Photo by Barton Jennings.

The BCR&N mainline is gone (most is now a hiking trail) and the IAIS mainline is only a single track, passing behind the busy downtown area, designated as the West Liberty Commercial Historic District and listed on the Na-

Iowa City Subdivision

tional Register of Historic Places. South of the mainline is the West Liberty Foods turkey processing plant. There is a short railroad siding to the west of town (Mileposts 221.4-222.2), as well as the West Liberty ECI (East Central Iowa Intermodal) at Milepost 226.7, an intermodal facility that opened on January 27, 1997.

224.0 COUNTY LINE – The railroad again bounces between Muscatine and Cedar Counties as it heads to the northwest, this time as it crosses a small stream in a patch of woods.

226.3 DOWNEY – Hugh D. Downey acquired the land at this location in 1853, and created the town of Downey when the railroad arrived here. On June 29, 1869, the eighty acres on which Downey was laid out was purchased by A. B. Cornwall, who had it re-surveyed. The small community never incorporated, but soon had a general store, carpenter shop, several stock buyers, a school house, and several churches.

Today, Downey is a rural community of several dozen houses. There is also a rail spur here to serve a small agricultural facility to the north.

227.6 COUNTY LINE – This is the county line between Cedar County, to the east, and Johnson County, to the west. **Johnson County** was named for Richard Mentor Johnson, a veteran of the War of 1812, a member of the U.S. House of Representatives and Senate for Kentucky, and the ninth Vice President of the United States, serving in the administration of Martin Van Buren. Johnson was the only vice-president ever elected by the United States Senate under the provisions of the Twelfth Amendment.

As with many counties in Iowa, it was actually created by the Wisconsin territorial legislature. (At the time, what is now Iowa was part of the Wisconsin Territory.) On December 21, 1837, the county was carved out of territory formerly in Dubuque County. However, there was not enough population initially to operate its own government and Cedar County officials performed the tasks for several years.

Today, the county's population is about 150,000, making it the fifth-most populous county in Iowa. The county seat is Iowa City.

231.1 MIDWAY – Midway is located west of the American Legion Road overpass where the railroad curves to the north. Look for the small triangle of grassland and trees to the south. Little information about Midway exists except that there was a switch here when the railroad was first built.

232.0 AMERICAN – Planning for Amtrak service from Chicago to the Quad Cities and on to Des Moines calls for a siding at American "to enable freight trains to hold out of the congested industrial switching and freight train classification at Iowa City, without creating undo delays to passenger and freight trains at Iowa City."

Just west of here and between Taft Avenue (Milepost 232.75) and 1st Avenue (Milepost 235.07) are a number of tracks serving several rail customers. Part of this area is planned to be an industrial park. Because of the rail work in the area, the Iowa Interstate and the City of Iowa City replaced the 1st Avenue grade crossing with a railroad overpass in 2016.

236.8 IOWA CITY – "They'll come to Iowa City. They'll think it's really boring." That's a quote from the *Field of Dreams* movie. However, for the rail enthusiast, the statement might not really be true.

Before the construction of the South Amana Yard and the reorganization of the railroad's subdivisions, the Iowa Interstate's Subdivision 1 (east to Blue Island, near Chicago) and Subdivision 3 (west to Newton, Iowa) met at the yard at Iowa City (IC). The Cedar Rapids & Iowa City can also interchange cars here, especially from their line south to Hills. The IAIS has a decent-sized yard, and there once was an engine service facility at Iowa City. Most of the yard and shop work was moved west to the South Amana Shops in 2012.

Iowa City Subdivision

Until October 2004 when it was moved to Cedar Rapids, Iowa City was also the corporate headquarters for the IAIS.

The Mississippi & Missouri Rail Road was completed from Davenport to Iowa City on December 31, 1855, some four months before the Mississippi River Bridge was finished. The first passenger train arrived in Iowa City to a huge celebration held at the state capitol on January 3, 1856. The Chicago, Rock Island & Pacific Railroad passenger station, located on the north side of the tracks just east of the Iowa River bridge, was built in 1898. It was the third depot in Iowa City.

CRIP station, Iowa City, Iowa. Photo by Barton Jennings.

The Rock Island used to have double track from Chicago ending at Iowa City. However, timetables from the 1960s and 1970s show that double track ended at West Liberty and that CTC signaling existed from there to Iowa City.

Iowa City was originally located in May 1839 by a commission charged with selecting a capital for the Iowa Territory, fulfilling the desire of Governor Robert Lucas to move the capital out of Burlington and closer to the center of the territory. When statehood was announced in 1846, Iowa City became the first state capitol. The state capital was here until 1857 when Des Moines was chosen as the new state capitol. The "Old Capitol'" is now a National Historic Landmark.

Iowa City was officially incorporated on January 24, 1853. While it is no longer the capital of Iowa, it is the county seat of Johnson County. Not long after the capital moved, Iowa City became the location of the University of Iowa, which later became the first public university in the nation to admit men and women on an equal basis. Related to university life, the ACT, "America's Most Widely Accepted College Entrance Exam," is headquartered in Iowa City.

237.1 IOWA RIVER BRIDGE – This nine-span deck plate girder bridge was built with piers that had room for a second track, but that second track was never constructed. This structure was built in 1901 by the American Bridge Company. The Cedar Rapids & Iowa City rail line passes beneath the IAIS at the east end of the Iowa River bridge, while U.S. Highway 6 passes under the west end.

The Iowa River is a 300-mile long tributary of the Mississippi River. The river flows generally southward and passes through Iowa City and the University of Iowa campus here. The Iowa River is known for flooding, in spite of efforts to stop it. Two recent problems were the June 2008 Midwest floods, and the Great Flood of 1993.

238.0 STADIUM – Until the 1950s, tracks that served the nearby University of Iowa football stadium were shown in Rock Island employee timetables. Today, the area is served on game day by the *Hawkeye Express* passenger train, delivering football fans from parking lots on the west side of town.

239.3 CLEAR CREEK BRIDGE – Clear Creek starts to the west, south of the Amana Colonies. It flows east to here, and then just downstream Clear Creek enters the Iowa River.

241.0 VERNON – This is an old 1660-foot long siding with the west switch removed. The *Hawkeye Express* passenger train is often stored here between football games.

Iowa City Subdivision

242.3 INTERSTATE 80 – The railroad passes under I-80 for the sixth time since leaving Chicago, Illinois.

242.9 HAWKEYE – Hawkeye is the location of Hawkeye Foodservice Distribution, a privately owned broadline distributor of foodservice products. Hawkeye was started by Joseph Braverman, who came to the area from Russia in 1917. He developed a small chain of grocery stores around Iowa City and then expanded into regional product delivery. After the flood of July 13, 1962, the company moved from downtown to this location, David Braverman's farm. By 2012, Hawkeye Foodservice was servicing restaurants, hospitals, health care facilities, schools, amusement parks and hotels in 11 states, and was one of the top 30 food distributors in the nation. In that year, US Foods announced plans to buy the company to allow it to expand into Iowa.

A siding exists here with a track into the Consumers Cooperative ag facility. Just to the west is a track into Beisser Lumber Company.

243.6 INTERSTATE 380 – I-380 extends from the I-80 interchange, just to the south, northward to Cedar Rapids and on to Waterloo, Iowa. It is about 75 miles long and was built during the 1980s.

244.6 TIFFIN – This location was originally established in 1867 as the community of Copi. However, the original owner of the land, Rolla Johnson, changed it to Tiffin, named for Tiffin, Ohio. It was incorporated December 27, 1906. About 2000 people live here.

The Rock Island had a siding to the north here in the 1970s. Heading west, the railroad starts a steady climb of a maximum of 0.8%, peaking at Homestead. The railroad follows Clear Creek, often visible to the south. This area includes a number of rolling hills with a mix of farmland and woods.

251.6 OXFORD – Oxford is one of those towns whose name came about almost by accident. The location was originally called "Tank" because there was a railroad water tank here. The actual town was founded in 1868 by P. C. Wilcox. However, there was no agreement on what to name the town. Because of this, the petition to formally establish the town was filled out with everything but a town's name. W. H. Cotter, the person who was to submit the petition, took the form home where his wife suggested Oxford, for the name of her childhood town in New York. Other neighbors also suggested names, all of which were written on pieces of paper. Reportedly, Fred Cotter, the three-year-old child of the Cotter's, drew a name from the suggestions and Oxford was selected. Oxford was incorporated on April 8, 1881.

The railroad once had a long siding to the north and a short siding to the south. There is still a short spur track to the south to serve the small grain elevator here. The Rock Island station was east of the Augusta grade crossing, on the north side of the mainline with a siding running behind the building. The building was one-story and featured semaphore train order signals.

254.8 COUNTY LINE – Look for the road crossing of Johnson-Iowa Road NW. Johnson County is to the east while Iowa County is to the west. **Iowa County** was named for the Iowa River, which flows through the county. The county was formed on February 17, 1843. Trivia time: Iowa County is one of seven counties in the United States that shares its name with its state, along with Arkansas County, Hawaii County, Idaho County, New York County, Oklahoma County, and Utah County.

Iowa County is a rural county with a population of 16,355 in 2010. The county seat is Marengo. The county includes the Amana Colonies, seven villages of German Pietists. They moved to this area in 1855 to remain isolated, and lived a communal life until the mid-1930s. Today, the villages are a major tourist attraction and have been a National Historic Landmark since 1965.

Iowa County was a big supporter of the construction of the Mississippi & Missouri Railroad. In 1858, Iowa County voted to aid in the construction of the railroad, pledging the amount of $100,000 in bonds, in addition to the land grants across the county already issued by Congress. Even with the funding, construction didn't take place for several years.

256.6 HOMESTEAD – The Iowa Interstate has a siding here, approximately 3000 feet in length. Some histories of Iowa County state that the first European settlers, Linneas Niles and John Burgett, settled near Homestead. What is known for sure is that a post office opened here in 1852 with the name Homestead, almost a decade before the railroad built through the community in 1860. Almost immediately, the railroad sold their share of Homestead to the Amana Society, giving them access to the railroad. Of the Amana colonies, this is the only one without the word Amana in its name. According to reports, in 1881, Homestead "contained a train depot, hotel, post office, grain elevator, meeting house, schoolhouse, general store, lumber yard, and a large distributing warehouse."

For fans of actor Ashton Kutcher, Homestead is the town cited by him to be his home. Actually, growing up, he and his family lived four miles out of town. After his family moved, Ashton moved into Homestead for a while.

259.0 YOCUM CONNECTION – On February 11, 2000, Yocum Connection, a full wye interchange between Iowa Interstate's Iowa City Subdivision and the Third Subdivision of the Cedar Rapids & Iowa City near Homestead (IA), was placed into service. Yocum Connection became the new primary interchange point for the two railroads, replacing the Hill Track in Iowa City (IA), a steep piece of trackage that extends out of the west end of IAIS' yard. Yocum Connection was originally where the Milwaukee Road's Sixth Subdivision of the Iowa Division between Cedar Rapids and Ottumwa (IA), which joined their line between Davenport and Kansas City, passed under the former

Rock Island mainline. Today, the CIC's portion is all that remains.

The east wye switch at Yocum is at Milepost 258.5. Prior to the construction of a full wye, the junction had only a single leg and was known as Crandic Junction. The junction is named after former IAIS President Fred Yocum.

IAIS 510 eastbound, Yocum Connection, Iowa. Photo by Barton Jennings.

259.6 SOUTH AMANA YARD – In 2010, Iowa Interstate Railroad announced the construction of a new locomotive service facility and yard on 62 acres just west of Yocum Connection. The new 30,000 square foot, $24 million shop building was designed around the fourteen 4400-horsepower General Electric ES44AC locomotives the Iowa Interstate began buying in 2008. According to the railroad, the new locomotives didn't even fit in the old shops. The new shop complex was designed to accommodate up to five locomotives and included a wash bay and station to change wheel assemblies. Additionally, the new building was equipped with overhead cranes and below-ground walkways, allowing crews to work beneath locomotives.

The shop opened in October 2012 and was dedicated as the Dennis H. Miller Locomotive Works. Dennis Miller was promoted to President and CEO of the railroad in 2002 and became Vice Chairman of the Board in March of 2012.

Besides the shop complex, the railroad also built three train-length yard tracks to handle the traffic on and off the Cedar Rapids & Iowa City, the railroad's largest source of traffic. Additionally, crew staffing was moved from Iowa City to here for the mainline trains – Council Bluffs to Blue Island (CBBI) and Blue Island to Council Bluffs (BICB). This allows locomotives to be swapped and for freight cars to be added and subtracted to the trains. The yard tracks allow this to be done without blocking the mainline of the railroad, a major change from when area operations were based in the small yard at Iowa City. As business has grown, some trains now originate or terminate here, using the station code of "SA" for the yard.

IAIS Dennis H. Miller Locomotive Maintenance Works, South Amana, Iowa. Photo by Barton Jennings.

IAIS shops, South Amana, Iowa. Photo by Barton Jennings.

IAIS 510, South Amana, Iowa. Photo by Barton Jennings.

Newton Subdivision
South Amana (Iowa) to Des Moines (IA)

The Iowa City Subdivision of the Iowa Interstate stretches from Milepost 260.0 (South Amana), to Milepost 353.2 at Des Moines. The eastern half of the route was built by the Mississippi & Missouri, while the western half was built by the Chicago, Rock Island & Pacific Railroad after the 1866 merger. The line was part of a plan to provide a connection to the Union Pacific mainline at Omaha. Later, it also provided the shortest connection to the Nebraska, Kansas, and Colorado parts of the Rock system.

This part of the railroad features another major project of the Iowa Interstate – the Newton Yard relocation. Originally located near the heart of town, it was moved out to the northeastern edge of town in the late 1990s. This was done to make room for a Maytag expansion for their new corporate headquarters and additional parking. The new yard includes the Lee Horst Transportation Center, which in addition to providing intermodal services, also includes a small shop facility. The facility is named in honor of Lee Horst, a former General Road Foreman on IAIS and career railroad man who passed on in 2002.

Like much of the rest of the Chicago to Council Bluffs mainline, traffic across the Subdivision features the two main trains – BICB (Blue Island to Council Bluffs) and CBBI (Council Bluffs to Blue Island). A switcher is also based in the Newton area.

259.6 SOUTH AMANA YARD – Details on this location are in the Iowa City Subdivision information on page 144.

262.1 SOUTH AMANA – South Amana was founded in 1856 as one of the Amana Colonies. South Amana received its name because it was the southernmost of the Colonies. Its population is about 200 and the community includes several craft and furniture companies and stores. The town is to the south on U.S. Highway 6.

267.3 MARENGO – Marengo was established in 1845 when a commission was formed to locate a new county seat for

Iowa County. The town was established on May 24, 1847, by E. C. Lyon, and named for the Plains of Marengo in Italy, the location where French forces under Napoleon Bonaparte defeated an Austrian army in the Battle of Marengo, fought on June 14, 1800. Marengo was officially incorporated on July 4, 1859, more than a year before the Mississippi & Missouri Rail Road built through the town in October 1860. The elevation here is 738 feet above sea level, but with the Iowa River just north of town, flooding does occur.

The current Iowa County courthouse is located on the north side of Marengo and was completed in 1893. It was placed on the National Register of Historic Places in June, 1980. The Iowa Interstate has a 5330-foot long siding at Marengo, located to the north of the mainline. On the north side of the tracks is the large Marengo Elevator complex ("We want to elevate your profits!"), a local grain and feed company. East of the elevator is a spur track into the closed Quad/Graphics printing facility. Quad/Graphics, the printer of *Model Railroader* and other similar magazines, closed this plant in 2014.

IAIS 510 eastbound, Marengo, Iowa. Photo by Barton Jennings.

268.6 BIG BEAR CREEK BRIDGE – This bridge consists of three different type of bridge spans. From the east, there are three ballast deck pre-cast concrete spans, a 110-foot long quadrangular through truss built in 1901 by the American Bridge Company of New York, and then a through plate girder span. The bridge is a total of 310 feet long.

The Big Bear Creek flows into the Iowa River about two miles north of here. Heading west, the Chicago, Rock Island & Pacific Railroad left the Iowa River floodplain and started to follow Big Bear Creek. Before the railroad arrived, Big Bear Creek was noted for the timber that lined the stream, rare in this area of grassy plains. At least one sawmill was built on Big Bear Creek to cut this timber for early settlers. The creek was also important as an all-weather source of good water. Several major trails followed Big Bear Creek.

273.9 LADORA – This is a musical town, named by music teacher Mrs. Scofield, for the musical syllables la-do-ra. Ladora was surveyed in September, founded by James A. Paine on October 25, 1867, and incorporated on December 27, 1879. The population of Ladora in 1880 was 285, it was 283 in 2010.

The first small depot, measuring 16' x 22', was built in 1869. A replacement station was built in 1877. The railroad once also had a siding and elevator track to the south. Today, there is still a spur into the concrete elevator shell. In the 1870s, Ladora shipped out mainly corn and oats, with wheat, hogs, and cattle also being shipped out on the railroad.

To the south near the elevator is the building of the former Ladora Savings Bank, now the Ladora Bank Bistro. The building states that "the wealth of this community embodies the richness of her soil, the integrity, frugality and diligence of her people." The building was designed by architect Charles B. Zalesky, who was a partner in an architectural firm in Cedar Rapids, Iowa. The building was dedicated on July 26, 1920, but the bank failed and closed on July

27, 1931. Over the years, the building has been used as a number of businesses, including a Red Cross office, several antique stores, a truck driver rest area, an attorney's office, and today's restaurant. It has also served as a community center and polling place.

Former Ladora Savings Bank. Ladora, Iowa. Photo by Barton Jennings.

Inscription on the front of former Ladora Savings Bank. Photo by Sarah Jennings.

The first area post office was opened in 1865 on the nearby Wilson farm. While Mrs. Scofield came up with Ladora, the post office in Washington, D.C., spelled it La Dora, thinking that it was French. The post office moved to the Rock Island depot in 1869.

277.1 U.S. HIGHWAY 6 – The railroad passes under the highway, the Grand Army of the Republic Highway. The highway stretches from Bishop, California to Provincetown, Massachusetts. It follows the Iowa Interstate across parts of Iowa.

278.1 BIG BEAR CREEK BRIDGE – The railroad crosses Big Bear Creek again, this time using a through plate girder and a through truss span. Heading westward, the railroad continues to follow the easy grade created by the stream.

279.9 VICTOR – Victor was first known as Wilson, named after one of its original land owners. On April 12, 1854, George W. Wilson purchased the land from the United States which now includes the site of Victor. Wilson was a friend and business associate of many of the leaders of the Mississippi & Missouri Railroad, so he knew of the route that construction would take. When Iowa County and the State of Iowa voted to help fund the railroad, there was a requirement to build at least one hundred miles of track west of Davenport by January 1, 1862. This would put the line near the west side of Iowa County, meaning that Wilson's property could be very valuable as a town site. After a meeting with the railroad, arrangements were made for a route through the property and the creation of a town. George Wilson began building a depot on November 15, 1861, to mark the location. Soon a general store and a lumber yard stood nearby.

The town of Wilson was officially founded by Joseph Blackburn on May 5, 1863, but was renamed Victor in 1865 for a nearby post office. The post office was established in 1854 and named for Victor, New York. Victor was incorporated on November 30, 1868. A grain elevator and a stockyard were built by the late 1860s, supporting the shipments of corn, wheat, oats, hogs, cattle, sheep and horses.

Victor grew quickly, having a population of 691 in 1880. In 2010, 893 people lived in the community which brags that it is what many "new urbanists" would like to create in bigger cities. A short siding still exists to the north that is used to serve several agricultural facilities.

280.0 COUNTY LINE – The county line is at the westernmost grade crossing in Victor, known as County Line Road. It separates Iowa County to the east and Poweshiek County to the west.

Poweshiek County was formed in 1843 and named for Fox Chief Poweshiek. The word Poweshiek means "the roused bear." Poweshiek was known as the "Peaceful Indian," having signed the treaty that ended the Black Hawk War in 1832, the "Black Hawk Purchase." This treaty opened the first lands in Iowa for settlement by the whites. This area was reportedly Poweshiek's favorite hunting and fishing territory. He often lived in a small village near the southwest corner of the county. He and the survivors of his tribe left Iowa in the winter of 1845-46 for the reservation in Kansas.

The county seat is Montezuma, even though the largest town in Poweshiek County is Grinnell. From here to the western border of the county, there is a line of small towns. Combined with those along I-80 just a few miles to the south, the county has a population of about 20,000.

Poweshiek County was another county that subscribed to bonds to help pay for the railroad's construction. The bonds reportedly guaranteed that the railroad would be built quickly, but no construction took place and the County Supervisors refused to pay. However, a lawsuit that went all the way to the U.S. Supreme Court forced payment and the creation of taxes across the county.

282.2 CUB CREEK BRIDGE – According to the *Bridgehunter* website, this is a deck plate girder bridge built in 1892. They show that the main span was built by the Lassig Bridge &

Iron Works of Chicago, Illinois, while the approach spans were built by the American Bridge Company of New York.

Cub Creek forms to the southwest in the rolling hills just north of Interstate 80. It flows into Big Bear Creek just across the field to the north.

282.5 CARNFORTH – There was once the small community of Manatt located here. It was created in 1884 when the Chicago & North Western built a line through here from Belle Plaine on its mainline to the coal mines at What Cheer and Muchakinock to the south. Almost immediately, a post office was established as Manatt in 1884. Several months later, a railroad executive renamed it Carnforth, reportedly from a town name he found in a book he was reading at the time. The post office also made the change at the time, but it closed in 1907.

In 1896, an attorney for the CRI&P submitted a description of the C&NW line as part of a service complaint. "The North-Western line which crosses at Carnforth is but little more than a coal road, built from Belle Plaine to the Muchakinock mines. There is but little freight originating on that line, and the gross freight charge on freight that could be tendered to us at Carnforth originating on the lines of the NorthWestern would not amount to $50 per year." After the mines closed, the line was abandoned in 1958.

Today, the north-south grade can barely be seen running through a small patch of woods to the south. The old Carnforth depot, originally built by the Rock Island, was relocated four miles east of Victor. Heading west, the grade continues a slow climb as it follows the Big Bear Creek.

283.9 LITTLE BEAR CREEK BRIDGE – This is another bridge that was built in 1892 when the line was upgraded for heavier trains. It was built by the Lassig Bridge & Iron Works of Chicago, Illinois. It consists of five deck plate girder spans.

Big Bear Creek turns to the northwest near here, and the railroad starts following Little Bear Creek as it heads west to Grinnell, where the stream starts.

287.7 BROOKLYN – Brooklyn is known as the Community of Flags. It first began lining streets with flags in 1991 to celebrate *The Des Moines Register*'s Annual Great Bicycle Ride Across Iowa. This event is the largest bike-touring event in the world and crosses Iowa each year from west to east. With the success of the flag display, more flags were displayed until the community was lined with them, including one giant flag visible from Interstate 80. To help pay for the project, the town has a Flag Store which sells flags, antiques and crafts, located across the street from the Brooklyn Opera House on Jackson Street. The Opera House was incorporated in 1910 and opened on February 28, 1911.

Brooklyn is also the boyhood home of John Wayne, who was born Marion Morrison in nearby Winterset. In 1909, he moved with his family to a home at 717 Jackson Street in Brooklyn. They soon moved to Earlham, but then back to Brooklyn in 1913. John Wayne attended first grade here before his family moved to California in May 1914. Today, the home is the John Wayne Historical Site and is noted by a historical marker about eight blocks north of the tracks.

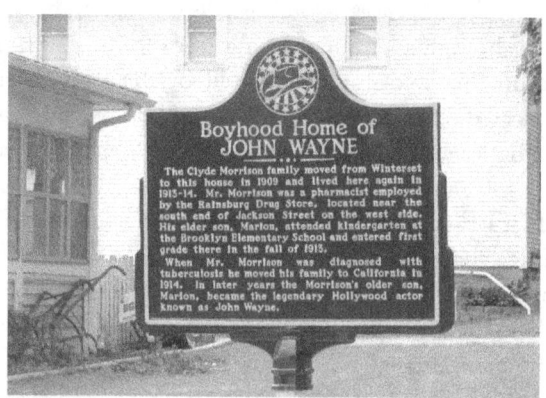

Marker at boyhood home of John Wayne in Brooklyn, Iowa. Photo by Sarah Jennings.

Newton Subdivision

The first community here was named Greenville, founded in 1849 by James Manatt. In 1854, the name of the town was changed to Brooklyn. A romantic version of the naming claims that Dr. Rueben Sears named it Brooklyn because the community was located between two brooks, Big Bear Creek and Little Bear Creek. Another version states that Dr. Sears named it for Brooklyn, New York; not quite as romantic.

With the Civil War starting up, construction on the Mississippi & Missouri Rail Road slowed. The railroad reached here on June 2, 1862, meaning it took twenty months to build the 21 miles of track from Marengo to Brooklyn. The following year the railroad reached Grinnell, and the company's name was changed to the Chicago, Rock Island & Pacific Railroad.

With the arrival of the railroad, Brooklyn began to grow, reaching a population of 1250 in 1870, the year after the town was incorporated on May 3, 1869. The town later stopped growing and today is the home of about 1500 residents. The Iowa Interstate has a 7835-foot long siding at Brooklyn, located on the south side of the mainline. There were once a number of other tracks serving local elevators and stock pens. Just to the south is Little Bear Creek.

IAIS 510 eastbound, Brooklyn, Iowa. Photo by Barton Jennings.

293.7 MALCOM – Malcom actually came late to the scene since the railroad was built through the area in 1863. In 1866, the town was laid out by Z. P. Wigton, reportedly named for a railroad surveyor. It was officially incorporated in 1872. It was never a large place and today has a population of about 300.

Malcom is the location of the historic P. P. Raymond Mansion. Mr. Raymond farmed outside of town beginning in 1856 and became relatively wealthy. He founded the town's first and only bank, P. P. Raymond and Sons, and built this house in 1874. It was listed on the National Register of Historic Places in 1985, which states that the house is a noteworthy example of the Second Empire style found in a small town. It is described as "a 2½-story frame structure that features a mansard roof with a concave slope, elaborate window hoods, window bays, and a turret."

In 1970, the Rock Island had a siding to the north and a short track to the south. Today, the Iowa Interstate has two tracks to the north to serve the Heartland Co-op. This facility can store 3,974,000 bushels of grain, and also handles many types of dry and liquid fertilizers, bulk and packaged chemicals, bulk and packaged seed, and bagged feed. In 1987, three cooperatives with facilities in Panora, Dallas Center, Minburn and Granger merged to create Heartland Co-op. The three cooperatives were Panora Farmers Cooperative, formed in 1947; Farmers Cooperative Company, formed in 1919 at Dallas Center; and Minburn Cooperative, created in 1945 and expanded by buying a plant at Granger in 1986. Over the next few years, several more elevators were bought.

In 1993, a newer Heartland Co-op was created by the merger of Alleman Cooperative Company, Mitchellville Cooperative, the former Avon Grain Company facilities, and the original Heartland Cooperative. The cooperative has continued to grow across the region by merging with and buying other elevators and cooperatives. Among these was the Gateway Cooperative in 2001. Gateway had acquired the Malcom Farmers Co-op Elevator in 1996.

297.3 ASCALON – The Rock Island had a siding to the north here until the 1980s. It was located between 90th and 80th Streets.

The word Ascalon comes from Ashkelon, a coastal city in Israel and the location of the Battle of Ascalon, considered the last action of the First Crusade. The word Ascalon is a popular one used in many computer games and fantasy. It is also the lance or sword that Saint George used to slay the dragon. Winston Churchill used the name for his airplane during World War II.

Ascalon was not listed in the February 1, 1910, *Rock Island Lines List of Officers, Station Agents, Etc.*, but it was listed in the 1967 *List of Stations*.

299.1 LITTLE BEAR CREEK BRIDGE – This bridge was built by the Rock Island and consists of three 44-foot long deck plate girder spans.

300.8 BERMANS – The spur to the south serves the scrapyard of Sam Berman & Sons, a long-time shipper on the railroad.

302.0 GRINNELL SIDING – This is the location of the station sign for the Iowa Interstate Railroad. It is near the Penrose Street grade crossing on the east side of Grinnell, and marks the 4110-foot long siding that still exists here for the use of the railroad.

302.7 GRINNELL – Grinnell is easy to spot due to the passenger station at the diamond with Union Pacific, added to the National Register of Historic Places in 1976. The Mississippi & Missouri Rail Road built from Brooklyn to Grinnell, a total of 15 miles, by October 1863. Within a few years, the Iowa Central built through Grinnell as a part of its line south to Albia, Iowa. It later became part of the Minneapolis & St. Louis (M&StL), stretching from near Albert Lea (MN) southward to Oskaloosa (IA) and Albia (IA), and then eastward to Peoria (IL). The Iowa Central became a part of the M&StL on January 1, 1912. By 1957, this was the Tenth

District, operating between Marshalltown and Oskaloosa, and the home of passenger trains #7 and #8. Grinnell was Milepost 268.8 on the M&StL.

For more than 40 years, the M&StL fought off numerous financial issues until being sold to the Chicago & North Western on November 1, 1960. Most of the railroad was quickly abandoned by the C&NW. However, this line was not duplicated by a better line, and was still part of the railroad when it in turn was bought by Union Pacific. UP operates the line from Marshalltown (IA) to Eddyville (IA).

At the diamond of the Iowa Interstate and Union Pacific is the former brick and stone station. Jointly built by the CRI&P and M&StL in 1892-93, the building has had wood additions added and a restaurant installed. Just to the west, the former Railway Express Agency brick building also stands, now used by the Grinnell Railway Express Model Railroad Club. Across the tracks to the southeast is a residence with a history tying it to the Brotherhood of Railway Trainmen. The building served as a bar and gathering place for train crews for several generations.

IAIS 510 eastbound, Grinnell, Iowa. Photo by Barton Jennings.

The former Grinnell Railway Express Agency Office. Photo by Sarah Jennings.

Josiah B. Grinnell was one of the partners who developed a townsite at this location in 1854, populated by settlers from New England and New York. While Stella was the original planned name for the community, Grinnell convinced the other partners to use his name instead. The idea of developing a community in the west reportedly came from his friend Horace Greeley, the famous editor of the *New York Tribune*. Grinnell was an energetic thirty-two-year-old Congregationalist minister. Seeking Greeley's opinion on an alternative outlet for his reformist zeal, Grinnell reportedly received the now famous advice, "Go West, young man, go West! There is health in the country and room away from our crowds of idlers and imbeciles. Go West and grow up with the country!" Grinnell at first looked at Missouri, but based upon the advice of Henry Farnam, one of the owners of the Chicago & Rock Island and the Mississippi & Missouri Rail Road, Grinnell chose Iowa as the site for his new community.

The town began to boom when the railroad arrived in late 1863, and the town was incorporated on April 28, 1865. By 1880 Grinnell had a population of around 2000, and became the largest community in Poweshiek County. Grinnell was also helped by the presence of Grinnell College, considered as one of the best of the small town liberal arts colleges in the United States. Grinnell College dates it history to 1843 when eleven Congregational ministers set out to proselytize on the frontier. As a part of this effort, they established Iowa College in Davenport in 1846. Several decades later, the school moved to Grinnell and unofficially became Grinnell College while still retaining Iowa College as its official name. The school had to essentially restart when it and much of the town was destroyed by a tornado on June 17, 1882. However, in 1889, the college made history when it and the University of Iowa played each other at Grinnell in the first football game played west of the Mississippi River. In 1909, the school officially became Grinnell College.

Today, Grinnell is also home to the new Spaulding Center for Transportation – Iowa Transportation Museum. Located downtown, it is named after the Spaulding Carriage and Automotive Works that once operated in Grinnell. The company was founded in 1876. In 1909, it announced its intentions to build a car even as it was already producing 10,000 carriages and wagons a year and employing up to 300 in its Grinnell factories. The Spaulding automobile was produced from 1909 to 1916. However, only one Spaulding is known to survive, owned by a Missouri collector.

303.0 GRINNELL FREIGHT HOUSE – The February 1, 1910, *Rock Island Lines List of Officers, Station Agents, Etc.* showed this name as a separate location from the passenger station. It

305.7 COUNTY LINE – The Iowa Interstate crosses the county line where it bridges over E. 156th Street North. Poweshiek County is to the east while Jasper County is to the west.

Jasper County was named after Sergeant William Jasper, a Revolutionary War hero. During the battle of Sullivan's Island in June 1776, the British pounded the American fort, eventually shooting down the flag pole bearing the Fort Moultrie Flag – a blue flag with a white crescent used by South Carolina forces. William Jasper, a member of the Second South Carolina Regiment, jumped out of the fort, walked the entire length in full view of the British, and then cut the flag from its pole. Climbing the wall, he fastened the flag to a cannon sponge-staff and planted it in the wall, all while in the face of deadly fire. For this feat, South Carolina President John Rutledge presented Jasper with his dress sword at a review held soon after the battle and offered him a commission. Jasper turned this down, instead preferring to serve as a scout for the American forces. Jasper was also recognized later for his scouting efforts against the British until he was killed at Savannah in 1779 while planting the colors of the Second South Carolina Regiment on the British lines. He was buried somewhere near the scene of the battle in a mass grave with many of his comrades.

308.7 TURNER – Turner was listed in the February 1, 1910, *Rock Island Lines List of Officers, Station Agents, Etc.* book, but by 1973, Rock Island track profiles show no tracks here. A 1901 map of Jasper County shows this location to be Turner Post Office.

The town of Turner was established by Othiol Johnson Turner after he arrived from the Cumberland Mountains of Kentucky and bought a large amount of acreage in 1870. A small community soon grew up around his "ranch" on the railroad, attracting a depot, a large general store, stock pens, a lumber yard, large grain elevator, post office, ice house, blacksmith shop and a pool hall, many owned by the Turner family. The Turners also continued to buy land in the area.

Besides the shipment of cattle and horses, a cheese factory was the other major rail shipper at Turner. The cheese factory provided a market for the milk of local farmers, and its products were shipped east and west to markets. For a while, this was also the home of the Turner Coal and Lumber Company.

It wasn't until April 19, 1899, that the town was officially platted as Turner, and some continued to use the name of Dixie, a name sometimes used since the Turners arrived in 1870. However, little remains today to mark the location of Turner. Most of the community burned in a fire that started in the cheese factory, and no tracks remain. Reportedly, only a single cement foundation remains to mark the town of Turner.

309.8 ROCK CREEK BRIDGE – This stream drains the fields on the rolling hills to the north. It then flows south under the railroad and then Interstate 80, before entering the North Skunk River several miles to the south.

311.9 U.S. HIGHWAY 6 – The railroad passes under the highway about two miles east of Kellogg. That is the North Skunk River to the south.

313.8 KELLOGG – Kellogg is easy to find – just look for the 3955-foot long siding to the south serving the Heartland Cooperative elevator with a 3,267,000 bushel grain storage capacity. The original grain elevator at Kellogg was built and owned by I. L. Patton. In 1909, the elevator was purchased by a group of farmers to form the first grain elevator co-operative, known as The Farmers Elevator Company. It eventually became the Farmers Cooperative of Kellogg and Pickering, which became a part of Heartland Cooperative in 2007.

This location was first known as Manning's Station, a regular stagecoach stop. Operated by Dan Manning, the complex included lodging in a series of long and narrow barracks. From there, it gets a bit complicated. On September 12, 1865, Enos Blair and Dr. Abraham W. Adair founded the town of Jasper City based upon the plans of the railroad to build west from Grinnell. However, when the railroad arrived during 1866, they named the station Kellogg after Judge Abel Avery Kellogg. Meanwhile, the post office was named Kimball for the railroad's Iowa Superintendent Abel Kimball. Because of this, there was a great deal of confusion about what to actually call the community. Kimball eventually turned down the honor of having the town named after himself and the town was called Kellogg when it was incorporated on February 6, 1874.

The railroad reached the town in the spring of 1866 and became the station at the end of the line, making it an important location. A turntable was installed southwest of the depot and some limited shop facilities were added to service the trains that started and ended here. The end of the line remained in Kellogg for some time, fueling the early growth of the town. However, construction began again in 1867 and the first train passed through Kellogg on July 1, 1867.

Kellogg was initially incorporated in 1873 and made a municipality in 1874, and by 1881 was the second most populated town in the county. However, it was never much larger than it is today, with a population of 599 in the 2010 census. A mill opened in 1878 and burned down just three years later, only to be replaced by another mill on the Skunk River making White Lily Flour and Silver Leaf Flour. In the 1930s, the Craven Broom Factory opened and shipped their finished product by rail. The Midwest-One Minute Factory was also here for some time and manufactured washing machines. However, today Kellogg remains essentially a farming community.

315.1 SKUNK RIVER BRIDGE – This three-span plate girder bridge crosses the North Skunk River, a tributary of the Skunk River. The North Skunk River has its headwaters in Marshall County, Iowa. The name Skunk River was an early interpretation of the Sauk and Meskwaki name of "Shecaqua." The name was supposed to refer to smelly skunks, but later interpreters said that the name was "Checaqua" which simply referred to any strong or obnoxious smell. Since the river was lined with wild onions, some feel that the stream should be called the Onion River.

320.0 NEWTON YARD – The CRI&P yard was originally located near downtown Newton, but the Iowa Interstate moved it during the late 1990s to the northeast side of town to make room for the new Maytag corporate headquarters. The new yard, station code "NT," included the new Lee Horst Transportation Center, which in addition to providing intermodal services, also included a small shop facility (used to store the QJ steam locomotives) and a wye. The facility is named in honor of Lee Horst, a former General Road Foreman on IAIS and career railroad man who passed on in 2002.

The Key Cooperative elevator is located just north of the small yard at the Newton Rail Center. The privately held firm, based in Newton, is involved with grain and feed as well as lumber and construction. Further to the northwest is the Renewable Energy Group Newton plant. This plant is a 30-million-gallon-per-year biodiesel production facility. It was originally engineered and built in 2006 by the Renewable Energy Group (REG) and owned by Central Iowa Energy, LLC (CIE). Production started in April 2007. REG and CIE consolidated in February 2010 with REG becoming sole owner/operator of the facility. REG started in the biomass-based diesel business two decades ago while operating under the umbrella of West Central Cooperative in Ralston, Iowa. It has expanded into an independent firm, based in Iowa.

Also in this area is TPI Composites. The construction of this wind turbine blade factory was announced in December 2007. TPI was founded in 1968 as Tillotson Pearson Inc., a manufacturer of high-performance sail and powerboats along with a wide range of composite structures used in other industrial applications. The firm, headquartered in Scottsdale, Arizona, is the largest U.S.-based independent manufacturer of composite wind blades.

Heading west, the railroad passes a number of warehouses and factories, many from the days when Maytag was a major part of the community. Today, a number of smaller companies use various parts of the facilities, including Ad-

Newton Subdivision

vanced Wheel Sales, one of the country's leading truck and trailer wheel suppliers.

322.5 NEWTON – Look for the Newton train station. It was opened in 1912 by the Rock Island, has been restored, and has been used as a private business.

IAIS 6988 2-10-2 passing the former Newton, Iowa, train station. Photo by Barton Jennings.

Newton is the county seat of Jasper County. When it was first platted in 1846 as the county seat, it was called Newton City. The town was incorporated on January 6, 1857. The names Newton and Jasper go together as both men were sergeants who served under Revolutionary War General Francis Marion.

In the late 19th century, Newton's growth was fueled by the development of coal mines in the region. The first significant mine in the area was the Couch mine of the Jasper County Coal and Railway Company, opened in the 1870s. Besides coal, Newton has been the home of a number of interesting events and businesses. For example, Newton is the home of Maytag Dairy Farms and was formerly home to the Maytag Corporation's headquarters until the Whirlpool Corporation acquired it in 2006. It is the location of Iowa Speedway, which each year hosts races operated by

NASCAR and the Indy Racing League. In 1969, boxer Rocky Marciano died when the small aircraft in which he was flying crashed two miles south of the Newton airport when it came out of low clouds and struck trees. Finally, Newton is the home of the International Wrestling Institute and Museum.

For many years, Newton was a regional railroad hub. Besides the east-west mainline, the CRI&P had a line to the south. In 1877, the Newton & Monroe Railroad Company was incorporated to build a line from "the main line of the Chicago, Rock Island and Pacific Railroad in the town of Newton, Jasper County, Iowa in a southerly direction to the town of Monroe in said Jasper County," using the authority of the previously incorporated Iowa, Minnesota & North Pacific Railway Company. Within a few years, 17 miles of track were in service between Newton and Monroe. It soon became part of the CRI&P. The line south of Newton was abandoned in 1936.

The Minneapolis & St. Louis had a line from Newton southeast to their mainline at New Sharon, Iowa. This line was the 16th Subdivision in *Employee Time Table No. 15*, dated December 6, 1959. It operated from Newton to New Sharon, Iowa, but was abandoned in 1962 by the Chicago & North Western (C&NW).

To the north was the regionally famous Fort Dodge, Des Moines & Southern Railroad. The FtDDM&S began as a small coal carrier which expanded and became a common carrier hauling freight, passengers, mail and express. While it started as a steam railroad, it converted to an electric interurban, trolley and bus operation, and finally to a diesel freight operation. After several reorganizations, the remains of the railroad were sold to the C&NW in 1968.

323.5 U.S. HIGHWAY 6 – The railroad bridges over U.S. Highway 6, which is 1st Avenue through Newton, with an 86-foot long through plate girder span.

324.1 U.S. HIGHWAY 6 – The railroad again bridges over U.S. Highway 6, which is also Iowa Highway 14 here.

325.1 INTERSTATE 80 – The railroad passes under I-80 for the seventh time since leaving Chicago, Illinois. U.S. Highway 6 and I-80 share the same roadway in this area.

326.4 CHERRY CREEK BRIDGE – The bridge that the railroad uses to cross Cherry Creek consists of three different sizes of deck plate girder spans. Cherry Creek starts less than ten miles to the north and flows southward into the South Skunk River.

328.6 METZ – In 1853, William Hitchler received a land grant of 140 acres from the federal government for what eventually became Metz, Iowa. Hitchler and his brother had arrived from Germany just a few years earlier, and slowly developed a community named Farmersville along an old stage route. After the railroad built through the area, a grain elevator, a creamery, and several businesses opened up near the depot, reportedly named Metz by Hitchler. Today, only a few houses and the Metz Community Church mark the location of the community. Look for it at the grade crossing with South 36th Street West.

Just to the north was once the Newton & Northwestern, created in 1902 from the Boone, Rockwell City & Northwestern Railway, the operator of several coal mines and a railroad to serve them. In 1912, the mines at Colfax ran out of coal and the line was soon abandoned from Midvale to Newton, including the route through Metz.

329.2 SOUTH SKUNK RIVER BRIDGE – The Iowa Interstate bridge includes a 154-foot Warren through truss span on the west end, with five shorter spans to the east. The truss bridge was built in 1900 by the American Bridge Company of New York, with the approach spans replaced in 1980 with the newer spans.

The South Skunk River starts in Hamilton County in north central Iowa and flows south through Ames before merging with the North Skunk River, making the branch about 185 miles long. The South Skunk has been researched since 1998 by the "Skunk River Navy," a student-led biological diversity study sponsored by Iowa State University.

333.7 COLFAX SPRINGS – Colfax Springs, a railroad station during the late 1800s and early 1900s, came about due to coal mining, but its product was healing water. During the fall of 1875, a crew was boring for coal a mile east of town for the railroad. They hit a steady flow of water, water which tasted of minerals. The water was tested by James R. Blaney, a Chicago chemist, who declared it to have a high mineral content and to be of great medicinal value. The spring immediately began to attract invalids and the sick who praised the water's healing powers.

Almost immediately, John F. Dixon, owner of the land on which the spring was located, built a small hotel and opened the first resort at what became known as Colfax Springs. The Rock Island also opened a station nearby to handle the large volumes of visitors who previously were dropped off at the downtown Colfax station, more than a mile away. In 1881, Dixon sold the land and hotel to Samuel W. Cole and his son, who then built a larger hotel they called the Cole Hotel, located "three blocks from the depot and situated in a natural grove." As business boomed, the hotel was sold and became the Grand Hotel.

By the late 1800s, Colfax Springs was being promoted as the "Carlsbad of America" and more hotels had been built to handle the sick and the conventions that the area was also attracting. A reported nine hotels and sanitariums, and nineteen mineral wells, were in operation at the community's peak. By 1910, an estimated 25,000 visitors, both invalids and conventioneers, visited Colfax Springs and Colfax each year. However, a combination of World War I, the use of several facilities for veteran care, and the influenza pandemic of 1918-1919 (which killed more people than the

Newton Subdivision

war itself), ended the springs business here. The railroad also soon closed its depot and moved all railroad business to the Colfax station.

To the north can be seen the trace of an old railroad grade through the woods alongside the South Skunk River. About two miles of the Rock Island were realigned by 1954.

334.7 COLFAX – Colfax began as a stagecoach station, located about ten miles west of Newton. Robert N. Stewart arrived in the area from West Virginia in 1864 and applied to Josiah B. Grinnell, congressional representative for the Fourth District, for a post office to be located at the stagecoach station. With the approval of the post office, two names were suggested: Sheridan or Colfax. At the time, Schuyler Colfax, a Representative from Indiana (1855-1869) who was chairman of the Committee on Post Office and Post Roads, was a big supporter of the Daily Overland Mail and his name was likely chosen for that reason. Later, Colfax was Vice President of the United States with President Grant (1869-1873). The Colfax post office officially opened on January 18, 1865.

Colfax, Iowa, station sign. Photo by Barton Jennings.

In April of 1867, Abel Kimball, the railroad's Iowa Superintendent, bought the land around Colfax and hired Charles C. Turner to survey it. On July 22, 1867, the plat of

Colfax was recorded with the railroad being the center of the town. Within several months, the railroad arrived and Colfax was suddenly more valuable and began to grow. The area's resort history was centered on the east side of Colfax at what was known as Colfax Springs, but the history is hinted at by the presence of Mineral Springs Park next to the tracks at the Iowa Interstate's station sign. To the north is the Colfax Livestock Sales complex, next to the Colfax Fairgrounds.

James Norman Hall, co-author of *Mutiny on the Bounty*, grew up in Colfax and includes tales of this time in several of his other books. For many years, Colfax was also the home of the Monroe Company, often described as the world's largest manufacturer of folding banquet tables. Founded in 1908 as the Close-To-Nature Company, a manufacturer of tents and other outdoor supplies, the company became the Monroe Company in 1935, specializing in making tables and chairs. This company closed in 2007, and after several attempts to save the company, its equipment and materials were auctioned off on April 30, 2016. The former factory buildings are located just to the north of the railroad at the Walnut Street grade crossing.

During the end of the Rock Island Railroad, there was a long siding to the south and a short siding to the north at Colfax. Today, the south siding stretches from Milepost 334.5 to 335.8. The north siding is now a long spur with a switch on the east end.

Colfax was also the eastern terminus of the Des Moines & Central Iowa Railroad. The DM&CI began operations as the Inter-Urban Railway, incorporated in 1899. By late 1902, the railroad connected Des Moines and Colfax, a distance of 23 miles. In 1906, the railroad built a 35-mile branch connecting Des Moines to Perry. In 1922, the railroad was reorganized as the Des Moines & Central Iowa Railroad. Service to Colfax was eliminated in 1941 and the line abandoned in 1946. Passenger service on the rest of the system was eliminated in 1949 and the remaining freight service handled by diesel into the 1950s. Its old grade was to the north. Also to the north was the grade of the Fort Dodge, Des Moines & Southern Railroad

The Coal Business

During the late 1860s, coal was discovered in the area on land owned by Joseph Slaughter, and quickly began to be used to heat houses and businesses in Colfax. The railroad took notice and began to support the industry. The history of Jasper County states that the "first large scale coal mine in Jasper County was the Watson No. 1 Mine," which was located five miles southeast of Colfax. It was served by the Rock Island using a long railroad spur. With the boom from the coal business, Colfax was incorporated on August 10, 1875.

From 1881 to 1900, the Jasper County Coal and Railway Company operated a number of coal mines north of Colfax. By 1902, the Colfax Consolidated Coal Company, formed in 1902, brought the mines of Colfax under a common operator. To serve existing mines and to open mine No. 8 to the southeast, they built their own railroad. The Colfax Northern Railroad (1901-1912), later the Colfax Northern Railway (1912-1926), connected the CRI&P with the coal mines to the southeast at Seevers. Seevers has been described as a coal mining town about three miles southeast of Colfax with a post office from 1903 to 1914. Colfax Consolidated Coal owned and ran Seevers.

A 1910 inspection of the Colfax Northern by the Iowa State Commerce Commission, Board of Railroad Commissioners, provided a number of facts about the railroad. It stated that the railroad "owns about five miles of track between Valeria and Colfax. It operates under lease about seven miles of track south of Colfax to certain mines numbered seven and eight. The business of the railroad is practically confined to the hauling of coal and the transportation of coal miners to and from said mines." Of special note was the miners train operated to and from the mines each day. The report stated that the "entire equipment of cars owned by said railway consists of four box cars used for transporting miners to and from their labors, one passenger car which runs from Colfax to Valeria, and two small engines. The cars used to transport miners consist of one forty foot car, two sixty foot cars, and one forty foot car about ready to be put into service. These cars are seated in the cheapest manner with ordinary boards." The condition of the miner's train was such that the mine workers union had filed a complaint with the state.

A later lawsuit involving ownership of part of the railroad property revealed further details. The lawsuit stated that the Colfax Northern Railway Company was incorporated in June 1912. The beginning of the railroad was built in 1897 by the Jasper County Coal Company, and later sold to the Colfax Consolidated Coal Company. When initially built, the line extended from Colfax to a coal mine about one mile south of Colfax. This mine was known as No. 5, and it lasted about four years before the coal was all mined. Another mine, known as No. 6, was opened about 3/4 mile east of No. 5 and the railroad was extended. Mine No. 6 lasted about eight years. Before this mine closed, Mine No. 7 opened and a short spur track was built to serve it. In 1905, Colfax Consolidated Coal Company opened Mine No 8 near Mine No. 7, which closed in 1913. Before that happened, mine No. 9 opened about a mile southwest of No. 8. The railroad was extended to serve each of these mines.

The coal business was so big in the Colfax area that two United Mine Workers locals were based here with a total combined membership of almost 600 in 1912. However, within a decade, the mines had played out and closed down. With the loss of the coal and the resort business, Colfax reverted back to being a farming town, and its population today is about 2000.

340.1 COUNTY LINE – The county line is on the east side of Mitchellville at the Jasper Road grade crossing. Jasper County is to the east while Polk County is to the west.

Polk County was named for James Knox Polk, the 11th President of the United States (1845–1849). Polk was born in Mecklenburg County, North Carolina, and later lived in and represented the state of Tennessee. Polk served as Speaker of the House (1835–1839) and Governor of Tennessee (1839–1841) before becoming president. Polk kept his word by serving only one term after accomplishing most of his goals. He died of cholera three months after his term ended.

Known as the "last strong pre-Civil War president" and the "least known consequential president" of the United States, his list of accomplishments is long. For example, Polk increased the size of the country more than any president except Jefferson, settling claims to Texas and the Oregon Territory, and by acquiring California and the Southwest. Polk signed the Walker Tariff that brought an era of nearly free trade to the country until 1861 and established a treasury system that lasted until 1913. He oversaw the opening of the U.S. Naval Academy and the Smithsonian Institution, the groundbreaking for the Washington Monument, and the issuance of the first postage stamps in the United States.

340.6 MITCHELLVILLE – This town was established in 1856 and platted in 1867 by Thomas Mitchell, often credited with being the first white settler in Jasper County. Mitchellville was incorporated as a city on September 30, 1875.

Mitchell's farm later became the Thomas Mitchell Park, owned by Polk County. Mitchellville is also the location of the Iowa Correctional Institution for Women. For the railroad, to the north is a short siding that serves the Heartland Co-op elevator. The population of the town is now less than 2500.

For trains heading west, they face one of the steepest grades on the line through Mitchellville. The grade is 1.0%, topping off at an elevation of 985 feet at Mitchellville.

Mitchellville, Iowa. Photo by Barton Jennings.

345.8 ALTOONA MERCHANTS/COLD STORAGE – This track to the north serves Merchants Distribution Services and Iowa Cold Storage in what is a planned industrial park.

346.9 ALTOONA – Altoona is one of those towns that has had numerous names, many at the same time. The first name used when the town was founded in 1868 was Petersburg. However, the name was changed to Altoona, based upon the Latin term "altus," meaning high, because this was the highest elevation on the Des Moines Valley Railroad. The post office founded in 1868 also used the name Altoona. However, the railroad called the station here Yant after the local landowner, Anthony Yant. The issue was settled on March 11, 1876, when Altoona was incorporated as a city.

During the late 1800s and early 1900s, coal was mined throughout the area, and several tracks were used to ship the coal on the railroad. However, like many of the other towns in the area, the coal ran out during the early part of the 1900s and the community went back to farming. Today, with a population of 15,000, Altoona also serves as a bedroom community for Des Moines.

Landus Cooperative operates the former Farmers Cooperative Company elevator at Altoona. Note the Altoona FC markings, with the slogan "Together We Can" up high on the elevator silos. The Iowa Interstate serves the elevator complex with a spur track off the siding. Altoona is also the location of Adventureland, an amusement park; Prairie Meadows, a horse racing track and casino; a Bass Pro Shops retail store (the first one in central Iowa); and a Facebook data center.

Altoona, Iowa. Photo by Barton Jennings.

Altoona is the connection with the Prairie City Line, the former Des Moines Valley Rail Road route. This IAIS line once extend to Pella, Iowa, about 35 miles southeast of here. In 1998, the line was cut back about 8 miles to Otley, and then another 15 miles to Prairie City in 2000. In 2015, most of the rest of the line was abandoned. This line has an interesting history, and actually dates prior to the CRI&P reaching Des Moines. On June 1, 1864, the Des Moines Valley Rail Road Company (DMV) acquired the Keokuk, Fort Des Moines & Minnesota Rail Road Company, which had already built between Keokuk and Eddyville (northwest of Ottumwa). By late August, 1866, the DMV had built to Altoona and on into Des Moines. When the CRI&P reached Altoona in 1867, it used the Des Moines Valley Rail Road to reach Des Moines.

By 1870, the Des Moines Valley Rail Road had been extended on to Fort Dodge, Iowa. In late 1873, the railroad was foreclosed on and sold to R. W. Hyman, R. C. Greer and J. A. Johnson, Trustees. The trustees divided the railroad, selling the line from Keokuk to Des Moines to the Keokuk & Des Moines Railway Company in 1874, and the line from Des Moines to Fort Dodge to the Des Moines & Fort Dodge Railroad Company. The Keokuk & Des Moines Railway Company was leased to the Chicago, Rock Island & Pacific Railroad Company in 1878. However, the lease was lost when the Rock Island filed for bankruptcy on April 20, 1915, but was regained when the CRI&P came out of receivership in June 1917. The line was technically sold to the Chicago, Rock Island & Pacific Railway Company on August 18, 1924.

Maps of Altoona from 1914 show the Rock Island depot just west of the Range Line Road (today's 1st Avenue) grade crossing, on the south side of the tracks. The maps show two mainlines to the north of the station as well as a siding, with a second siding around the south side of the station. Just to the north was the "Inter-Urban Railway."

Information about the Iowa Interstate's Prairie City Line can be found on page 279 of this route guide.

351.5 DIVISION LIMITS – During the early 1970s, this was the limits between the Rock Island's Illinois Division and Des Moines Division.

352.5 PLEASANT HILL – Pleasant Hill was incorporated as a city on May 12, 1956, but has been a settlement since the mid-19th century when the railroads built through this area.

This is the Fairfield Drive grade crossing, but Rock Island records show no facilities here. Iowa Interstate documents indicate that East Des Moines yard limits begin near here at Milepost 352.7.

353.0 FOURMILE CREEK BRIDGE – The Iowa Interstate bridge consists of five deck plate girder spans. Built about 1900 by the American Bridge Company of New York, each span is 44 feet long. This is one of a number of streams in the area that flow into the Des Moines River to the south.

353.2 EAST DES MOINES – This is the official western limits of the Newton Subdivision of the Iowa Interstate. It is also the west yard limits for IAIS' East Des Moines, and the east yard limits for UP Des Moines. The Iowa Interstate operates over tracks belonging to Union Pacific from here west to Milepost 355.9. Trains originating and terminating in the Des Moines area often use the code of "DM" to indicate the location.

Union Pacific

The Iowa Interstate operates over trackage owned by Union Pacific between Mileposts 353.2 and 355.9. This track was originally part of the Rock Island, built in 1867. However, 108 years later the railroad entered its third and final bankruptcy. A strike by the railroad clerks in August 1979 basically ended the railroad. In early 1980, the bankruptcy court determined that the Rock Island could not be successfully reorganized, and a sale of all company assets was ordered.

In 1983, the Chicago & North Western acquired what was known as the Spine Line – Rock Island's north-south line between the Twin Cities of Minnesota and Kansas City. As a part of the purchase, the C&NW acquired the Des Moines terminal trackage, thus the 2.7 miles of the east-west Chicago to Council Bluffs route. On April 25, 1995, the C&NW became part of Union Pacific, making this short piece of the original Rock Island a part of Union Pacific, a goal of the 1860s and again in the 1960s.

354.4 IOWA HIGHWAY 46 – IA-46, locally known as SE 30th Street, bridges over the eastern end of Des Moines Yard. To the south is UP's Short Line yard, their primary Des Moines facility. This yard was known as East Des Moines Yard when the Rock Island operated it. Today, UP owns the yard while the Iowa Interstate has trackage rights through the area. The two railroads also interchange cars here. The yard has more than 30 tracks, not counting engine and other company service tracks.

355.6 SHORT LINE JUNCTION – Short Line Junction was once the crossing of the Rock Island's north-south mainline from Kansas City to Minneapolis and the Rock's east-west mainline from Chicago to Council Bluffs. Today, the north-south line is Union Pacific's Mason City Subdivision, or "Spine Line," a name the track received while being operated by the Chicago & North Western. The name Short Line Junction came about with the construction of the "Short Line" from Carlisle to Allerton, Iowa, in 1911-1913. This section of track was formally purchased by the Rock Island in 1922.

The junction once had wye tracks in all four corners and crossovers between the two east-west main tracks. Currently, the wyes on the east side of the junction remain to allow Union Pacific trains to get to Short Line Yard, and the east-west line is single track. A track in the northwest quadrant now connects the Spine Line to the Iowa Interstate for UP trains moving in that direction.

Short Line Junction was once protected by a two-story brick tower (built in 1926), located in the northwest corner of the diamond. The tower, once featuring Rock Island emblems, has been torn down. Rock Island trains were not the only ones controlled by the tower. Over the years, the tracks of several railroad companies converged and crossed within the tower's jurisdiction, including Chicago, Burlington & Quincy; Chicago Great Western; Chicago & North Western; Ft Dodge Des Moines & Southern; and Wabash.

Just to the east of the junction is Short Line Yard. This large yard once featured a roundhouse and turntable, special passenger train servicing tracks for the "Rocket" trains, and other facilities for the railroad. Few of these facilities still exist and Union Pacific now operates the yard. Union Pacific will also occasionally detour from Short Line Junction westward to Council Bluffs over the Iowa Interstate.

355.9 DES MOINES – The switch at this location connects to the Union Pacific's Spine Line. Today, Union Pacific operates over the tracks of Iowa Interstate from Short Line Junction westward for about 2.7 miles (milepost 355.9 to 358.6) to their Perry Branch. Tracks west of here belong to the Iowa Interstate, but are also UP's Perry Subdivision, using trackage rights over the line to reach several industrial leads.

This is the west end of the Union Pacific Des Moines yard limits.

IAIS 712 eastbound at Mitchellville, Iowa. Photo by Sarah Jennings.

Council Bluffs Subdivision
Des Moines (Iowa) to Council Bluffs (Iowa)

The Council Bluffs Subdivision covers the Iowa Interstate route between Des Moines (Milepost 358.7) and Council Bluffs (Milepost 487.3). The Council Bluffs Subdivision was constructed originally by the Chicago & Rock Island, starting at the east end in mid-1867. The railroad reached Des Moines in 1867, and Council Bluffs on May 11, 1869. Most of the line between Atlantic and Council Bluffs was realigned as the Atlantic Cutoff in 1953, with the old route soon abandoned. The line changed hands after the 1980 bankruptcy of the railroad, first being operated by the Iowa Railroad, and then to Heartland Rail Partners, and eventually the Iowa Interstate starting in 1984.

The Iowa Interstate operates local switchers out of Des Moines and Council Bluffs and sees the railroad's two main trains – BICB (Blue Island to Council Bluffs) and CBBI (Council Bluffs to Blue Island). It is also not uncommon for Union Pacific to detour trains between Shortline Junction at Des Moines and Council Bluffs.

355.9 DES MOINES – The switch at this location connects to the Union Pacific's Spine Line and is the west end of the Union Pacific Des Moines yard limits.

356.2 DMU–C&NW–FTDDM&S CROSSING – The tracks of the Fort Dodge, Des Moines & Southern Railway (FtDDM&S) ran immediately west of the north-south Spine Line and then curved west to head to Bell Yard, crossing the Rock Island mainline here.

This location was also known as East DMU Junction. A line breaks off to the north and follows the Iowa Interstate to the Des Moines River where the line ends. The line is the former Des Moines Union (DMU). It should be noted that Grenville M. Dodge, Union Pacific's chief engineer during the construction of the transcontinental railroad, served as the DMU's first president.

Iowa Interstate Railroad: History Through the Miles

357.0 CRI&P ROUNDHOUSE – A March 1884 Sanborn Insurance Map shows that the Rock Island had a large roundhouse to the north of the tracks just east of today's grade crossing with East 7th Street. Several car repair shop buildings were also here.

Just to the west of the grade crossing, and also to the north, the same map shows a CRI&P "Freight Depot." The map shows that the Rock Island was six tracks wide here at the time, with the north track serving the freight depot.

357.1 WABASH STATION – To the north, located at 120 East 5th Street, is the former Wabash station, shown by some to be the East Side Union Depot used by CGW, CB&Q, CRI&P, and Wabash. Built of brick, an 1891 Sanborn map shows the building as the "W. St. L. & P. R.R. Pass. Depot" and located on the mainline of the Wabash, St. Louis & Pacific Railway Company. Today, the building is connected to an adjacent building.

Former Wabash station, Des Moines, Iowa. Photo by Sarah Jennings.

The Des Moines, Iowa Falls & Northern/FtDDM&S two-story brick station, built about 1902 and located at 625 E. Court Avenue, is located just north and east of the Wabash building. Originally built as a freight house, it was rebuilt in 1933 to include a passenger station for the interurban line. It later was rebuilt in the 1980s as a restaurant and was placed on the National Historic Register. In 2017, the building houses the offices of the Iowa State Bar Association.

Former Des Moines, Iowa Falls & Northern/FtDDM&S station, Des Moines, Iowa. Photo by Sarah Jennings.

A March 1884 Sanborn Insurance Map shows that the Rock Island had a "Passenger Depot" a block further west, also to the north of today's Iowa Interstate tracks and across the tracks from the Merchants' Union Barbed Wire Company building.

357.5 DES MOINES RIVER BRIDGE – The Iowa Interstate and Union Pacific cross the Des Moines River on a 625-foot long bridge built by the American Bridge Company of New York sometime after 1901. This bridge, consisting of eight spans (five 80-foot long plate girder spans and three 75-foot long plate girder spans), replaced a four-span lattice truss bridge. It was built for two main tracks, but only the north track exists today.

To the north is the former Des Moines Union Railway bridge, now used as a pedestrian bridge over the Des Moines River. The DMU opened in 1886 and was owned by the Wabash and the Milwaukee Road. It also served the Chicago Great Western and the Burlington railroads. There were once several other rail bridges to the south, about where Elm Street and Market Street are today, operated by other railroads such as Wabash and CB&Q.

Des Moines River bridge, Des Moines, Iowa. Photo by Sarah Jennings.

357.8 CRI&P DES MOINES – On August 29, 1866, the Des Moines Valley Rail Road Company arrived in Des Moines. About a year later on September 9, 1867, the first Rock Island passenger train arrived, making it the second railroad to reach Des Moines.

Of the two major stations built in Des Moines – Union Station and CRI&P Station – this is the only one still standing. The Rock Island Railroad built their station is 1910, housing the headquarters of the Iowa Division. Besides the Rock Island, the Minneapolis & St. Louis also used the station for many years. During the 1940s, the M&St.L moved to their own station on 9th Street. They ended passenger service to Des Moines in 1959. By March of 1969, the Rock Island was down to only four trains daily at Des Moines. Train #18, the northbound *Plainsman*, arrived at Des Moines at 1:05 pm. Just five minutes later at 1:10 pm, the

Corn Belt Rock, #10, arrived heading eastbound. Things got busy again later in the afternoon when #17, the southbound *Plainsman*, arrived at 4:25 pm and #7, the westbound *Cornhusker*, arrived at 4:35 pm. The last passenger train serving Des Moines was a Rock Island train, discontinued in 1970, one year before the creation of Amtrak.

The Rock Island Station still stands. The freight station section to the east houses several restaurants and bars, while the main station to the west houses the Business Publications Corporation in 2017. Restoration plans continue for the building with additional businesses moving into its space. Some plans for Amtrak service to Des Moines also include using the station for passenger service again.

Former Rock Island station, Des Moines, Iowa. Photo by Sarah Jennings.

Des Moines Union Station was to the north, across 5th Street, facing the court house. Railroads that used the Union Station were the Milwaukee Road, Wabash, CB&Q, and Chicago Great Western. None of these four railroads operated a major mainline through Des Moines. The Milwaukee Road operated a branch line northwest to Spirit Lake, Iowa, along with a spur north to Madrid, Iowa, connecting with its main line between Chicago and Omaha. The Wabash operated a branch line southeast to Moberly, Missouri, connecting with its main line to St. Louis. The Burlington had two branch lines into Des Moines – the Albia & Des Moines Subdivision and the Des Moines & Osceola Subdivision. The Albia line connected to the CB&Q Chicago-Omaha mainline at Albia, Iowa, southeast of Des Moines, while the Osceola line connected to it to the southwest, making essentially a loop through Des Moines. Finally, the Chicago Great Western operated from Kansas City to Oelwein, Iowa, and then on to Chicago and Minneapolis. Their trackage went south of downtown Des Moines and used CB&Q tracks to reach Union Station.

In 1905, approximately 50 passenger trains a day served Union Station, making it the largest "union" station in Iowa at the time. However, by the 1950s, passenger service to Union Station was almost gone. 1950 saw the Burlington Route begin serving a small station at 6th and Market Streets, several blocks to the southwest. The CB&Q ended passenger service to Des Moines in 1967. The Chicago Great Western also left Union Station in 1950, moving to their small station at 9th Street and Clifton Avenue, several blocks to the west. The CGW ended passenger service to Des Moines in 1962. In 1953, the Milwaukee Road discontinued passenger service to Des Moines, and the Wabash operated the last train to Union Station in 1959. Union Station was torn down in the 1960s and is today a parking lot.

Another station once existed in Des Moines in the 1900s. The C&NW had a station at East 4th Street and Locust Street. Des Moines was located on a Chicago & North Western branch line down from Ames, Iowa, on its main line between Chicago and Omaha. The C&NW ended passenger service to Des Moines in 1954 and later tore down their station.

Des Moines, incorporated on October 18, 1851, is the state capital of Iowa, and county seat of Polk County. In 1846, Fort Des Moines was established at this location and named for the nearby Des Moines River. The word "Des

Moines" is a much-altered French version of the name for the local Moingwenas tribe, a part of the Illinois Confederacy. The French were in this area in the late 1600s and traded with "The Moins."

358.3 DMU CROSSING – Located just west of the 12th Street grade crossing, this area was known as West DMU Junction, and was the western connection with the Des Moines Union Railway.

According to a Sanborn map dated 1884, there were actually two roundhouses in this area. To the south of Market Street at Eleventh Street, where a large parking lot now exists, was a CB&Q roundhouse. The Wabash had a roundhouse to the north of the tracks at 14th Street, with the tracks also shown as belonging to the "DNW&StL," likely the St. Louis, Des Moines & Northern Railway.

The same map showed that during the 1880s, there were actually numerous passenger and freight stations throughout the Des Moines area. From the 1884 Sanborn map, stations were at East Elm between 4th and 5th Streets (CB&Q); the northwest corner of 2nd and West Elm (CB&Q); north side of West Vine between 3rd and 4th (CRI&P); middle of West Market between 3rd and 4th (Des Moines & Ft. Dodge); and across from the south side of the courthouse square between 5th and 6th Street (an unnamed interurban line).

A few of the other major rail structures in 1884 were a roundhouse two blocks south of the Rock Island and on the west bank of the Des Moines River (CB&Q); a Wabash freight house on the southeast corner of Seventh and West Cherry; and an unnamed fright depot on the southeast corner of 3rd and West Market Streets. Besides these major buildings, the railroads had a number of other facilities including sawmills, lumber yards, bridge timber yards, and grain warehouses. What Sanborn called the "Town of Fort Des Moines" was a busy railroad hub in 1884.

358.6 C&NW JUNCTION – The Chicago & North Western once crossed the Rock Island at this location, located where the grade crossing with SW 16th Street now exists. In this area is a small yard, known by some as Fleur Yard, that is used by the Iowa Interstate to service local customers. The Des Moines Switcher (DMSW) often works out of here.

Just west of here, the Raccoon River is directly to the south. The Raccoon River flows into the Des Moines River just south of downtown Des Moines. While the river is only thirty miles long, it has three branches that range between 72 and 196 miles long. The North Raccoon River is by far the longest at 196 miles long. It starts in northwest Iowa and flows south to not far from here where it merges with the other two branches. The Middle Raccoon River is 92 miles long and starts in west-central Iowa and flows generally to the southeast before merging with the South Raccoon River and then the North Raccoon River. The shortest of the three at 72 miles long, the South Raccoon River starts in farmland to the south of where the Middle Raccoon River forms and also flows to the southeast to form the Raccoon River.

360.9 GRIMES LINE JUNCTION – This is a new junction, as the branch used to parallel the Rock Island just to the north all the way from downtown Des Moines. Known as the Grimes Line, this 11-mile branch travels northwest through Clive to the outlying suburb of Grimes, Iowa. The line is actually owned by Norfolk Southern (yes, NS reached Des Moines from the south, via the old Wabash at one point), but IAIS is the contracted operator of this former Milwaukee Road Line. The reason for this arrangement is that the line is isolated from the rest of the NS system by a long stretch of BNSF trackage rights acquired after the original Wabash main into town was abandoned.

The Grimes Line once went much further, but was abandoned north of Grimes during the 1970s. The Iowa Interstate's Des Moines switcher is responsible for servicing customers along this route, with the primary customers be-

Council Bluffs Subdivision

ing Pitt Des Moines (a steel fabricator) in Clive and Beisser Lumber in Grimes. Details about this line are found on page 283.

361.1 WALNUT CREEK BRIDGE – This bridge is a Warren through truss with all verticals, built in 1897 as a double track bridge. The Warren truss span is 113 feet long, and the entire bridge is 157 feet long. The Iowa Interstate is quickly replacing older bridges along the line to handle the heavier modern freight cars. There are plans to replace the Warren truss span with a 114-foot through plate girder span in 2017.

This stream starts to the west of the Interstate 80 belt on the west side of Des Moines. Walnut Creek has one of the most urbanized watersheds in Iowa, with approximately 60 percent urban land use and 40 percent agricultural land use. Walnut Creek flows into the Raccoon River just to the south.

361.8 UNION PACIFIC HOLLINGSWORTH INDUSTRIAL LEAD – The Union Pacific employee timetable shows that this line to the south is 1.4 miles long.

362.6 CRI&P WEST DES MOINES – Under the Rock Island, West Des Moines was the west end of two main tracks.

362.8 C&NW JUNCTION – Union Pacific's West Des Moines Industrial Lead and Waukee Industrial Lead both leave the Iowa Interstate mainline here. The track from here east to Short Line at milepost 354.5 is Union Pacific's Perry Subdivision.

363.0 WEST DES MOINES – West Des Moines was originally a railroad junction town known as Valley Junction. A station was established here in the 1860s, although a school was built here by 1849. Valley Junction was incorporated on August 16, 1893, and renamed West Des Moines on January 1, 1938. Valley Junction originally boomed as a trading community, especially after the Chicago, Rock Island & Pacific Railroad built their area switching facilities and repair shops here. In 1936, these facilities were moved out of Valley Junction and into Des Moines, and soon the town became West Des Moines.

The original passenger depot built by the Rock Island when the area was Valley Junction still stands and is used as a business. Located in Railroad Park across Railroad Avenue from the tracks, the depot is accompanied by CB&Q caboose 13939.

West Des Moines is one of Iowa's largest and wealthiest cities, and Des Moines' richest suburb. In 2008, it ranked 94th in *Money* magazine's list of the "100 Best Places to Live and Launch."

Former Rock Island depot in West De Moines, Iowa. Photos by Sarah Jennings.

CB&Q caboose 13939 in Railroad Park, West Des Moines, Iowa.

366.3 COMMERCE – In 1960, Commerce was annexed by the larger West Des Moines. The town of Commerce Mills was laid out in August of 1871 by A. J. Jack, on what was described as a gentle slope overlooking the valley of the Raccoon River. Within a year, A. J. Jack built a dam and flour mill on the river. The mill led to the development of several other businesses, including a grain dealership and stockyards. In 1881, the post office shortened its name from Commerce Mills to Commerce.

367.0 INTERSTATE 35 – The railroad passes under I-35, the ninth-longest of all Interstate Highways and the third-longest north-south Interstate Highway. It stretches 1568 miles from Laredo, Texas, to Duluth, Minnesota.

367.8 COUNTY LINE – The county line between Polk County (to the east) and Dallas County (to the west) is about three quarters of a mile west of where the Iowa Interstate passes under Interstate 35. **Dallas County** was created in 1846 and was named for George Mifflin Dallas, a U.S. Senator from Pennsylvania and the 11th Vice President of the United States, serving under James K. Polk at the time. The county seat is Adel.

369.7 SUGAR CREEK BRIDGE – Sugar Creek forms to the north of Interstate 80 near Waukee, Iowa. The 116-foot long bridge consists of several short I-beam spans with ballast deck timber spans on each end. There are plans to replace and lengthen this bridge to 180 feet long as a part of a drainage plan.

Just to the east at Milepost 369.5, the Iowa Interstate replaced the former timber trestle over another small stream with a two-span precast concrete bridge in 2012.

372.8 BOONEVILLE – Booneville was named for William and Susannah Boone, the original owners of the property where A. J. Lyon established the town in 1871. There is a 6030-foot siding here between Mileposts 371.5 and 372.7. It is often used to store cars for the local grain elevator. The former CRI&P wooden depot has been moved to Main Street and is used as a residence.

At Booneville is another Heartland Cooperative facility. This one has 1,830,000 bushels of grain storage capacity, handles various types of fertilizers, and sells gas and diesel fuels. It does have a railroad loadout. This facility was once the Booneville Cooperative Elevator Company, formed in 1949. It was merged into Heartland in 1991.

373.0 RACCOON RIVER BRIDGE – This bridge, built in 1900, consists of four through truss spans, all between 145 and 155 feet long. The Raccoon River is only about 30 miles long, but it is created by three smaller rivers, the North, Middle, and South Raccoon Rivers, which are each 72 to 196 miles long. Des Moines obtains its drinking water from the Raccoon River just before the Raccoon River empties into the Des Moines River.

Heading west, the railroad follows the Raccoon River for the next five miles.

376.6 VAN METER – Several sources say that this area was known as Tracy, but it soon took the name Van Meter after the town was laid out in 1869. The name Van Meter came from Henry G. & Jacob Rhodes Van Meter, the owners of two area grist mills. The mill operated by Henry G. Van Meter was located about three miles west of De Soto on the bank of the South Raccoon River. The location was originally the Glover & McPherson sawmill, built in the mid-1850s. Henry G. & Jacob Rhodes Van Meter bought the mill in 1859 and rebuilt it as a grist mill. Jacob Van Meter's grist mill was on the Raccoon River just northwest of town. This mill was built about 1866 and was designed to grind both wheat and corn. Van Meter was officially incorporated on December 29, 1877.

With the arrival of the railroad, Van Meter became a timber town. For many years, railroad ties and cordwood was loaded near the station. However, as the farms grew and the lumber alongside the rivers was cut, the business went away.

During the late 1800s, there were two major industries at Van Meter – coal and brick. Coal mining began during the late 1860s when some coal was mined for local blacksmith use. In 1878, Boag & Van Meter began sinking a shaft about 250 feet deep, located just to the west of town, to mine two large seams of coal. In 1879, the mine's engine house burned down and new machinery was installed, leading to the sale of the mine and the coal lease to J. L. Platt and J. M. Thompson and their Chicago and Van Meter Coal Company. With the mine reopened, it employed fifty men and produced about 1000 bushels of coal a day. Much of the coal was used locally or sold to the railroad, but some was shipped west to Omaha.

A sister company, the Platt Pressed and Fire Brick Company, was created in the early 1890s to use the clay waste from the mine, as well as the coal, to make brick. Reportedly, by 1900, all of the coal from the mine was used to make brick. The mine played out and closed in 1902.

Van Meter was the boyhood home of Baseball Hall of Fame Cleveland Indians pitcher Bob Feller, "The Heater from Van Meter." Feller started with the Indians at the age of 17 and pitched from 1936 until 1956 with four years off during World War II when he was in the U.S. Navy as a Chief Petty Officer assigned to the *USS Alabama*. Feller was listed as the "greatest pitcher of his time" by the *Sporting News*, called "the fastest and best pitcher I ever saw during my career" by Ted Williams, and "probably the greatest pitcher of our era" by Stan Musial.

The house at the corner of Elm and Mill Streets serves as the Bob Feller Hometown Museum. Today, Van Meter is a small farming community with no major industries. It has a population estimated to be about 1200. In early June of each year, Van Meter hosts Raccoon River Days, a community-wide celebration which includes everything from a parade and BBQ contest to a baseball tournament and a talent show.

The North and South Raccoon Rivers merge just west of here. In the 1970s, the Rock Island Railroad had a short spur track at Van Meter. Today, the IAIS simply passes through with their mainline.

378.5 BULGER CREEK BRIDGE – Bulger Creek starts on the east side of Earlham and flows east, and then into the South Raccoon River just north of here. Heading west, the Iowa Interstate departs the Raccoon River and starts to follow Bulger Creek. This bridge consists of two 55-foot deck plate girder spans.

379.8 DESOTO – De Soto was founded when Thomas Hemphill, Henry G. Van Meter, and Jacob Rhodes Van Meter made available land for the Chicago, Rock Island & Pacific to build a depot and water tower. A town was also platted in 1868 by Captain A. J. Lyon, the County Surveyor, using the name De Soto to honor a railroad official. It was incorporated on May 24, 1875.

For many years, De Soto was a stock shipping center with several buyers shipping animals east towards Chicago. The depot was located just west of the Osage Avenue grade crossing and between the tracks. While some reports state that the Rock Island bought a great deal of land at De Soto, there was never much here and today the town houses about 1000 residents.

Just west of town the railroad passes under U.S. Highway 169 at Milepost 380.1. The highway is just short of 1000 miles in length and starts in Virginia, Minnesota, and stretches south to Tulsa, Oklahoma.

380.5 BULGER CREEK BRIDGE – This 110-foot long Warren through truss bridge was built in 1944.

381.4 BULGER CREEK BRIDGE – This bridge was built by the Rock Island Railroad with two 53-foot deck plate girder spans. The elevation here is about 920 feet, fifty feet higher than Van Meter.

382.5 COUNTY LINE – The railroad has turned to the southwest and to the north is Dallas County. **Madison County** is to the south and was created on January 13, 1846, named for James Madison, the fourth president of the United States. The county has a population of about 16,000 and the county seat is Winterset, the birthplace of John Wayne. Multiple reports state that Hiram Hurst was the first settler in the county, arriving in April 1846. The sources also say that he came from Andrew County, Missouri, with at least one stating that he fled Missouri due to being "a suspected murderer, arsonist and hog thief."

Madison County, and its bridges, have been the subject of a book, movie and musical.

385.5 WINEAR – South of Winear (also known as Quarry Junction) was once one of the last lines built by the CRI&P. By 1912, there was already a several-mile-long line here that served the Iowa Portland Cement quarry and works. Iowa Portland Cement was formed in 1910 and immediately built a plant in Des Moines, Iowa, shipping rock by rail from the quarry here. Hawkeye Cement Company bought the company in the 1920s and then sold it to Marquette Cement Manufacturing Company in 1940. In June 1979, Monarch Cement bought the plant and quarry.

In 1958, the Rock Island built a new 11-mile line from Winear to Winterset, the birthplace (1907) of John Wayne. This line replaced a much longer line that looped around the south side of Des Moines to serve Winterset. The line was abandoned in the early 1980s when no company acquired it after the railroad closed down. The old grade can still be made out as a line of trees across a number of fields.

Just east of the wye at Winear was once another track to the south, as well as a short siding to the north. With the west siding switch west of Ivy Avenue (Milepost 385.3), this group of tracks served the limestone quarry on the property of S. A. Robinson. It was reported that this quarry once had steam derricks, drills and a crusher plant. Today, there are no side tracks and just a number of holes from all of the quarry activity in the area.

For trains heading west, they are climbing one of the steepest grades on the line. The elevation at De Soto was 885 feet, while it will be 1105 feet at Earlham. That is an average of 0.6% with some grades of more than 1.0%.

387.5 EARLHAM – Earlham was established in 1869 following the arrival of the CRI&P. The town was named for Earlham College, a Quaker college in Richmond, Indiana. Earlham was incorporated on April 26, 1870. The father of John Wayne bought a local drug store here in 1910, so Earlham is another boyhood home of John Wayne.

In 1912, there was a track that ran several miles to the south to serve a stone quarry on the property of the Earlham Land Company. The quarry produced dimensional blocks, rubble, and crushed stone from limestone described as being white to buff in color. The plant had its own crusher plant and workers used steam derricks and drills to move and cut the stone. Early reports list at least seven quarries within several miles of Earlham working this same type of limestone.

The March 1916 Sanborn Insurance Map shows what the railroad was like in that year. In town, the CRI&P depot was on the north side of the tracks at Chestnut. Across the tracks to the south was a large stockyards complex. On the house track to the north of the depot were a number of shippers, including a "poultry, butter & eggs" facility, three coal yards, a lumber yard, and a grain elevator.

The Iowa Interstate has a 6005-foot long siding, and a second track to serve the Landus/FC grain elevator and feed mill, to the south. Farmers Cooperative Company (FC) was created out of the Farmers Elevator Company in 1944, making it the largest farmer-owned local agriculture cooperative in Iowa. Based in Farnhamville, Iowa, they have three manufacturing feed mills across central and northwest Iowa – Earlham, Greene and Larrabee. These mills manufacture nearly half a million tons of complete feed annually. The complex became part of the Landus Cooperative with the April 1, 2016, merger with the West Central Cooperative of Ralston, Iowa.

The town of Earlham is mainly to the north, and today has a population of 1450.

391.0 COUNTY LINE – The railroad heads to the northwest after leaving Earlham for Council Bluffs. Because of this, the railroad heads back into Dallas County just west of the Pitzer Lane grade crossing.

391.4 DEXTER - GERDAU – There is a short siding and a spur track to the south.

391.8 INTERSTATE 80 – The Iowa Interstate bridges over Interstate 80 just west of the Gerdau track. This is the eighth time that I-80 and the Iowa Interstate Railroad have crossed each other since Chicago.

393.1 DEXTER – Dexter is another town created as the CRI&P built through this area. The town was created in June 1868 as Marshalltown, but quickly changed its name when it discovered that the name was already being used in Iowa. The name Dexter came from a well-known trotter horse who had recently set a record for a mile race. It was incorporated that way in 1871.

Dexter was once the home of the Dexfield Amusement Park, located about three miles north of the town center. Dexfield was the first amusement park in Iowa, opening in 1915 and named for the communities of Dexter and Redfield. The park featured a swimming pool, pavilion, merry-go-round, ballfield, and many more attractions. It was the place to be for people living in western Iowa, at least until the end of the 1920s and the Depression years. The park finally closed after opening for a few weeks around July 4th in 1932. An attempt to reopen the park in 1933 ended with an infamous event, the July 23, 1933, shootout between members of the Barrow gang and police from across Iowa.

Bonnie and Clyde and their partners who made up the Barrow Gang had been in a series of robberies and shootouts over the previous month. The gang had decided to hide in the woods near the old Dexfield Amusement Park. During the night of July 23-24, 1933, a police posse from Dexter, with support from other law enforcement agencies from as far away as Des Moines, engaged in a gun battle with the Barrows. Every member of the outlaw gang was shot, with several dying. Bonnie and Clyde were able to leave the scene on foot, steal a car, and escape, only to be killed ten months later. However, the gang's photographer, Blanche Barrow was captured and jailed. Unique for any shootout with the Barrows, no police were killed.

Fifteen years later, Dexter was the scene of a less deadly event, but one which may have decided the Presidency of the United States. On September 18, 1948, a national plowing match was being held in Dexter. President Harry Truman was in attendance and made a speech attacking the 80th Congress for its record in regard to the American farmer. The speech is credited with gaining Truman the farm vote and possibly being the most important speech of his 1948 Whistle Stop Campaign.

The Iowa Interstate passes through the southern part of Dexter where it has a siding to the north to serve the Heartland Co-op elevator. This is the former Grainco facility, acquired on December 29, 2010. This complex has 2,800,000 bushels of grain storage capacity, a bagged feed facility, and the ability to load railcars.

The *New York Times* once called Dexter the "One Horse Town" after the source of its name. Today, the town proudly promotes the phrase by claiming that it is "The Original One Horse Town." The population of Dexter was 611 at the 2010 census, and little has changed since.

Dexter, Iowa. Photo by Barton Jennings.

Dexter, Iowa, "One Horse Town" sign. Photo by Sarah Jennings.

393.8 COUNTY LINE – Dallas County is to the east and to the west is Guthrie County. **Guthrie County** was created on January 15, 1851, and named by Theophilus Bryan, sheriff and later county judge of the county. He named it in honor of his friend Captain Edwin B. Guthrie, a commanding officer of a company of Iowa volunteers who died in the Mexican-American War in 1847. The county seat is Guthrie Center. In 2010, the population of the county was 10,954, and no community or town had more than 1700 residents.

395.8 COUNTY LINE – For westbound trains, the railroad is heading to the southwest and crosses the county line just north of 350th Street. The railroad has been basically following the county line and exits Guthrie County and enters Adair County. **Adair County** was created in 1851 from parts of Pottawattamie County and named for John Adair, eighth Governor of Kentucky and member of both the U.S. House and Senate. Adair also served in the Revolutionary War and War of 1812. The county has a population of about 8000 and its county seat, Greenfield, is the largest town in the county with 2000 residents.

Greenfield was not the original county seat. When the county was created, Summerset (now Fontanelle) was selected in 1855 by a panel of three commissioners. When Greenfield was created, it almost immediately caused an effort to move the county seat. Multiple petitions, votes and court rulings kept the seat in Summerset. In 1874, a vote approved the move but was challenged in court. Nevertheless, more than 200 citizens of Greenfield marched to Fontanelle, loaded the county's records and furniture into 75 wagons, and hauled them to Greenfield. Despite the orders of the sheriff, Greenfield became the effective county seat, made official a month later when the Supreme Court of Iowa approved the vote.

398.3 STUART – Stuart was originally a small Quaker community named Summit Grove. The first settlers arrived about 1850, and were made up of Quakers from Indiana and Ohio.

Shortly after the arrival of the Quakers, Charles Stuart, an agent for a scales company, made a stop in the community. Later Captain Charles Stuart, a veteran of the Civil War, purchased land near the present-day Stuart. When the Rock Island built through the area, Captain Stuart and the railroad officials worked closely to lay out the town and ensure that Stuart would be the site of the division station and machine shops. The plat of the town was filed for record on September 29, 1870, and the Town of Stuart was incorporated on February 6, 1877.

With the arrival of the railroad, a number of crude buildings were built to handle the rail maintenance work. Soon, the original wooden railroad shops and terminal buildings were replaced by brick and stone. The engine house was enlarged over the years to accommodate as many as 38 locomotives. There were also large machine, blacksmith and boiler shops, making Stuart the only large shop on the Rock Island Line between Silvis, Illinois, and Omaha, Nebraska.

The brick train depot, which is still standing today, was built in 1879 with material from a demolished depot at Rock Island, Illinois, and from parts of the original 1869 station. As was standard at the time, the station contained both a ladies' and a gentleman's waiting room, as well as a ticket office and a baggage room. Today, the station, the only remaining railroad structure in Stuart, is on the National Register of Historic Places, placed there in 1980. Look for the Hotel Stuart, across Front Street from the depot, also listed on the National Register of Historic Places. For years, this was the hotel of choice for travelers visiting Stuart. Note the restored hotel sign stating that the hotel is "Strictly Modern."

Former Rock Island station in Stuart, Iowa. Photo by Barton Jennings.

Restored Hotel Stuart sign, Stuart, Iowa. Photo by Barton Jennings.

Council Bluffs Subdivision

During the Panic of 1893, the railroad began considering the movement of the shops from Stuart to the Des Moines area, near the junction with the north-south line from Kansas City to Minneapolis. In 1896, the official word went out that a decision had been made to move the division station to Valley Junction. Although the move wasn't made immediately, on September 24, 1897, the Rock Island declared that the "railroad shops at Stuart will be cleaned out by Saturday night." With the removal of the shops, more than 400 people moved from town during the next week. This depopulation moved the center of Stuart's activity from the shops near the south end of town to the north end of town where other businesses existed.

With the removal of the railroad shops, the number of tracks at Stuart greatly reduced. However, in 1973, there were still a siding and several industry tracks to the south, and several house tracks to the north of the mainline. However, today, there are only parts of the siding and a short spur track into the Koster Grain feed mill to the south. Koster Grain was created in 1977 in Maple River, Iowa, and has grown from that grain elevator into a regional feed provider for turkeys, horses, cows, and other livestock.

Reportedly, one of the more exciting happenings to occur in Stuart was the robbery of the First National Bank by the infamous Bonnie and Clyde on April 16, 1934. Bonnie and Clyde were killed about a month later on May 23rd in Sailes, Louisiana. The bank building is now the home of the Stuart Police Department.

399.1 COUNTY LINE – Heading west from Stuart, the railroad turns back to the northwest and leaves Adair County and re-enters Guthrie County. There is a switch to the track to the south that serves a new industrial park and several shippers, including Wausau Supply.

401.5 EAST MENLO – To the north is the Flint Hills Resources Ethanol Plant, a 120 million gallon per year plant. This ethanol production facility began operating in September 2008 and was known as the Hawkeye Renewable Ethanol Plant. Hawkeye, according to the company's website at the time, "is a privately owned, Iowa based renewable energy company which uses locally produced corn to manufacture and distribute ethanol in the United States." Flint Hills Resources acquired the plant in 2010. The plant has a five-track yard as well as a three-track loading facility.

403.2 MENLO – Menlo is another railroad-based community and is located at the west switch of the Flint Hills Ethanol Plant. It was originally founded in 1869 as "The Switch." To recognize that this was the only community on the line in Guthrie County, the name became Guthrie Switch, then Guthrie. To avoid confusion with nearby Guthrie Center, the town was renamed Menlo. The name Menlo is believed to come from Menlo, Ireland. The town was incorporated in 1881. Signs into town state, "A town of few and friend of all." The town's population is approximately 350 and there is a short spur track into a small grain storage facility.

At one time, Menlo was a junction with a branch to the north to Guthrie Center. On November 25, 1879, the Guthrie & North Western Railroad Company was incorporated to build from near Guthrie (Menlo) "on the main line of the Chicago, Rock Island and Pacific Railroad" northward through Guthrie Center to "some other point on the northern or western boundary of the State of Iowa to be hereafter determined." The railroad built 14 miles of track from Menlo to Guthrie Center by 1880 and was soon leased to the Chicago, Rock Island & Pacific Railroad Company. The line soon failed financially and was sold to the CRI&P under foreclosure for $200,000 on September 3, 1890. In 1969, the line was abandoned. The old grade can be seen curving off to the north at the west end of the railroad curve on the west side of Menlo.

Heading west, the railroad climbs over several sandy ridges. It peaks at an elevation of 1304 feet at Milepost 407, and begins a descent of as much as 0.8% until Milepost 412.

Council Bluffs Subdivision

408.8 MIDDLE RIVER BRIDGE – The Middle River starts in southwestern Guthrie County and flows generally eastward, passing through Adair, Madison, and Warren Counties. Most of the route through Warren County has been straightened and channelized to protect the south side of Des Moines from flooding. It eventually flows into the Des Moines River southeast of the City of Des Moines, 125 miles downstream from where it begins.

The railroad crosses the Middle River on a single-track bridge consisting of three deck plate girder spans measuring a total of 210 feet long. The bridge carries a builders plate stating, "Built by the American Bridge Co., Lassig Branch, Chicago, Ill, 1901." Just southeast from this bridge the South Fork Middle River flows into the Middle River. Heading west, the railroad follows the South Fork to near Adair, Iowa.

410.1 CASEY – Casey was named for one of the railroad contractors building the CRI&P. The town was founded on January 12, 1869, and incorporated in 1880. In July of each year, the community hosts the Casey Fun Days, a mix of community activities, including a parade, cook-outs, and more. Casey gained even more fame in 2015 when its city hall burned down, part of a scheme to cover the theft of more than $250,000 by the city clerk. This was a big expense to the community, especially since its entire population is less than 500.

There is a short siding to the south at Casey that serves a small elevator and fertilizer complex. This facility started as a local elevator cooperative, but was sold to the West Central Cooperative in 2001, giving them 1.1 million bushels of grain storage and dry fertilizer warehouse storage. West Central Cooperative started as the Farmers Cooperative Association of Ralston in 1933, and became the West Central Cooperative in 1979. They own and manage almost thirty facilities across western Iowa.

412.8 SOUTH FORK MIDDLE RIVER BRIDGE – The railroad continues to follow the South Fork. This bridge consists of two deck plate girder spans, each 56 feet long. Just west of this bridge marks the location of the start of the Adair track realignment.

413.6 SOUTH FORK MIDDLE RIVER BRIDGE – This bridge consists of three deck plate girder spans. One is 80 feet long while the other two are 52 feet long. Throughout this area, the railroad curves back and forth through a number of fields as it climbs grades of almost one percent as it approaches Adair.

416.3 COUNTY LINE – Look for the small private grade crossing that marks the county line between Guthrie and Adair Counties. Heading west, the railroad again leaves Guthrie County and enters Adair County.

416.9 ADAIR – Adair, with a population of about 800, sits on the county line between Adair and Guthrie Counties with part of the town in each. Look for the yellow "smiley-face" water tower to find Adair. If you are on the nearby Interstate 80, you will also see signs that read, "Welcome to Adair; it'll make you smile." Some businesses in town also use the slogan of "The happiest town on Earth."

The Rock Island Railroad built through today's Adair in 1868. To get through the area, the railroad had to cross the ridge that forms the watershed divide between the Missouri River and the Mississippi River. Recognizing this, the railroad initially called the area Summit Cut, and the railroad still peaks here today at 1407.54 feet of elevation. Adair is reportedly the second highest town in Iowa. The name Summit is still used as the name of the township in Adair County.

The book *History of Adair County, Iowa, and its People, 1915 – Volume I* states that the first settlers in Summit Township and the town of Adair were Azariah Sisson and his son, William A., who arrived here in June, 1869. The book also states that William A. Sisson was a "train dispatcher for the Chicago, Rock Island & Pacific Railroad at Atlantic for about two years." The first building at what became Adair was reportedly built in 1868 to serve as the headquarters for the engineers and surveyors building the railroad. Later, the building was used as a maintenance-of-way section house.

As the population slowly grew, area government was organized and Walnut Township was split to create Summit Township. About the same time, the community of Adair was laid out in the summer of 1872 on the property of George C. Tallman. The county recorder officially received the plat on August 20, 1872. The growth was initially slow, but the railroad built a depot at Adair during the summer of 1873 and a lumber yard soon located nearby. Adair was incorporated in 1884.

The name Adair, used by both the town and the county, honors General John Adair, a general in the War of 1812 who later became the 8th governor of Kentucky. John Adair first gained notoriety when he joined the South Carolina state militia and served in the Revolutionary War. He was captured by the British at the Battle of Camden (August 16, 1780) and escaped after several months, but was soon recaptured. After being released during a prisoner exchange, Adair was commissioned as a lieutenant in the South Carolina militia. After the war, he was elected as a delegate to South Carolina's convention to ratify the United States Constitution. During the Northwest Indian War in 1791, John Adair was promoted to captain, and then major. He became a general during the War of 1812. After moving to Kentucky, Adair served in the U.S. House of Representatives, then as Governor of Kentucky, and finally a term in the U.S. Senate.

In 1973, the Rock Island Railroad indicated that there were no tracks here except for the mainline. Today, the Landus Cooperative has an elevator in Adair. The elevator was until 2016 the West Central Cooperative elevator, known as Adair Feed & Grain. The website stated that the Adair Feed and Grain Company was a "family owned and operated business that we started in 1961." It was purchased in 1991, gaining the cooperative access to the Iowa Interstate Railroad and new markets.

In late 2015, the members of the West Central Cooperative of Ralston, Iowa, and the Farmers Cooperative Company of Ames, Iowa, approved a merger between the two cooperatives. The merger became effective on April 1, 2016, creating the Landus Cooperative, the seventh largest grain company in North America based on storage capacity. The Cooperative states that it has approximately 7000 member-owners and has facilities in more than 70 communities in Iowa and Minnesota. The new cooperative has shuttle-loading facilities on all seven major Iowa rail lines, and is based in Ames, Iowa. This elevator is located on the east side of town and is a traditional elevator complex as well as covered warehouse space, connected by an overhead auger system that crosses the railroad's mainline. The complex has its own tracks, a small yard, and a small 4-axle Plymouth locomotive.

Adair Track Realignment

As part of the Rock Island's massive line rebuilding of the late 1940s and early 1950s, the company relocated about 6.6 miles of track near Adair in 1954. The track alignment through Adair between the two overpasses (2nd Street and White Pole Road) was not significantly changed, but the tracks either side of Adair were changed greatly.

On the east side of Adair, it is easy to see the old alignment as it is used by the Adair Feed & Grain complex. East of the mill's trackage, the line wandered around the hillsides to the north before crossing the new grade about Milepost 414.9, east of the Hickory Avenue grade crossing. Most of this part of the old grade is still used as local farm roads. Heading on east, the original grade continued to head to the southeast and briefly back into Adair County before turning to the northeast, crossing Gibbon Avenue and a small stream. The original grade then continued to the northeast across a number of fields, bridged the South Fork Middle River just south of the current bridge at Milepost 413.6, and rejoined the new alignment near the Juniper Avenue grade crossing at Milepost 413.1.

Heading west from Adair, the track realignment started immediately, heading straight and passing under Interstate 80 instead of sharply curving to the south. The original line then curved west and crossed the new alignment just west of today's Cedar Avenue grade crossing near Milepost 418.5. It then closely followed the old highway past the Jesse James Historical Site before the two alignments rejoin west of Turkey Creek at Milepost 419.7. Only a few signs of this former grade are visible today, as most of it has been included in area farm fields.

417.9 INTERSTATE 80 – The railroad passes under I-80 just west of Adair. This is the ninth time that the railroad and Interstate meet. When discussing why the railroad industry lost much of its dominance in the freight and passenger business, the government support of highways is generally mentioned. The fact that Interstate 80 was built in direct competition with the Rock Island Railroad is clear from the number of meetings along the route. It is also probably not a coincidence that the railroad began to quickly fail financially after the highway was built, going from a financial condition where the railroad could be basically rebuilt in the 1950s to going into bankruptcy in the 1970s, less than a decade after the Interstate was completed.

419.0 JESSE JAMES HISTORICAL SITE – About 1.5 miles west of Adair is the Jesse James Historical Site. It is not visible from the railroad, but is on the north side of the low ridge to the north. This monument is at the site where the James-Younger Gang staged the first robbery of a moving train on the evening of July 21, 1873. To rob the train, the gang derailed the Rock Island train by pulling one rail out just before the train got to it. This resulted in the train rolling onto its side, killing the engineer (John Rafferty) and fireman (Dennis Foley), and injuring a number of the passengers. The James Gang, dressed as members of the Ku Klux Klan, then robbed the survivors as they crawled out of the wreck. The gang was after a $75,000 gold shipment, but it was delayed, and the gang got away with only $3,000 in money and jewelry.

In 1954, the Rock Island Railroad erected a large steam locomotive driver wheel with a plaque stating: "Site of the first train robbery in the west, committed by the notorious Jesse James and his gang of outlaws – July 21, 1873." A short section of display track is also located at this small roadside park.

Sign at Jesse James Historical Site near Adair, Iowa. Photo by Sarah Jennings.

Each year on the third weekend of July, Adair celebrates "Jesse James Days," complete with parade and a re-enactment of the train robbery.

419.3 TURKEY CREEK BRIDGE – This bridge consists of three deck plate girder spans – one fifty feet long and two 24 feet long. To the north is the former U.S. Highway 6, now White Pole Road. What is now known as the White Pole

Road started with a Good Roads Convention in Des Moines on March 8-9, 1910. The plan was for citizens along a River-to-River road (Davenport to Council Bluffs) to build and maintain their own road. Ten thousand farmers volunteered to build the road, not costing the state any money. While the original road went north of here, a road between Atlantic and Des Moines was also built through the support of the White Pole Auto Club. The original White Pole Road was then designated in 1910 and followed along the Chicago, Rock Island & Pacific Railroad from Des Moines to Council Bluffs. Much of the route later became U.S. Highway 6 and remained that until the construction of Interstate 80 in the 1960s. In this area, communities have begun to promote the historic route as a tourist attraction. Here, it is described as a 26-mile scenic and historic byway that runs parallel to Interstate 80 between mile markers 76 and 100 and connects the communities of Adair, Casey, Menlo, Stuart and Dexter, Iowa.

White Pole Road sign near Dexter, Iowa. Photo by Sarah Jennings.

Heading west, the railroad follows Turkey Creek downhill as far as the west side of Wiota at Milepost 435. Along this route the railroad passes through farmland and a number of windmills.

419.72 = 420.59 MILEAGE CONVERSION – This mileage conversion, provided in Rock Island Railroad documents, is due to the line changes around Adair. The new line was much straighter, which eliminated about a mile of track. The Iowa Interstate provides the information in a different manner by stating that the distance from Milepost 420 to Milepost 421 is 400 feet, and the two mileposts can clearly be seen near each other.

420.6 COUNTY LINE – Heading west, the railroad goes from Adair County into Cass County. Look for the road into the windmills on the north side of White Pole Road to the north. **Cass County** was established in 1851. Previously, it had been a part of Pottawattamie County. The county was named after Lewis Cass, a Michigan senator and a Democratic presidential candidate of 1848. The county has a population of about 14,000, with more than half living in the county seat of Atlantic.

425.7 ANITA – In 1900, maps show that the Rock Island depot was at the south end of Walnut Street on the north side of the mainline. There were two sidings to the north of the depot. The northernmost siding still exists and is used to serve the Wiota/Anita Elevator Company. The Iowa Interstate has a 4980-foot siding to the south of the mainline at Anita.

Anita is located on property once owned by Lewis Beason, who had it surveyed and platted in 1869, the same year the railroad built through the property and a post office was established. In a dinner with railroad officials, Lewis Beason was offered to have the railroad station named after him, but he suggested the name of his wife's niece, Anita Cowles of San Francisco.

In 1870, Beason sold the property to Franklin H. Whitney, B. F. Allen, and John P. Cook, who promoted the town and sold lots. As the town grew, it was incorporated on June 10, 1875. The Pearl Grist Mill was built in 1877, and the farming of potatoes became the major crop in the Anita area. Today, Anita has about 1000 residents and is probably best known for the nearby Lake Anita State Park, located just south of town.

432.5 WIOTA – Wiota was created in 1872 as a depot on the Chicago, Rock Island & Pacific Railroad Company, located on the property of Franklin H. Whitney, one of the owners of nearby Anita. B. F. Allen, a partner in Anita, also was apparently a partner in this venture. A post office opened at Wiota in 1873, although a town site wasn't recorded until November 13, 1877, and it wasn't incorporated until 1884. In 1900, maps show two sidings to the south of the mainline of the Rock Island. The farthest south track served a number of industries, including from east to west, corn cribs, stock yards, three elevators, and a coal dealer. The depot was on the south side of the main track at the end of Centre (Center) Street. Today, there is only a mainline at Wiota, and a short house track into the Wiota Elevator. This elevator uses the old Rock Island depot as their office and scale house.

Former Rock Island depot, Wiota, Iowa. Photo by Sarah Jennings.

The name Wiota has a confusing history. If it comes from the Sioux word "wa-ota," it relates to the passage of time, such as "many snows" or "many moons" or "many suns." It could have also come from the Winnebago and Iowa languages where "niota" means "much water." Many seem to think the second is more likely as the area has a tendency to flood.

While Wiota initially grew quickly, it peaked early and never grew very large. In the 2010 census, the population was 116. Few signs of the many businesses that once existed here can be found today.

West of Wiota, the railroad continues to follow Turkey Creek. Because of this, the railroad crosses a number of small streams from the hillsides to the north. During 2017, the Iowa Interstate had plans to replace many of the small ballast deck timber trestles with new precast concrete spans. Modernizing these bridges reduces their maintenance needs and increases the weight capacity of the railroad.

436.0 HAMPTON ROAD – The railroad passes under Hampton Road and then turns to the north, finally leaving the Turkey Creek watershed.

437.2 U.S. HIGHWAY 6/71 – The railroad curves to the west through a deep cut. Above, U.S. Highways 6 and 71 bridge over the railroad. As stated elsewhere, U.S. Highway 6 is the Grand Army of the Republic Highway, and exists from Bishop, California to Provincetown, Massachusetts. It has followed the Iowa Interstate Railroad across much of Iowa. U.S. Highway 71 is a north-south road between International Falls, Minnesota, at the Canadian border, south to a junction with U.S. Highway 190 between Port Barre and Krotz Springs, Louisiana. The two roads share the same route from Interstate 80, just a few miles north of here, to the east side of Atlantic, Iowa.

440.0 ATLANTIC – Atlantic, using station code "AT," is the county seat of Cass County and the home of more than 7000 residents, the largest town served by the railroad since Des Moines. When the town was founded in 1868, the residents determined that they were about halfway between the

Council Bluffs Subdivision

Atlantic and Pacific oceans. They flipped a coin to determine which ocean the town would be named after. However, the Rock Island Railroad planned to establish a town here also and the planning engineer had already chosen the name Avoca. The local residents got their way when the town was incorporated on November 26, 1869, and the name Avoca was used for a station name on the original line further west.

The Iowa Interstate has a 6200-foot siding here between Mileposts 439.5 and 440.8. There is a siding to the north, plus two more tracks often used to store freight cars. On the south side of the IAIS mainline at about the center of the small yard is the restored CRI&P station, now offices for the Chamber of Commerce, located at 102 Chestnut Street. The station has also housed a small restaurant. The station was built of brick in 1898 and is listed on the National Register of Historic Places. The depot was built in the Renaissance Revival style, and according to the National Register application, "the Atlantic depot's design is unusual and does not fit any of the standard Rock Island plans."

Former Rock Island station, Atlantic, Iowa. Photo by Sarah Jennings.

The report includes a great deal of information about the design of the station. It states that the "interior of the depot is dominated by function. In the custom of the day, separate waiting rooms were provided for men and women in the one-story wings. The west room – currently the freight room — was the men's waiting room, while the east ladies' waiting room eventually became the one public room." The report also describes the office area of the station by stating that the "central area of the building contains the restrooms and the ticket/dispatcher office on the ground floor and the roadmaster's office on the second floor. The upstairs cannot be reached from the interior but is only accessed by a staircase and exterior entrance on the south — downtown side — of the building." The west end of the building was the baggage and express room, separated by an open breezeway. The National Register application stated that "sometime during the 1950s, the breezy, covered walkway between the depot and the express buildings was filled in with wood frame partitions and heated." This area has been opened up today to restore the depot to its original look.

Sign on former Rock Island station, Atlantic, Iowa. Photo by Sarah Jennings.

Maps from about 1900 indicate that the railroad had a water tower east of the depot. Further east was also a building labeled as "Freight." North of the small yard was property marked as "Warehouse Lots" with several tracks serving the area. At the east end of town at Hazel Street was a track that curved to the north, crossed the East Nish-

Council Bluffs Subdivision

nabotna River, and served the National Starch Company facility.

Atlantic is an important location for the Iowa Interstate Railroad. It is the home of the Atlantic Switcher, based out of a new railroad office at the west end of the yard near the Locust Street grade crossing. It will become even more important with the construction of a new ethanol plant just north of town on the Atlantic Spur.

IAIS 715 at Atlantic, Iowa. Photo by Barton Jennings.

Atlantic Northern & Southern Railway

Please pay close attention to this bit of railroad history. In 1906, the Atlantic Northern & Southern Railway was created. The company built a line northward from the west side of Atlantic to Kimballton, Iowa. It then extended the south end of the line through downtown Atlantic, and then southward to Villisca on today's Amtrak *California Zephyr* route, all in Iowa. Little information is available on this line. In a 1910 Official Guide, the only route being operated was the one to Kimballton. A local history flyer notes that the line reached Grant (formerly Garfield, Iowa) on the southern line on December 27, 1910. Apparently, the railroad failed in 1913 and it was broken into two parts.

The part of the line that headed north from near today's Atlantic Spur switch became the Atlantic Northern Railway. This road was formed in 1913 and operated from Atlantic to Kimballton. It was abandoned in 1936. The second part, the line south to Villisca, was sold to the Atlantic Southern Railway, which was abandoned in 1915, according to the Iowa DOT railroad abandonment records. For researchers, the name of this short-lived railroad causes confusion, as there was already another railroad here named Atlantic Southern.

West of the Locust Street grade crossing, and located at the west end of the Atlantic Yard, can be seen a faint grade curving off to the south. This route, the Atlantic Southern Railroad Company, was incorporated on November 22, 1879, "to construct, maintain, and operate a railroad, with single or double track, extending from a point on the Main Line of the Chicago, Rock Island and Pacific Railroad at or near the City of Atlantic in the County of Cass, and State of Iowa, in a southerly direction through the town of Lewis in said County, to some point on the southern or western boundary of the State of Iowa, to be determined, to Griswold, with the necessary side tracks, turn outs, station grounds, stations and other buildings, which it may be found necessary in such maintenance and operation." It quickly built a line from Atlantic southward to Lewis (nine miles) that year, and then six miles further south to Griswold the next year. There it connected with a CB&Q line that came north from the mainline at Red Oak, Iowa. The Atlantic Southern Railroad was soon acquired by the CRI&P. It was abandoned in November 1942, 63 years after the railroad was founded.

Atlantic Cutoff

The Iowa Interstate route west of Atlantic, known as the Atlantic Cutoff, is actually a new line opened on September 14, 1953, by the Rock Island. John Dow Farrington became the chief operating officer of the CRI&P in 1936, and began a series of modernizations across the system, including everything from new passenger and freight equipment to improved rail lines. Among these was the Atlantic Cutoff, a mostly straight line westward from near Atlantic to Peter, where the Rock Island utilized eleven miles of Chicago Great Western track to reach Council Bluffs. This route, involving 35 new and 12 rehabilitated miles of track, saved about 10 miles of distance via Avoca. When the new line was completed, the railroad abandoned the line between Shelby and East Council Bluffs, and Atlantic and Walnut, by November of the same year.

In materials put out by the railroad, the Cutoff was described as the "last and largest of a series of line changes made in the last 16 years under the railroad's improvement program." The opening celebration was held at Atlantic and featured Farrington driving a silver spike to officially complete the project. Early records of the railroad indicate that the route of the Cutoff was actually the proposed route for the original line, as presented by Grenville M. Dodge. However, the difficulty of construction and possibly the financial encouragement by existing communities led the railroad to build the original line to the north.

440.7 EAST NISHNABOTNA RIVER BRIDGE – The Nishnabotna River is a tributary of the Missouri River and generally consists of two parallel rivers in Iowa: the East and West Nishnabotna Rivers. The East Branch is about 100 miles long and flows in from the northeast, while the main river is only about a dozen miles.

The bridge includes two 55-foot, three 50-foot, and four 44-foot deck plate girder spans. The bridge was built in 1902 by the American Bridge Company.

440.8 ATLANTIC SPUR SWITCH – Known by the Rock Island as Audubon Junction, today this location is the connection with the Iowa Interstate's Atlantic Spur. When the railroad was acquired by the IAIS, the line existed to Audubon, about 25 miles north. However, the line beyond Moorman (about 3 miles from here) was abandoned in 1995. Originally, this route was the Atlantic & Audubon Railroad Company, incorporated in 1878 to build northward into Audubon County. It was eventually sold to the Chicago, Rock Island & Pacific Railroad Company. Details about this line can be found on page 289.

This is the location of the start of the Atlantic Cutoff. Where the railroad curves to the southwest, the original line continued straight ahead to the northwest. The new line, instead of following several winding streams, now cuts straight across a series of rolling hills, creating a series of grades between 0.8% and 1.0%. Note the lack of grade crossings due to the cuts and fills.

441.6 BUCK CREEK BRIDGE – This new bridge was built as part of the Atlantic Cutoff. It includes two 60-foot spans and one 80-foot span, all deck plate girder designs. Buck Creek starts about five miles north of here and flows into the East Nishnabotna River just to the south.

446.5 INDIAN CREEK BRIDGE – This bridge has a 100-foot deck plate girder span across the stream with an 80-foot deck plate girder span approach on each end. Indian Creek forms on the west side of Audubon, Iowa, and flows to the southwest to here, and then south into the East Nishnabotna River. Indian Creek has a history of flooding and it has been channeled along parts of its route.

Just east of this bridge at Milepost 446.1 is a bridge over 555th Street. The bridge consists of a 60-foot deck plate girder span, with shorter spans on each end. This bridge was installed here in 1952 as part of the Atlantic Cutoff. However, the main span was actually built in 1902 by the American Bridge Company and relocated here during the construction.

447.4 COUNTY LINE – The county line between Cass County, to the east, and Pottawattamie County to the west, is just west of the county road overpass. **Pottawattamie County**

Council Bluffs Subdivision

is somewhat unique in that it has two active courthouses, one in the county seat of Council Bluffs, and one in Avoca. 62,000 of the county's 95,000 residents live in Council Bluffs. Avoca only has 1500 residents. The county was named in 1847 for the local Indian tribe. The word Pottawattamie reportedly means "keepers or makers of the fire."

449.6 WALNUT CREEK BRIDGE – This bridge consists of three deck plate girder spans, each 60 feet long. Walnut Creek starts about ten miles to the north and flows southward just a few miles west of the East Nishnabotna River. It eventually turns west and enters the West Nishnabotna River.

450.6 510TH STREET – Less than two miles south of here is the site of the March 8, 1944, crash of a B-24 Liberator bomber. On that day, a training exercise turned bad when a midair collision resulted in one plane crashing, killing all seven crewmen aboard the plane. A model B-24 weather vane serves as part of a memorial to the crew. The memorial was reportedly first built in 1994 by a troop of Boy Scouts from Walnut, Iowa.

B-24 Liberator bomber crash memorial. Photo by Barton Jennings.

453.7 GRAYBILL CREEK BRIDGE – Graybill Creek starts a few miles to the north and flows to the south and into the West Nishnabotna River. The bridge consists of three deck plate girder spans – an 80-foot span in the middle and 60-foot approach spans.

455.0 HILLIS – Hillis was a short stretch of double track on the Rock Island's Atlantic Cutoff; there was no community here. The second track, located between Mileposts 454 and 457, was located to the north of the mainline. A set of crossovers existed in the middle at Milepost 455.6 and were known as Hillis. Today, a siding still exists here to the north, but it is only 4190 feet long and is located between Mileposts 454.7 and 455.5.

The name Hillis probably came from the Hillis family which included Isaac L. Hillis, one-time mayor of Des Moines. The family was long involved in politics, and several members were early surveyors in Indiana and Illinois. Some members of the family also invested in area railroads.

459.3 HANCOCK JUNCTION – This is the junction with the Oakland-Hancock spur that serves the Scoular elevator in Hancock. The spur is all that is left of a former CRI&P line, running north-south, that once crossed here. On November 22, 1879, the Avoca, Macedonia & Southwestern Railroad Company (AM&SW) was incorporated to buy the Avoca, Harlan & Northern Railroad and extend it further south. While the line was chartered to build south of Macedonia, it only built 17 miles of track from Avoca to Carson by 1880. As with many railroads like this, the CRI&P soon acquired the company and the line acquired the name of the Carson Branch. The track between Oakland and Carson was abandoned by the CRI&P in 1954. The line north of Hancock was abandoned in 1979.

Hancock is about a mile north of the IAIS mainline. The AM&SW caused the creation of Hancock when the Carson Branch was completed in 1880. Established by F.

H. Hancock, it was officially incorporated on May 16, 1891. Details about the spur can be found on page 293.

Just east of the switch, the Iowa Interstate bridges over the Hancock Spur and U.S. Highway 59. Highway 59 is part of the NAFTA Corridor Highway System, starting at the Mexican border at Laredo, Texas, and ending at the Canadian border north of Lancaster, Minnesota. It connects to major roads at both borders to provide highway transportation into the other two countries.

459.4 WEST NISHNABOTNA RIVER BRIDGE – The Nishnabotna River is a tributary of the Missouri River and generally consists of two parallel rivers in Iowa: the East and West Nishnabotna Rivers. Like the East Branch, the West Branch is about 100 miles long while the main river is only about a dozen miles. The name Nishnabotna comes from a Native American word meaning "canoe-making river." C. W. McCall mentioned the river is some of his music, referring to it as being "a yard wide and a foot deep." McCall knew the area since his albums were recorded in nearby Omaha.

Many people probably don't know who C. W. McCall is, however during the 1970s this advertising executive from Western Iowa was a radio favorite. Bill Fries started writing advertising for the Old Home Bread brand of the Metz Baking Company. To sell the bread, he wrote about the adventures of a truck driver, C. W. McCall, his dog Sloan, and the truck stop where he always ate the bread. Many of the stories were based upon his home in Audubon, Iowa, and several won Clio Awards, the advertising industry's equivalent of an Emmy. So popular were his stories that he began recording albums and toured as C. W. McCall. It should be noted that Chip Davis, the creator of "Mannheim Steamroller," wrote the music to Fries' lyrics. After retiring from music, Bill Fries moved to Ouray, Colorado, and served three terms as mayor.

The West Nishnabotna River bridge includes four 90-foot long spans, one 100-foot span, and one 78-foot span, all deck plate girders.

461.8 400TH STREET – As stated elsewhere, when the Atlantic Cutoff was built, there were few at-grade crossings with roads. With the cuts and fills of the line, most crossings include a bridge. Several of them, like this one, are wooden bridges built by the railroad to take rural farm roads across the tracks.

463.6 SILVER CREEK BRIDGE – This bridge has a 100-foot span over the water with approaches 70 feet long. All spans are deck plate girder designs. Silver Creek, or Big Silver Creek as it is known by some, flows south into the West Nishnabotna River. It is a long stream, stretching most of the way north-south across the state.

466.6 MIDDLE SILVER CREEK BRIDGE – This bridge consists of three deck plate girder spans – 60 feet, 79 feet, and 80 feet long. The western part of Silver Creek forms to the north near Shelby on the original route, and flows south into Silver Creek near Silver City.

471.6 KEG CREEK BRIDGE – This deck plate girder bridge includes four spans with lengths of 100 feet, 90 feet, and two of 60 feet. Keg Creek is another north-south running stream that drains western Iowa. This one drains into the Missouri River near Pacific Junction, Iowa.

474.7 PETER – Peter was once a junction location, as the Rock Island joined with the Chicago Great Western for access on into Council Bluffs as a part of the Atlantic Cutoff. CRI&P track charts show the Rock Island ownership of the tracks ended at milepost 474.68, and the tracks west of here were owned by the Chicago & North Western, originally Chicago Great Western.

The Chicago Great Western built this line as their Fort Dodge to Council Bluffs route, completed in 1903. The C&NW abandoned the CGW line in 1971, leaving the Rock Island on the line. Today, it is Iowa Interstate Railroad. The siding here, located on the south side of the mainline, was abandoned in 1999.

476.3 MCCLELLAND – McClelland was founded in 1903 when the Chicago Great Western built their line to Council Bluffs through land owned by W. H. McClelland. When the railroad was built, there were no towns in the area, so the railroad supported the growth of McClelland as a water stop and a source of freight and passenger business. The 1910 *First Annual Report of the Chicago Great Western Railroad Company* stated that the "Iowa Townsite Company was organized July 5, 1901, with a capital stock of $10,000 all issued and owned by the Chicago Great Western Railroad Company." The Iowa Townsite Company established a town site at McClelland. The town quickly included a lumberyard, depot, three general stores, a drugstore, hardware store, two saloons, a livery stable and blacksmith shop, and a grain elevator. A post office opened in 1904 and the town of McClelland was incorporated on December 14, 1904.

The *1913 Annual Report* of the CGW stated that a new 22' x 55' frame depot had been built at McClelland to replace the "former depot destroyed by fire." For many years, McClelland was the location of a siding. Today, a short spur track is all that remains. Likewise, McClelland has seen a drop in its population, with only 150 residents today. The street to the south of the tracks is Railroad Street. Iowa Interstate trains heading west drop down grades of 0.5% all the way to Council Bluffs from here.

McClelland is starting to feel the nearby growth in the Council Bluffs-Omaha area. Several new subdivisions and a number of rural houses have been built in the area over the past few years. Downtown McClelland has the feel of a small community with several parks, including the Ellison Gardens near the grain elevator buildings.

481.5 GILLIATT – Look for the road crossing with Gilliatt Avenue. Howard Gilliat of London, England, was on the Finance Committee of the Chicago Great Western during the late 1890s. It is likely the name came from him as he raised a great deal of funds for the construction of the company.

Gilliatt was another town site created by the Iowa Townsite Company. The 1910 report stated that there was "purchased for this purpose 2,177 acres of land at a total cost of $161,460.92. Sales have been made aggregating $136,031.84, and there remains unsold 199.77 acres of land and town lots, with an estimated selling value of about $50,000.

482.6 U.S. HIGHWAY 6 – This three-span deck plate girder bridge (50 feet, 82 feet, and 81 feet) crosses U.S. Highway 6, a road that has followed the railroad across Iowa. The bridge was built in 1968.

484.6 LITTLE MOSQUITO CREEK BRIDGE – This bridge crosses the creek and McPherson Avenue with a series of deck plate girder spans with a timber trestle/I-beam mix on the west end. The bridge was built in 1901 and the approaches were replaced in 2013 and 2014. The railroad has been following Little Mosquito Creek downhill for the past few miles. Just to the west, Little Mosquito Creek flows into Mosquito Creek. Also to the west is Interstate 80.

485.0 CRI&P OWNERSHIP – Rock Island track charts show that from this point west, the tracks revert back to CRI&P ownership. Other documents state that this happened at Milepost 486.34.

486.0 COUNCIL BLUFFS YARD LIMITS – This is the east end of the yard limits for Council Bluffs.

486.2 MOSQUITO CREEK BRIDGE – This bridge also crosses Valley View Drive using a series of deck plate girder

Council Bluffs Subdivision

spans. The bridge has been rebuilt several times as Valley View has been widened.

Mosquito Creek starts near Earling in west-central Iowa. It flows south to here, with I-80 using the valley it created. South of here about ten miles, it flows into the Missouri River.

486.4 RIGG – Some documents state that the tracks reverted back to CRI&P ownership here. However, it likely happened just off the west side of the bridge over BNSF, as the original CRI&P line ran along the west side of the former Milwaukee Road line and crossed the Chicago Great Western at the end of the bridge.

486.6 BRIDGE OVER BNSF – This bridge, consisting of one 120-foot through plate girder span, crosses the former Milwaukee Road route, now BNSF. Just west of the bridge, the railroad went from single track to double track for the approach into Council Bluffs, Iowa.

The Chicago Great Western once went straight at the end of the bridge and curved to the west to stay on the north side of the Rock Island's Council Bluffs yard. The Rock Island originally came in from the north, located on the west side of the former Chicago, Milwaukee, St. Paul & Pacific Railroad route now used by BNSF. It then followed the current route into Council Bluffs.

487.1 HARRY LANGDON BOULEVARD – The railroad passes under the Harry Langdon Boulevard overpass and then curves sharply to the northwest on a curve that varies between three and four degrees, pretty sharp for a mainline. Just to the south, the former Milwaukee Road line, now BNSF, makes a similar curve.

Harry Langdon was a vaudeville and silent films comedian star, considered to be one of the four best comics of the silent film era. He later worked in sound movies, but his wide-eyed, childlike character failed to make the transition and he had to change to a henpecked-husband character.

Langdon was born in Council Bluffs on June 15, 1884, and worked local medicine shows and stock companies before he was twenty. He was in vaudeville by 1906 and making movies by 1923. He worked with a number of the early stars, even being briefly partnered with Oliver Hardy. Harry Langdon has a star on the Hollywood Walk of Fame. Council Bluffs celebrated "Harry Langdon Day" in 1997, and Harry Langdon Boulevard was named in 1999.

487.15 = 497.39 MILEAGE CONVERSION – This mileage conversion, provided in 1973 Rock Island Railroad documents, is due to the line changes created by the Atlantic Cutoff. However, the Rock Island didn't use the mileage conversion in their *Des Moines Division Employee Timetable No. 2*, dated December 29, 1974, or their March 18, 1979, *System Employee Timetable No. 1*. In both of these cases, the mileage conversion was done west of the Omaha, Nebraska, station. This was easy to do as the Rock Island operated over Union Pacific track between Council Bluffs and South Omaha.

The Iowa Interstate Employee Timetable also fails to mention this mileage conversion, likely since it ends in Council Bluffs.

Finally, the Federal Railroad Administration (FRA) shows that the mileage conversion takes place between the Interstate 80 overpass (Milepost 487.30) and the 16th Avenue grade crossing (Milepost 499.11), based upon their grade crossing database.

Because of these conflicts in where the mileage conversion happens, the reference points in the Council Bluffs area will include all known mileposts from these various sources.

487.2 EAST SWITCH COUNCIL BLUFFS YARD – This yard was known as Bluffs by the Rock Island Railroad in the 1970s. The Iowa Interstate employee timetable states "East and west main switches may be left lined and locked for the last position used."

Council Bluffs Subdivision

487.3 INTERSTATE 80 – For the tenth time since Chicago, the Iowa Interstate and Interstate 80 cross each other. Here, I-80 uses two separate bridges some distance apart. To the north, the Iowa Interstate has a paved parking area that supports their intermodal container yard.

CBIS Improvements Project

Starting in 2013, Interstates 80 and 29 were rebuilt in this area, a project known as the Council Bluffs Interstate System (CBIS) Improvements Project and that included significant changes in the railroad system in Council Bluffs. A notice posted by the Surface Transportation Board on October 30, 2013, provided a great deal of information about the railroad changes involving four different railroads: BNSF, CBEC Railway, Iowa Interstate, and Union Pacific. According to the filed plan, there were a number of steps involving building new tracks and abandoning others to simplify rail operations in the area.

There were several major parts of this project that directly impacted the Iowa Interstate, or happened next to the line. In this area, the BNSF Bayard Subdivision was rebuilt with a wye to the south as a new connection to the CBEC Railway and the MidAmerican Energy Company's Walter Scott, Jr. Energy Center. This new line allowed the abandonment of several miles of track owned by CBEC Railway and impacted several trackage rights agreements involving the different railroads.

The other major project involved the former BNSF-IAIS diamond at Milepost 488.7. Here, the diamond was removed and the BNSF Council Bluffs Subdivision from the south was curved to the west to join the IAIS and BNSF Bayard Subdivision. At IAIS Milepost 489.30 near S. 7th Street, a new connection was built to the north that connected with BNSF Milepost 492.65 on the Council Bluffs Subdivision. This allowed the abandonment of almost a mile of track, track that once looped to the north of the diamond and passed by the former CB&Q depot on South

Main Street. As a part of this change, the Iowa Interstate also received trackage rights over BNSF to reach the CBEC.

Obviously, the CBEC Railway is a major part of these changes. The CBEC Railway is basically a power plant railroad with no operations of its own built to reach out to multiple railroads in the Council Bluffs area. The railroad was built in 1997 and is owned by the MidAmerican Energy Company. The power plant burns coal and the railroad allows BNSF, UP and IAIS to bid on contracts to deliver the coal. There are several other customers on the line, including an ethanol plant.

487.8 BLUFFS – This is the name and milepost used for the Council Bluffs Yard in the CRI&P *Des Moines Division Employee Time Table No. 2*, dated December 29, 1974, and the *Rock Island System Employee Timetable No. 1*, dated March 18, 1979. On a 1973 track profile, the milepost is shown as 498.0.

The Iowa interstate uses the name Council Bluffs (CB) for the entire area. Business can be busy here as the Iowa Interstate interchanges freight with BNSF, Union Pacific, Canadian National, and Kansas City Southern. The Council Bluffs Yard is the western terminus for the Iowa Interstate Railroad. Because of this, the yard includes the needed locomotive and freight car servicing facilities. North of the mainline, the first few tracks are used for the railroad's intermodal container service and includes a large paved pad, officially located at 2722 South Avenue in Council Bluffs. The railroad likes to brag that this is the "only intermodal facility in the state of Iowa." Further north are several yard tracks used for general freight service, a shop building, several service tracks and an above-ground turntable. The railroad's local office is also located in this area.

Immediately to the south is the site of the former Milwaukee Road yard, and then a bit farther the former Wabash yard. Both of these yards were used by the Council Bluffs Railway until the company was purchased by the Iowa Interstate in 2006. This complex includes 93 acres of rail yards

Council Bluffs Subdivision

and six miles of main line track. For the Iowa Interstate, parts of the property are in use for carload activities and transload services, while some property remains for future expansion and industrial development.

This yard complex started with the Milwaukee Road and Wabash railroads, but its more recent history dates back to the Iowa Southern Railroad which operated more than sixty miles of former Wabash, later Norfolk & Western Railway, track between Council Bluffs and Blanchard, Iowa. In 1988, the Iowa Southern abandoned the line to Blanchard, but kept the switching business in Council Bluffs. In 1989, the Iowa Southern was bought by National Railway Systems, which created the Council Bluffs & Ottumwa Railway to operate the yards and tracks in town. In May 1991, the railroad was again sold, this time to OmniTRAX, which created the Council Bluffs Railway. In July 2006, the railroad and property was sold to the Iowa Interstate Railroad.

Along with the Council Bluffs Railway came a connection to tracks owned by CBEC Railway that lead to the Mid-American Energy, Council Bluffs Energy Center (CBEC). This coal-fired power plant sits on the east bank of the Missouri River, several miles south of here.

Also in this area are two large grain elevators – Hansen Mueller Council Bluffs Elevator and Bartlett Grain. The closest is Hansen-Mueller, a grain industry leader based in Omaha, Nebraska. The company is a grain merchandiser, buying and selling commodities such as corn, soybeans, wheat, oats, and a number of feed ingredients and byproducts like dried distillers grains (DDGs) and soy hull pellets.

Bartlett & Company is a family-owned company based out of Kansas City. It was founded in 1907. They have facilities and offices in 11 states and Mexico and their principal businesses are grain merchandising, flour milling, feed manufacturing and cattle feeding. This is their Council Bluffs South elevator.

488.7 BNSF CROSSING – Until 2016, there was a crossing for the BNSF line from Pacific Junction at this location. The crossing was removed in 2016 as part of a project to realign tracks in the area. Involving BNSF, IAIS, CBEC, and the Iowa Department of Transportation, BNSF was rerouted down their Bayard subdivision, and joint trackage is now used between 16th Avenue and 7th Street. Just west of here a new crossover was built between the Iowa Interstate line and BNSF to the north.

Abandoned crossing is part of track realignment project in Council Bluffs, Iowa. Photo by Sarah Jennings.

With the mileage conversion, the diamond would be at Milepost 499.0. There were once three diamonds here. From east to west, they were once Norfolk & Western, CB&Q (BNSF), and Milwaukee Road. From here to the end of the Iowa Interstate at the Council Bluffs Pool Yard, details are provided for all grade crossings and features.

Area Railroad Historical Sites

Just a few blocks to the north is the former Council Bluffs Carnegie Library. Today, this building is used by the Union Pacific Railroad Museum, opened in 2003. A block east of here was the old Chicago Great Western station, located at the intersection of 15th Avenue and South Third

Street. It was used as an office building until being torn down in 2016.

Several blocks further north (605 Bond Street, now 3rd Street) is the Historic General Dodge House, built in 1869 for Grenville M. Dodge. Dodge held many positions during his life, including Ulysses S. Grant's intelligence Chief in the Western Theater, commander of the XVI Corps during the Atlanta Campaign, U.S. Congressman, and railroad executive who helped build the Union Pacific Railroad's transcontinental line. The mansion was designed by Chicago architect William Boyington, architect for the first LaSalle Street Station, the famous Chicago Water Tower, the original Chicago Board of Trade building, Joliet Prison, and many other regional buildings. Built on a hill overlooking Council Bluffs, the house was used by the Dodge family until sold in 1943. It went through several owners before being acquired by the Historical Society of Pottawattamie County in 1964 for $30,000, the same price for which the house was built. Today, the house is listed as Council Bluff's only National Historic Landmark, and tours are available.

Former home of Grenville Dodge, Council Bluffs, Iowa. Photo by Sarah Jennings.

488.8 16TH AVENUE – 16th Avenue runs east-west just south of the former Rock Island depot. The Iowa Interstate tracks cross through the middle of the intersection between 16th

Avenue and South Main Street. Just to the west is the location of the Rock Island station. In 1870, the Rock Island Railroad Company built a large hotel and dining hall at their station to support the passenger traffic. The FRA shows this grade crossing to be at Milepost 499.11.

488.9 CRI&P STATION – With the mileage conversion, this is Milepost 499.2. The former Chicago, Rock Island & Pacific station, located next to the tracks on South Main Street, is now the RailsWest Railroad Museum. The existing frame depot was replaced in 1899 with a Romanesque Revival structure, built as two one-story brick buildings with pink granite trim connected with a massive Spanish tile roof. The larger building contained the passenger waiting rooms and offices, with baggage rooms in the smaller building. The Rock Island used the same design to construct its depots in Iowa City and Ottawa, Illinois, and similar materials were used to build the depots in Wilton, Anita, and Atlantic, Iowa.

Former CRI&P station, Council Bluffs, Iowa, now used by the RailsWest Railroad Museum. Photo by Barton Jennings.

The CRI&P arrived in Council Bluffs on May 11, 1869, a day after Union Pacific and Central Pacific met at Promontory Summit, Utah. This means that they lost much of the business opportunities since the C&NW had arrived 2½ years earlier. For years, Council Bluffs was a major terminal town as the Chicago railroads attempted to gain the Union Pacific interchange business from the west. The Chicago & North Western; Chicago, Milwaukee, St. Paul & Pacific; Illinois Central; Chicago, Burlington & Quincy; Chicago Great Western; and Wabash all competed for this business against the Rock Island. History reports state that by 1883, Council Bluffs boasted eight railroad depots, numerous roundhouses, and six freight depots.

From the late 1930s until the 1970s, the Rock Island shared the depot with the Chicago, Milwaukee, St. Paul & Pacific Railroad. A major change occurred in 1954 when the breezeway was filled in between the two separate buildings. Another change happened in May 1970 when passenger service ended and the women's waiting room was converted into offices while the men's waiting room was used for freight storage. The Rock Island ended operations altogether in March 1980 and the building was deserted until 1985 when the City of Council Bluffs leased the building to the Historical Society of Pottawattamie County and the Greater Omaha Society of Model Engineers. The building was placed on the National Register of Historic Places in July 1995.

RailsWest Railroad Museum

Today's museum dates back to the lease by the Historical Society of Pottawattamie County and the Greater Omaha Society of Model Engineers. The station was restored, including the replacement of much of the roof and wood trim. The interior was also restored, removing many of the modernizations that had taken place over the years. The freight room is now used by the Greater Omaha Society of Model Engineers and houses their HO scale model railroad. The passenger area features a number of displays about railroad industry, and displays the former ticket office as the RailsWest Railroad Museum.

Outside is a collection of railroad equipment. The display features two steam locomotives: UP 814 and CB&Q 915. Union Pacific 814 is a 4-8-4 built by ALCO (Schenectady) in 1937 with construction number 68822. The Chicago, Burlington & Quincy locomotive started as Burlington & Missouri River Railroad (B&MR) #44, a 4-6-0 built by the railroad's Havelock Shops in 1901. When the B&MR became part of the CB&Q, it became locomotive #915.

Besides the steam locomotives, there is a 1953 Plymouth Locomotive Works 45-ton Model 5700 center cab switch engine that once was used by Iowa Power & Light. There are also several cabooses on display. One is CRIP caboose #17130, formerly used in the Tucumcari Pool, and later owned and operated by Union Pacific as #24548. The CB&Q wooden caboose (waycar) #13855 is much older, having been built in November 1917, and donated to "the citizens of Council Bluffs" during October 1964. Union Pacific boxcar #462536 completes the freight collection.

The passenger fleet includes Union Pacific Railway Post Office (RPO) #5908, with its complete interior, built in 1963 by Budd. More glamorous is CBQ heavyweight lounge-solarium-observation car *Omaha Club*. This car was used on the Ak-Sar-Ben, a Lincoln, Nebraska, to Chicago train. The third passenger car is a Chicago & North Western cafe/lounge built in 1949 by American Car and Foundry. Car #7801 was used for trains that operated between Chicago and the west coast, also operating on Union Pacific and Southern Pacific.

Council Bluffs, Iowa

The name Council Bluffs dates back to the Lewis and Clark expedition, when Patrick Gass used the term in his journal about a meeting with the Otoe tribe on August 2, 1804. The location was actually on the Nebraska side of the Missouri River about twenty miles upstream. The area was next settled during the early 1830s when the Chippewa, Ottawa and Potawatomi moved here after leaving the Chi-

Council Bluffs Subdivision

cago area as a condition of the Treaty of Chicago. The St. Joseph's Mission was built here in 1839 by Pierre-Jean De Smet. De Smet also produced the first detailed map of the Council Bluffs area and the Missouri River valley system.

This area was a popular route across the Missouri River and a number of early settlers heading west passed through what became Council Bluffs. Henry W. Miller ran several businesses here and the community became known as Miller's Hollow. Miller's success in his business efforts is evident by his membership in Iowa's first state legislature. He was also foreman for the construction of the Kanesville Tabernacle. When the Mormons arrived in the mid-1840s, they named the community Kanesville, for Thomas L. Kane, who obtained for them Indian land along the Missouri River. Kanesville later became the beginning of the Mormon Trail to Utah. Few Mormons remained in Kanesville after the 1852 exodus to Utah, and the growth of the community due to the California Gold Rush. In that same year, the town was renamed Council Bluffs, and it was incorporated on January 19, 1853.

Council Bluffs became even more important when it was declared to be the official starting point of the transcontinental railroad by President Abraham Lincoln. More than a half-dozen railroads built to Council Bluffs from the east, and by the 1930s, Council Bluffs was the country's fifth largest rail center. The junction of all of these railroads and the Missouri River also made the city a major grain center, and then a center of food processing. Today, Council Bluffs is the county seat of Pottawattamie County with a 2010 population of 62,230.

489.0 SOUTH 6TH STREET – The FRA shows this grade crossing to be at Milepost 499.22. This is the first grade crossing west of the former Rock Island station.

489.1 SOUTH EXPRESSWAY STREET – Also known as Iowa Highway 192, the railroad passes under the highway and then has a grade crossing with South 7th Street. The

FRA shows these Mileposts to be 499.33 and 499.34. The Expressway was built to bridge over the many railroad operations in this area.

Rock Island System Employee Timetable No. 1, dated March 18, 1979, had a statement for trains here that stated "do not exceed 5 mph over crossover between 8th and 7th Streets." At the time, the Rock Island mainline still consisted of two tracks through Council Bluffs.

489.2 SOUTH 8TH STREET – The FRA shows this grade crossing to be at Milepost 499.42. To the north is an IAIS track that heads into the Ready Mix Concrete plant.

489.7 INDIAN CREEK BRIDGE – Indian Creek flows in from the north and is the route used by several railroads coming into Council Bluffs. It has been channeled through this area and more than a half-dozen railroad bridge spans cross it nearby. The Iowa Interstate bridge, like most in this area, is a through plate girder span. It is 48 feet long and was built by Lassig Bridge & Iron Works. A bridge for the second track is immediately to the south, and a second span is just a few feet further south.

On a 1973 Rock Island track chart, this is Bridge 5000 located at Milepost 500.0.

489.7 ILLINOIS CENTRAL CROSSING – With the mileage conversion, the diamond would be at Milepost 500.1. There were a number of interchange tracks in this area as all eight railroads attempted to connect with each other.

489.8 C&NW-BN CROSSING – This crossing was noted in a number of Rock Island employee timetables. There is still a connection in the northwest quadrant.

489.9 SOUTH 16TH STREET – The FRA shows this grade crossing to be at Milepost 500.01.

490.0 WEST COUNCIL BLUFFS YARD LIMITS – This location is noted in the Iowa Interstate Railroad employee timetable. It is also where Union Pacific-owned track begins heading west, at a milepost shown to be 500.27 in documents using the mileage conversion.

To the north was once a railroad office known as the Transfer Station, a base to swap train crews. To the west is the Council Bluffs Pool Yard. The term pool is an old term from when the CB&Q, C&NW, and Rock Island agreed to pool the business coming off Union Pacific as a way to standardize rates between Chicago and Council Bluffs. This unofficial monopoly worked as long as more railroads didn't show up, and it was eventually broken by the Wabash. However, it did start the consolidation of yards and facilities in Council Bluffs.

Just west of here at Twenty-First Street was the Union Pacific Council Bluffs Station, which once included the Transfer Depot and Hotel. This large and ornate station included a dining room and facilities to transfer passengers between the many railroads serving Council Bluffs. The station was built in 1877 and enlarged the following year. Because of the many railroads in town, the south wing of the Depot was home to five freight express companies.

The need for this station came about because in 1875, the U.S. Supreme Court decided that Union Pacific's eastern terminus was Council Bluffs. The station and hotel closed in 1929 as Omaha became the major station location. Near where the station once stood at 9th Avenue and South 21st Street is the Golden Spike, a 56-foot tall golden concrete spike erected in 1939 with the premiere of the film *Union Pacific*. It marks the location of Milepost 0.0 on the original main line of the transcontinental railroad.

The Golden Spike, Council Bluffs, Iowa. Photo by Sarah Jennings.

Peoria Subdivision
Bureau Junction (Illinois) to Peoria (Illinois)

This line was once the Chicago, Rock Island & Pacific's Third Subdivision of the Illinois Division. It was built by the Peoria & Bureau Valley (between Bureau and Peoria) by early November, 1854. When completed, it was immediately leased to the Chicago & Rock Island. When the Rock Island entered its court-ordered liquidation at the end of March 1980, several different operators managed the Bureau-Peoria line. Initially, the Elgin, Joliet & Eastern provided service, then segments were operated by Burlington Northern (Peoria to Henry) and B&O/CSX Transportation (CSXT) from Bureau south to Henry (when BN ended service north of Mossville). CSXT leased the line from Bureau to Henry from International Mining Company (IMC) to keep the business from the Goodrich chemical plant just north of Henry. To keep competition to the plant, Goodrich created the Lincoln & Southern Railroad and bought the line on south toward Peoria. In 1987, the L&S leased the operating rights over their line to Iowa Interstate (the Mossville-Henry portion had no revenue freight trains from October 1981 until IAIS began operating the line). In 2006, Iowa Interstate signed a sub-lease on the northern half of the line from CSXT and took over operations on February 4th. Today, the IAIS operates the line with a local out of Bureau, plus a number of coal and grain trains as well as general freight for interchange in Peoria. Recently, Norfolk Southern has been a significant participant in this interchange business in efforts to avoid congestion in the Chicago area.

Over the last few years, a great deal of business has developed on the Bureau to Peoria line. Most of this business is agricultural in nature, with a large percentage of it being shipped by ADM between their Cedar Rapids (IA) facilities and their Peoria distillery and Illinois River barge loadout. Other sources of agricultural traffic include corn syrup received from the Keokuk Junction Railway, organic corn and wheat shipments from the Illinois & Midland forwarded to CSX Transportation at Chicago, and shipments to ethanol energy companies such as Aventine Renewable Energy and Patriot Renewable Fuels.

Metal can also be seen moving over the line, generally to or from Keystone Steel & Wire or one of the nearby scrap dealers. A few on-line customers also ship or receive chemicals, fertilizers, plastics, and other products that go into consumer or agricultural production. The Tazewell & Peoria Railroad handles Iowa Interstate's switching and interchange work at Peoria.

For the railroad, trains heading towards Peoria are heading railroad-south. The easiest reference is that the Illinois River is to the east of the railroad all the way from Bureau to Peoria.

114.2 BUREAU – For information on Bureau, go to page 88 in the Iowa Interstate Blue Island Subdivision section.

114.7 HENNEPIN CANAL BRIDGE – The Hennepin Canal, also known as the Illinois and Mississippi Canal, was first proposed in 1834 as a waterway between the Mississippi River at Rock Island and the Illinois River near Hennepin. Congress authorized preliminary surveys on the project in 1871, construction began in 1892, and the first boat went through in 1907. The canal was never much of a success since it was built to older standards, and by the 1930s was used primarily for recreational traffic. The canal was open free to boat traffic until 1951. Today, the canal is a water and hiking recreational facility and is listed on the National Register of Historic Places.

This three-span through plate girder bridge crosses the Hennepin Canal between Locks 2 and 3. The three-span through plate girder sits on solid piers at each end, and uses two assembled steel piers for the center span. The bridge received major maintenance in 2016, removing the north approach span. The Bureau Junction wye switch is at the north end of this bridge. The south approach span has also been rebuilt, using an I-beam design.

115.1 BUREAU CREEK OVERFLOW BRIDGE – This through plate girder bridge measures 105 feet long and was built by Bethlehem Steel Company in 1948. This stream drains the area between Big Bureau Creek and the Hennepin Canal.

115.2 BIG BUREAU CREEK BRIDGE – Bureau Creek is the stream on which Michel and Pierre de Beuro had their trading post, located not far downstream at the junction with the Illinois River. Bureau Creek starts about ten miles north of Mendota, Illinois, and flows south for about 75 miles in total length.

This two-span through plate girder bridge was built in 1947 by the American Bridge Company of New York. It is a total of 220 feet in length.

116.3 UNDER I-180 – I-80 is a transcontinental highway that runs from downtown San Francisco, California, to Teaneck, New Jersey. It is the second longest Interstate Highway in the United States (after Interstate 90), and closely follows the route of the historic Lincoln Highway, the first road across America. In Illinois, it stretches between Chicago westward to the Quad Cities on the Mississippi River. I-180 breaks off of I-80 and heads south, ending near here. Officially, the south end of I-180 is to the east across the Illinois River at Hennepin, Illinois.

118.2 COUNTY LINE – This is the county line between Bureau County, to the north, and Putnam County to the south. **Bureau County** was organized out of Putnam County in 1837 with its county seat at Princeton. It was named for Michel or Pierre de Beuro, who ran a trading post from 1776 until 1790 near where Big Bureau Creek empties into the Illinois River. The county's population is less than 40,000.

The southern part of Bureau County includes part of the Military Tract. In May 1812, an act of Congress was passed which set aside bounty lands as payment to volunteer soldiers who participated in the War of 1812. The bounty land in Illinois is located in the western part of the state between the Illinois and Mississippi Rivers. Of the 5.4 million acres included in the tract, approximately 3.5 million acres was deemed fit for cultivation and was set aside for military bounties. The tract was surveyed in 1815-1816 and opened to settlement. At the time, the land was a mix of forest and wild prairie. Today, major parts of the county are planted in corn or soybeans.

After losing land to Bureau County, **Putnam County** is the smallest county in Illinois. The county was formed in 1825 out of Fulton County and named for Israel Putnam, a general in the American Revolution. Putnam fought with distinction at the Battle of Bunker Hill. Prior to that, he was a member of Roger's Rangers during the French and Indian War and also served in the regular British army, being promoted to major in 1758. Putnam also participated in England's expedition against Cuba in 1762. It is believed that Putnam returned to New England with Cuban tobacco seeds that he planted in the Hartford area, resulting in the development of the renowned Connecticut Wrapper agricultural product.

122.1 PUTNAM – Putnam was originally the name of a "paper town" that was staked off on September 3, 1835. It was located east of the Illinois River but nothing significant was ever built there. This Putnam was originally known as Snachwine Station when the Peoria & Bureau Valley Railroad built through the area.

The Snachwine Tile factory produced drain tile here. An early newspaper stated that the "works are situated two miles north of the village of Snachwine on the C. R. I. & P. Railroad. The works cover an area of four acres, and consist of quarry, sheds, engine house, kilns for burning, tile machine, etc. They are owned and operated by Winship Bros. & Reed." According to newspaper reports, the factory opened in 1878. In February 1881, the name of the post office was changed to Putnam to agree with the railroad.

The spelling of Snachwine conflicts with the more modern spelling of Senachwine, which is the name of the Township. The area is named for Chief Senachwine (Sen-noge-wone), war chief of the Potawatomis. Senachwine lived 1744-1831 and assisted American troops with their war against Black Hawk and the Sauks. Later, he was considered a traitor by some of his tribe for working with the white solders, especially after their tribe was pushed west. About one-half mile north of the village of Putnam is a series of burial mounds known by some as the Indian Burial Ground. Reportedly, thousands of tribal members are buried in these mounds, scattered over less than ten acres. During the 1930s, the area was opened as a park on the property of Walter Winship and George Wheeler. Today, the area is closed and again located on private property.

For the railroad, trains heading south face a short but steep climb to reach Putnam. For almost two miles, the grade is 0.64%. Trains passing through Putnam pass through the middle of the Rumbold & Kuhn Putnam Elevator. While not served by the railroad, this facility is big, holding 2,488,000 bushels of corn and beans. In the 1960s, the CRI&P had a siding to the west and a spur track to the east. There was once a depot between the mainline and the siding to the west.

Heading on south it is easy to understand the need for an elevator at Putnam. The next few miles are through field after field, often planted with rows of corn or soybeans.

125.3 COUNTY LINE – This is the county line between Putnam County to the north and Marshall County to the south. **Marshall County** is another county that was formed from parts of Putnam County, this time in 1839. It was named in honor of John Marshall, Chief Justice of the United States Supreme Court, who died in 1835. Marshall is a relatively small county, stretching 35 miles east-west and ten miles north-south, with about two-thirds of the county east of the Illinois River.

Its county seat is Lacon, located across the river from Sparland and for a number of years it was a political center for the area north of Peoria. For example, *The Illinois Gazette* of Lacon reported that on November 1, 1848, the "Hon. A. Lincoln addressed a numerous assemblage of our citizens from all parts of the county" as part of a campaign for General Zachary Taylor for President. During the Lincoln-Douglas debates, both visited Lacon on October 17, 1854, but neither reportedly made a speech. Two years later they returned and were billed to make speeches, but for some reason neither spoke. On September 29, 1856, Lincoln rode a train from Peoria to Lacon to attend a series of rallies.

In the 2010 census, the county had a population of 12,640.

126.1 GOODRICH – There is a wye here to serve several industries on the river to the east. The south switch is at Milepost 126.3. This was the location of the Goodrich chemical plant that helped save this line after the Rock Island bankruptcy. Today, the line serves United Suppliers (agricultural products), Mexichem Specialty Resins, and Emerald Performance Materials.

127.7 HENRY – Welcome to the "Best Town in Illinois by a Dam Site," the slogan of the town based upon the town's distinction of having the first lock and dam built on the Illinois River, completed in 1870 at a cost of $400,000. Its population is about 2500.

The area on the west side of the Illinois River is generally at a higher elevation, meaning that it floods less. Thus, over the years, most development occurred on this side. This included Henry, initially surveyed in 1834 and named after General James D. Henry. James D. Henry was an Illinois militia officer who rose to the rank of general during the Black Hawk War of 1832. In 1825, Henry was indicted for murder in Edwardsville, Illinois, but was never tried and eventually became sheriff in Springfield. When the Winnebago War broke out in 1827, Henry acted as adjutant for four companies of volunteers. In 1831, Henry was one of several officers who conducted raids against the Indians that led to the Black Hawk War. After the war, Henry moved to New

Orleans because of his "disease of the lungs" which caused his death in 1834.

According to a 1928 Sanborn insurance map, Henry was a very busy place at that time. Just south of the Western Avenue grade crossing, there was a coal dock, stockyards, and the W. W. Dewey & Sons elevator, built in 1880. A metal-sheathed grain elevator sits in the same location today. South of 3rd Street, there was a Standard Oil Company facility, another coal dock, and then a wood dock for team service. The railroad depot sat on the east side of the tracks across from the elevator, on the north corner of 3rd Street and Railroad Avenue. A block to the south once stood several railroad section and tool houses. Today, the railroad has a short spur track and a long siding on the west side of the mainline with no local customers.

Heading south, the railroad runs beside Illinois Highway 29, passing through farmland and a few small communities.

Grain elevator next to tracks in Henry, Illinois. Photo by Barton Jennings.

Henry, Illinois sign. Photo by Barton Jennings.

131.6 CROW CREEK BRIDGE – Crow Creek starts about ten miles west of Henry, flows east and then turns south to here. It enters the Illinois River just downstream in the Cameron National Wildlife Refuge.

134.7 SPARLAND – Just north of Sparland the train passes Goose Lake, and Wightman Lake to the south. Both are part of the Illinois River. The river is part of the cause for the settlement as it was founded on higher lands to avoid area flooding. The county seat of Lacon was built on the east bank of the Illinois River, with Sparland being the railroad stop for trains to and from Peoria. Lacon did have its own rail service, on a Chicago & Alton branch from Streator, Illinois. The Hamilton, Lacon & Eastern Railroad Company was created on March 7, 1867, and built almost 20 miles of track from Wennona, Illinois, to Lacon before being sold to the Chicago & Alton Railroad Company on April 5, 1870. The line was completed in 1871. The line then was merged with the Chicago & Alton Railway Company to create the new Chicago & Alton Railroad Company on March 14, 1906. It was abandoned in the 1970s.

The first settler in the area, Franklin W. Graves, arrived about 1830. He sold his farm in 1846 and headed west to California as a part of the Donner Party, dying that winter while snowbound in the Sierra Nevada Mountains. Graves sold his farm to George Sparr before he left to head west. On June 13, 1855, the heirs of Sparr laid out a town in this area, naming it Sparland. It was described as having "two ranges of blocks under the bluff west of the railroad track, running parallel with the track." A depot was also soon built.

Some maps from 1860 show the town as West Lacon, and the Peoria & Bureau Valley Railroad apparently knew it as Lacon Station. The July 2, 1868, issue of the *Henry News Republican* stated that "Sparland, Marshall County is a smart little place, situated on the Chicago & Rock Island railroads on the Peoria branch." The article went on to state that the "shipments of wheat from this section is small compared with other grains, for the reason that the flouring mill uses nine tenths of the amount of grain grown in the vicinity. The amount of grain shipped from this point within the past year were 300,000 bushels of corn, 150,000 bushels of oats, 40,000 bushels of wheat, 20,000 bushels of rye, and 1500 bushels of barley; 65,000 barrels of flour, 260 cars of stock – embracing cattle and hogs. The passenger receipts for the same period amount to about $19,000."

A detailed description of the grain elevator was also provided. It said, "The elevator here was erected in 1853, and is the property of the railroad company. It is 150 feet long and two stories high; engine house and sheller room 60 x 50 feet. The sheller is capable of shelling 3000 bushels a day. The elevator will contain 40,000 bushels. The engine – a 25 horse power – and the sheller and machinery are owned by C. F. Hitchcock. The storage cribs for corn are 160 x 25 feet, will contain 20,000 bushels and cost from $2400 to $4000. They were built in 1867."

There is a short spur to the east into an old elevator complex. There was once a siding to the west.

138.6 COUNTY LINE – To the north is Marshall County and to the south is Peoria County. **Peoria County** was formed in 1825 out of Fulton County, including most of the valley area along the Illinois River. The county was named for the Peoria, an Illiniwek people who lived there. During the early 1800s, the counties of Mercer, Warren and Tazewell were created from parts of Peoria County. Today, the county's population is almost 200,000 and its county seat is Peoria, the home of Caterpillar.

140.3 COON CREEK BRIDGE – Coon Creek is another small stream that drains the hillsides to the west and flows east to the Illinois River. The railroad crosses the stream using a 44-foot long deck plate girder span. Not far to the south is the Chillicothe Sportsmen's Club shooting range to the east and a former gravel quarry to the west.

141.3 SPRING CREEK BRIDGE – Spring Creek wanders through the marshy land in this area. Look for the long ballast deck timber structure.

141.6 SENACHWINE CREEK BRIDGE – The railroad crosses the creek using two 60-foot deck plate girder spans. Senachwine Creek forms west of Sparland, flows south to near here and then turns east to the Illinois River.

Just south of the bridge is the north switch to the siding at Chillicothe, used for sand loading by Galena Road Gravel Company. Almost immediately, the Iowa Interstate passes under the BNSF Chillicothe Subdivision, the former mainline of the Atchison, Topeka & Santa Fe (ATSF) between Chicago and Galesburg, Illinois. There was once a connecting track between the ATSF and the IAIS just south of these bridges. The south switch is just north of Wood Street (shown as Moffitt Street on some maps) at Milepost 142.1.

142.6 CHILLICOTHE – Chillicothe has long been a railroad town, with the Rock Island Railroad through downtown

Peoria Subdivision

and the Santa Fe flying overhead north of town. The Santa Fe has historically been the busier of the two railroads as this is their Transcon line – today the major BNSF route between Chicago and Los Angeles, via Kansas City and Albuquerque. The track from Kansas City to Chicago is actually about the last mainline ATSF track built, being completed in 1888 to reach eastern railroad connections. Chillicothe was important due to the nearby crossing of the Illinois River, and it became a crew change point. The ATSF once had a sizeable yard, roundhouse and station (known for some time as North Chillicothe) here, but today it is a shell of itself with just the main tracks and a few yard tracks to the north. With the use of diesels, crews no longer changed here and the community lost its Amtrak service in 1996 when Amtrak moved the *Southwest Chief* to the former CB&Q mainline, today's BNSF Mendota Subdivision.

West of Chillicothe is a major rail enthusiast attraction – Edelstein Hill. It is one of the steeper grades on the line and is used to climb out of the Illinois River valley. Another railroad attraction is the Chillicothe Historical Society Railroad Museum at Cedar and 3rd Streets in the old Rock Island depot. The depot, built in 1889, was acquired by the historical society and dedicated on May 21, 1987. In August of that year a 1929 Santa Fe caboose was obtained and displayed alongside the depot. There is some conflict about the history of this caboose, but most sources say this was originally ATSF 2051 built by the railroad in 1942, rebuilt in 1967 and renumbered 999130.

Former Rock Island depot, Chillicothe, Illinois. Photo by Barton Jennings.

Heading south in 1926, the Rock Island passed the Hunter Lumber Company coal dock on the southeast corner of Pine Street and North 3rd Street; Johnson Oil Refining Company south of the Willow Street grade crossing to the east; and the Guyer Grain Company, owned by the CRI&P, located just north of the depot at Cedar Street. The railroad runs along the east shoulder of 3rd Street.

The first house in Chillicothe was built in 1830, and with growth in the community, a survey was made in July of 1836. Chillicothe, named for a local Shawnee Indian chief, grew as the first major river port and railroad station north of Peoria. Chillicothe officially became a town in 1861, and a city in 1874. The grain business was one of the first commercial industries in town. At first it moved by steamboat, but the two railroads soon stole the business away and opened up new markets across the country. Besides grain, the town also once had a pottery company, a soda bottling plant, the Western Yeast Company, McGrath's Sand and Gravel, two cheese companies, two cigar factories, and a steam laundry company.

For a small town, there does seem to have been a number of famous people who lived in the community. Lance

(Henry) LeGault (the actor who played Colonel Roderick Decker on *The A-Team*), Johnston McCulley (pulp author who originated the Zorro stories), and David Ogden Stiers (Major Charles Emerson Winchester III on *M*A*S*H*) all once lived in Chillicothe.

144.1 COUGHLIN – Coughlin, where Rome is located on many maps, was once a flag stop on the line. A siding once existed on the west side of the mainline. The north switch was just south of Cloverdale Road.

145.6 ROME – Rome is a community of about 2000 located on Goose Lake, a part of the Illinois River. Wayne Nelson of the *Little River Band* grew up in Rome. During the early 1900s, the railroad had a mail crane at Rome. The railroad runs on the west bank of the Illinois River for the next few miles when heading south.

149.4 RENCH ROAD – Look for the Cat Building AC engine facility to west. The railroad once had several tracks into the facility at Milepost 148.9. Caterpillar built its Technical Research Center in Mossville in the 1960s, and then built their Building AC assembly facility here as well. A co-operative Ameren/Caterpillar generation plant and a small industrial park also sits near the factories.

151.1 MOSSVILLE – The railroad once had a siding to the west which wrapped around a depot, known as Mossville Station. There was also a mail crane here in 1910. There is still a spur track here, rebuilt in 2015 to hold cars needing repair. Mossville is unincorporated, but includes a number of small communities in the area. Heading towards Peoria, the communities get larger and closer together.

Mossville was created when the railroad built through here in 1854. William S. Moss and Isaac Underbill owned land in the area and created the community to take advantage of the new transportation.

155.0 SANKOTY – Look for the grade crossing with Sankoty Lane; the railroad once had a siding to the west named Sankoty. Today, Sankoty is a small residential community with a number of houses on the river. As small as the community is, the name actually impacts a larger region. The Sankoty (sometimes written "San Koty") Aquifer is located in central and northwest Illinois, and is used by a number of communities for drinking water. The sand that creates the aquifer was named in 1946 for this railroad siding.

156.5 NARROWS SIDING – The February 1, 1910, *Rock Island Lines List of Officers, Station Agents, Etc.*, showed a siding here with the name of Narrows Siding. The name of Narrows comes about because the river is tight against the bluffs on the west side of the river, forced there by the flow of Ten Mile Creek coming into the river from the east. This leaves only a small strip of land for the railroad and highway.

157.0 IAIS EAST PEORIA YARD LIMITS – This is the north yard limits for Peoria. It is just south of the private grade crossing at Milepost 156.95.

157.5 IAIS WEST PEORIA YARD LIMITS – This is the official ownership line with the Tazewell & Peoria Railroad (TZPR), owned by the Genesee & Wyoming. The railroad was created on November 1, 2004, to lease the lines of the Peoria & Pekin Union Railway (P&PU). The P&PU is the terminal railroad in the Peoria area and is owned by Union Pacific, Norfolk Southern and Canadian National. It also interchanges with and is used by BNSF; the Toledo, Peoria & Western; Iowa Interstate Railroad; Keokuk Junction Railway; and Illinois & Midland Railroad, another Genesee & Wyoming company that was once known as the Chicago & Illinois Midland Railway. Most interchange work is conducted at Creve Coeur Yard in east Peoria.

The Iowa Interstate uses "PE" as the code for Peoria, no matter the actual origin or destination in the terminal.

Most interchange actually takes place at Creve Coeur Yard, also known as East Peoria Yard.

Tazewell & Peoria Railroad

Although this is the south end of Iowa Interstate's Peoria Subdivision, their trains typically head on to Creve Coeur Yard in East Peoria to do interchange work. Because of this, details about this Tazewell & Peoria Railroad route are included here. The mileposts shown to Bridge Junction are those used by the Rock Island Railroad. Tazewell & Peoria Railroad mileposts will also be stated. From there to Creve Coeur Yard, calculated mileposts for the Rock Island Railroad are used to show the distances. Where known, TZPR mileposts will also be used.

Describing the tracks of the Tazewell & Peoria Railroad can be difficult as some are mainlines while others are basically industrial leads or yards. The September 21, 2004, ruling of the Surface Transportation Board (STB) describes the lines involved. They included the route from Peoria to here, which was described as "approximately milepost 0.0 (at or near Peoria, Illinois, Union Station) to approximately milepost 3.87N (at or near Iowa Interstate Junction, Illinois)."

A second route described included the route across the Illinois River to Wesley Junction near Creve Coeur Yard, and on to Pekin, Illinois. This route was described as being "approximately milepost 0.0 (at or near Peoria, Illinois, Union Station) to approximately milepost 9.2 (at or near Pekin, Illinois, IC Junction)."

Two other routes were also included in the lease. The third mainline is from Bridge Junction west to connect with Union Pacific and the other railroads near Bartonville. The route was described by the STB as "approximately milepost 0.0 (at or near Peoria, Illinois, Peoria Wye) to approximately milepost 5.1W (at or near P&PU Junction, Illinois)." The fourth route was the Creve Coeur Yard area from Wesley Junction east, described as "approximately Wesley Junction, Illinois, to approximately East Peoria, Illinois (approximately 1.7 miles of track; milepost designations are not available)."

157.8 LORENTZ AVENUE – This is TZPR Milepost 5.09. Just to the north is a southbound siding switch, once part of a series of sidings between here and downtown Peoria. The small yard here is known as North Limit Yard.

157.9 McCLUGAGE BRIDGE – The railroad passes under the McClugage Bridge, the crossing of the Illinois River by U.S. Highway 150. There are actually two bridges, the south bridge was built during the 1940s as a two-lane steel cantilever bridge and upgraded in the early 2000s. A new matching three-lane bridge was built just to the north for westbound traffic. The bridges are named for David H. McClugage, mayor of Peoria from 1937 to 1941.

158.4 SLOAN STREET – This is the road into the New-Indy IVEX Specialty Paper complex. This mill was built in 1913 by Judson M. Bemis, an Illinois farmer, as the Illinois Paper Company. It was originally built "with a paper mill and a small bag factory to produce white coated flour sack paper and consumer size flour bags," according to the company's website. It became the Bemis Brothers Bag Company during the 1920s, and then was bought by Forest Resources in 2005. It then became IVEX Specialty Paper, which was acquired by New-Indy JV Corporation in July 2015. New-Indy is a joint venture that was formed in 2012 by the Kraft Group and Schwarz Partners. Today, IVEX Specialty Paper is a leader in machine crepe papers used in the multiwall bag industry, and it produces a wide range of colored papers.

158.5 FAIRHOLM AVENUE – The south switch to the small yard and siding is just north of this grade crossing, TZPR Milepost 4.39.

158.8 KOMATSU SWITCH – To the east is the large Komatsu assembly plant, often known as Komatsu Dresser Haulpak. Peoria is the headquarters of the Mining Division of Komatsu-America. This Komatsu assembly plant is the home of some of the largest electric-drive mining trucks in the world, with some holding up to 360 tons of ore. The railroad is often used to haul parts of the trucks to their destinations, or to ports for export, as they are too big to assemble and move as one piece.

Komatsu is the world's second largest manufacturer and supplier of earth-moving equipment. These trucks started when Haulpak started building off-highway trucks in 1953. It then became part of Wabco, which was then bought by American Standard Company (known for bathroom fittings) in 1968. In 1984, Dresser Industries acquired the operation, then partnered with Komatsu which led to full Komatsu ownership in 1994. Within a decade, the Haulpak name was phased out and now they are simply Komatsu.

159.2 GRANT STREET – Grant Street marks the south end of the Komatsu facility, and is TZPR Milepost 3.67.

159.7 CAROLINE STREET – This is the road into the Detweiller Marina, a small-boat marina on Peoria Lake, a part of the Illinois River. Peoria Lake is naturally created by the narrow channel through Peoria. This is TZPR Milepost 3.22.

This was the junction with the Pioneer Industrial Railroad. According to the company's website, "on February 18, 1998, Pioneer Railcorp through its wholly-owned subsidiary Pioneer Industrial Railway Co. (PRY), began operating approximately 8.5 miles of railroad in Peoria County, Illinois when the Peoria & Pekin Union Railway Co. (PPU) assigned its lease with the owner, the Peoria, Peoria Heights & Western Railroad (PPHW) to Pioneer Railcorp. PPHW is owned by the City of Peoria, Illinois and the village of Peoria Heights, Illinois. The railroad's principal commodities are steel, and lumber." However, within a few years trail activists started demands for abandonment of the railroad and the creation of a trail. Since the line was actually owned by the City of Peoria, they could use political pressure to tear the railroad out. By the end of the 2004 lease, although the railroad was profitable and was essential for several local businesses, the railroad was gone and a slow process to build several miles of trail at a cost of nearly $10 million began, being named the Rock Island Greenway. A short spur track still exists here.

159.8 PEORIA JUNCTION – This is the junction with the line known as the Peoria Line which operated between Peoria and Rock Island. Today, it is a few miles of industrial trackage. To the east was once a Rock Island rail yard which stretched almost to the Illinois River bank.

160.0 PEORIA – This was the milepost location of Peoria in the March 18, 1979, employee timetable. The station here, known as the Evans Street Station, was built by the Rock Island to replace the downtown station in 1967. The last regular passenger train before the creation of Amtrak left from here on May 29, 1978. On August 21, 1977, the schedule for this train was a departure at 6:45am as train #12. It was scheduled to arrive at Bureau at 8:13am, at Joliet at 10:06am, and then Chicago at 11:20am. It would return in the evening as train #11, departing Chicago at 6:15pm, Joliet at 7:16pm, Bureau at 9:02pm, and arrive at Peoria at 10:40pm.

Evans Street Station sign, Peoria, Illinois. Photo by Barton Jennings.

Peoria Subdivision

Evans Street Station, Peoria, Illinois. Photo by Barton Jennings.

Just north of the station is a grade crossing with Morton Street, TZPR Milepost 1.41. Besides the station, the former CRI&P turntable also still exists here in the adjacent park. Near the station is Constitution Gardens, described as a "unique commemoration of the Bicentennial of the United States Constitution; a living legacy to the founding of the republic and a 50-acre oasis in the midst of the city landscape." However, the City of Peoria has reportedly sold the property to a developer for a series of apartment buildings.

160.7 INTERSTATE 74 – The railroad passes under I-74, an interstate highway between I-80 at Davenport, Iowa, and I-75 at Cincinnati, Ohio. There are also a few disconnected sections of I-74 in North Carolina.

161.0 PEORIA – This was the station milepost for Peoria in the 1967 CRI&P station list. It was known as the Rock Island Fulton Street Station, built in 1891 and expanded with a freight depot in 1899. This was not the first station used, as the Peoria & Bureau Valley Railroad arrived on November 9, 1854.

The two-story railroad station and adjacent one-story freight house were built next to the Illinois River, with trains coming through downtown Peoria on Water Street. Besides the Rock Island, the Minneapolis & St. Louis Railway used the Rock Island Station until the late 1930s. This left the station with four passenger trains, the twice-daily Chicago-Peoria Rockets #501-504. About the same time, in 1939, the station's clock tower was removed.

Peoria Fulton Street Station, Peoria, Illinois. Photo by Barton Jennings.

Passenger service to the station ended in 1967 when the railroad moved its operations to the new Evans Street Station a mile north. The next year, the station building was turned into a training center for the handicapped. The building was acquired by the City of Peoria in 1976 and listed as a National Historic Landmark in 1978. Today, the building is known as the River Station and has housed a series of restaurants and bars.

Other Peoria Stations

By the late 1870s, Peoria was the home of more than a dozen railroads and a tangle of tracks throughout town. To end the lawsuits and congestion, four of the city's railroads created the Peoria & Pekin Union Railway in 1880, designed to eliminate many of the duplicate facilities in Peoria. To coordinate the many passenger trains, the Peoria Union Station was built at the foot of State Street in 1882 and operated by the Peoria & Pekin Union Railway. The brick, two-story building, measured 404 feet by 55 feet and contained forty-two offices for the railroads and a number of other facilities such as a dining room, mail room, and an express office. By 1920, 110 passenger trains operated to and from Peoria daily. However, this dropped to 80 three years later and continued a steady decline over the next several decades, with a pause during World War II. The last passenger train, the *Peorian*, departed Union Station on June 25, 1955, operated by the Peoria & Eastern, a part of the New York Central. After that, the station was used as warehouse space by the nearby post office. It burned in August 1961.

A third major station once existed in Peoria, the terminal of the Illinois Traction System (ITS – Illinois Terminal Railroad after 1937). The original ITS freight house, car barn, and power house were between Walnut and Chestnut (State) Streets, and Water and Washington Streets. After the railroad stopped service to Peoria, the passenger station was saved and today is used by the Peoria Election Commission and is located on the corner of Walnut and Adams. This area was at the end of the ITS bridge across the Illinois River.

The City of Peoria

Peoria is the oldest European settlement in Illinois, established in 1691 after French explorers first passed the location while exploring the Illinois River. The first settlement was known as Fort Crevecoeur, founded on January 5, 1680, by French explorers René-Robert Cavelier, Sieur de La Salle, and Henri de Tonti. The term Crevecoeur was chosen as it means "Fort Broken Heart," describing the challenges of exploring and building the fort. The fort was located on the east bank of the Illinois River near the present site of Creve Coeur, a suburb of Peoria. On April 15, 1680, Henri de Tonti left the fort for Fort St. Louis at Starved Rock. The next day, the remaining seven men burned Fort Crevecoeur and fled to Canada with the remaining supplies. Soon, Tonti was pushed from the area by nearly six hundred Iroquois warriors.

Tonti returned in 1691 and established Fort Pimiteoui, which soon became a trade center that lasted for almost a century. With the land coming under English control, and then that of the new United States, the French moved from the area. In 1813, Fort Clark was built to help protect the territory during the War of 1812. In 1825, the County of Peoria was organized and the fort was officially renamed Peoria after the Peoria tribe.

From the beginning, the Illinois River was the base of transportation for Peoria. In 1829, the first steamboat, *Liberty*, arrived in Peoria. By 1844, there were a reported 150 steamboat companies operating on this part of the Illinois River. With the arrival of the first railroad in 1854, freight and passengers quickly moved to the new transportation mode, although barge service is still popular on the Illinois Waterway.

Through the late 1800s and early 1900s, Peoria was a base of manufacturing. It was once the home of the world's largest bourbon distillery plus several more, a Pabst brewery, Keystone Steel and Wire, corn processing facilities, slaughterhouses, an animal feed plant, several chemical plants, and just about every small factory that could exist. Peoria is also home of Caterpillar, one of the thirty companies comprising the Dow Jones Industrial Average, and several assembly plants are in the area.

Peoria is known for being pretty average based upon its location and demographics, which helped create the Vaudeville phrase, "Will it play in Peoria?" Today, Peoria is the largest city on the Illinois River and is the county seat of Peoria County. It is the seventh largest city in Illinois (120,000 in the city and 375,000 in the metropolitan area).

161.2 PEORIA – BRIDGE STREET – This location was named in the February 1, 1910, *Rock Island Lines List of Officers, Station Agents, Etc.* book. This was the junction to the former Toledo, Peoria & Western bridge across the Illinois

River. Just to the south was the Illinois Traction System bridge which led to their downtown station, once located not far to the northwest.

The name Bridge Street isn't found on modern maps of Peoria, but it once was located where the railroad passes under the William Kumpf Boulevard Bridge. Bridge Street was also known as Franklin Street.

A switch still exists here for a line that runs along the Illinois River. It runs through the ADM (Archer-Daniels-Midland) processing facility and their barge dock. Early maps show that the line was the Chicago, Rock Island & Pacific mainline, moved to make room for the Union Station complex. To the south, the line appears to have been owned by the Minneapolis & St. Louis.

161.5 PEORIA – CITY – This is another name from the February 1, 1910, *Rock Island Lines List of Officers, Station Agents, Etc.* book. The former **Peoria Union Station** was just to the west where the WTVP building now stands. Just on the river side of the station was the Peoria & Pekin Union freight house. Plans show that outbound freight was on the river side of the building while inbound freight was on the station side.

Mileposts for the Tazewell & Peoria Railroad lines start here as Union Station was Milepost 0.0. This can cause some confusion as mileposts increase in each direction along the route from Evans Station to Iowa Junction. IAIS trains heading to the Creve Coeur Yard or the Norfolk Southern East Peoria Yard continue down this route to Bridge Junction to cross the Illinois River into East Peoria.

As discussed elsewhere, the Peoria & Pekin Union was basically a terminal railroad that connected the many freight and passenger train operations together. This eliminated the need for duplicate facilities, investments none of the railroads wanted. The P&PU was organized on September 28, 1880, and began operations on February 1, 1881. The four founders of the P&PU were the Wabash, St. Louis & Pacific (Wabash); Indiana, Bloomington & Western (Peoria &

Eastern/New York Central); Peoria, Decatur & Evansville (Illinois Central); and Peoria & Jacksonville (Chicago & Illinois Midland). In 1954, ownership of the P&PU was spread among six railroads. These were the Nickel Plate (15.00%), Illinois Central (38.53%), New York Central/Peoria & Eastern (17.30%), Chicago & North Western (12.50%), Pennsylvania Railroad (8.34%), and Chicago & Illinois Midland (8.33%). By the time the P&PU was leased to the Genesee & Wyoming in 2009, the ownership was down to Canadian National, Norfolk Southern, and Union Pacific.

For those interested in all of the details, there is a great article in *Bulletin 158* of the Railway & Locomotive Historical Society entitled "Peoria Switching and Terminal Railway: The Peoria & Pekin Union" by Paul H. Stringham.

161.8 PERSIMMON STREET – Located at TZPR Milepost 0.28, there is a switch for a small yard and siding to the south. The Illinois Highway 116 Illinois River bridge crosses the middle of the yard.

162.2 EDMUND STREET – The south switch to the small yard is just north of here. Edmund Street (TZPR Milepost 0.78) is the main entrance into the ADM facility.

162.5 SOUTH STREET – Located at TZPR Milepost 1.11, this was the stockyard area in Peoria. Between here and the Illinois River were a series of slaughterhouses and stock pens. In this area were such companies as E. J. McDonough (slaughterhouse and hog barns), Wilson Provision Company (food packaging), E. Godel & Sons (packinghouse), Faber & Company (slaughterhouse), and Henry H. Shufeldt & Company ("Packers of Food Products").

Just south of here is the wye to the Peoria & Pekin Union Illinois River Bridge. This is the route to the P&PU Creve Coeur Yard and the Norfolk Southern East Peoria Yard.

162.7 BRIDGE JUNCTION – This is a large wye that connects the tracks in Peoria to the bridge over the Illinois River, thus reaching the many rail facilities in East Peoria. The Peoria & Pekin Union once had two roundhouses at Bridge Junction. The first was a large roundhouse in the middle of the wye, originally built with 30 stalls and later extended to 34. The second roundhouse was just to the west of the wye, served by a lead that cut across the south legs of the wye. These two facilities served not only the P&PU, but also the many railroads that used Union Station and the other facilities of the P&PU. The P&PU dieselized in 1952, ending their need for their three roundhouses and coaling facility. Over the next few years, the remaining railroads that served Peoria dieselized and the railroad decided to close the roundhouses and consolidate their offices and engine servicing facilities at the Creve Coeur Yard. The new engine facility opened on August 11, 1957.

Today, in the center of the wye where the larger roundhouse once stood is Greenbrier Castings. In 1990, the American Allied Freight Car Company was forced to move due to area highway construction, and they built a new facility here in 1991. Allied Freight Car was later bought by Greenbrier.

The area just to the north of the wye and away from the river was once a large P&PU yard. It is still known as their 90-Yard and is used for local work, although it once also handled freight interchange business for several railroads.

Just south of the wye and just before the Illinois River Bridge, the railroad has a diamond with the old CRI&P line that runs along the river.

163.1 PPU ILLINOIS RIVER BRIDGE – This is at least the third bridge here. The first was built as a Pratt through truss with a turn span, replaced in 1911 with a newer bridge designed and built by the McClintic-Marshall Company of Chicago. This bridge included a single-leaf, Strauss-type bascule bridge designed and built by the Strauss Bascule

Bridge Company of Chicago. Bascule bridges are hinged on one end and the other end lifts up to clear the waterway.

The current bridge was built 1983-1985 by American Bridge. The Illinois River bridge is 1080 feet long and includes a 460-foot long vertical lift polygonal Warren through truss bridge for commercial navigation. The approaches to the lift span consist of a number of deck plate girder spans – three on the Peoria end and four on the East Peoria end. The bridge was built as two-track, but only the south track is in service.

There is a switch to the second track at the south end of the bridge known as the Illinois River Bridge Interlocking. On April 28, 2003, the railroad issued the following notice that should explain the many tracks here.

"The rail east of the Illinois River Bridge (IRB) Interlocking through and including Wesley Junction has been reconfigured as follows:

The northern rail on the levee, from the East Home Signal of the IRB Interlocking to the yard, has been designated as yard track and will be referred to as the 'West Lead.' This piece of track is now non-signaled yard track, and provides access to Caterpillar SS, and yard tracks 32 through 41.

The portion of yard track formerly known as the 'East Peoria Lead' will now be referred to as the 'East Lead,' and is also non-signaled yard track.

When issuing yarding or departing instructions to trains, the Yardmasters will specify either East or West Lead.

The southern rail on the levee east of the IRB interlocking will be known as 'Main Track 1.' This remains signaled Main Track, and provides access to and from the East Lead, Nickel Plate Main, and the Single Main."

The Illinois River separates Peoria and East Peoria, and it also is the county line between Peoria County and

Peoria Subdivision

Tazewell County. **Tazewell County** was organized and the boundaries officially established on January 22, 1829. The name came from either Littleton Tazewell, or his father Henry Tazewell. Littleton Tazewell served in the U.S. Senate and later as the governor of Virginia in 1834. Henry Tazewell was also a prominent Virginia politician and had Tazewell County, Virginia, named after him. The county seat and largest city is Pekin.

163.9 WESLEY JUNCTION – According to the records of the Nickel Plate Road (Wabash, later Norfolk & Western and today Norfolk Southern), which operated over the P&PU from Wesley Junction to Peoria Union Station, the distance is 2.4 miles. Wesley Junction is the large wye that connects Creve Coeur Yard with the Peoria to Pekin mainline. The Creve Coeur Yard, located immediately east of the Wesley Junction, serves as an interchange yard for many of the railroads, and the base of operations for the Tazewell & Peoria Railroad. The yard is about 1.5 miles long and ends at Washington Street and Farm Creek, where the line continues as a joint Norfolk Southern and Toledo, Peoria & Western line at East Peoria. For those who are interested, the first water-powered mill in Tazewell County, a grist-mill, was built on Farm Creek in 1827.

Creve Coeur Yard, also known as East Peoria Yard, was built in 1906 as a hump yard, but was converted to a flat-switching yard in 1911 with a capacity of 3170 cars. When it was completed, the freight work was split between here and Yards 90 and 91 near Bridge Junction. In 1957, a new diesel shop was built at the west end of the yard just east of Wesley Junction.

The name Wesley Junction comes from the community of Wesley City, which once existed nearby. Wesley City grew on the Illinois River around an old French trading post which was built in the 1770s. As the area was being settled, the community was first platted in 1836. A grist and sawmill had been built nearby by a Methodist preacher and a few of his followers, and they pushed the name Wesley City to honor Methodist leader John Wesley.

Over the years, the Illinois River flooded and eroded the lands that made up Wesley City, and the community moved to higher ground and took the name "Crevecoeur" when it incorporated on May 5, 1921. In 1960, Mayor Carroll Patten led an effort to change the spelling to "Creve Coeur" and the rest is history.

IAIS 707, Peoria, Illinois. Photo by Barton Jennings.

Milan Branch
Rock Island (Illinois) to Milan (Illinois)

The Milan Branch is today one of the longest non-mainline parts of the Iowa Interstate Railroad. The track is known as the Milan Branch by the IAIS, but also as the Milan Spur. This line departs from the west end of the original Rock Island downtown yard, curves along the Mississippi River and heads south to Milan, Illinois, serving a small number of shippers, and ends at the Southwest Rock Island Industrial Park near Interstate 280.

The line started life as the Rock Island & Mercer County Railroad Company, chartered on April 29, 1876, to construct a railroad "from the village of Milan, in Rock Island County and State of Illinois to Section sixteen (16) in Richland Grove Township in Mercer County in said State." This placed the end of the line at the various coal mines then developing near Sherrard and Cable, Illinois. Over the next few years, the railroad expanded to serve more coal mines, but came under the control of the Rock Island & Peoria Railway (RI&P) by the late 1890s. The Rock Island & Peoria Railway had been chartered on October 9, 1877, to build a rail line "from the City of Rock Island in the State of Illinois, to the City of Peoria in said State." On June 10, 1903, the Rock Island & Mercer County Railroad (RI&MC) was fully purchased by the Rock Island & Peoria Railway. The two railroads connected at Milan and the RI&P was able to use the tracks of the RI&MC between there and Rock Island.

The next day, June 11, 1903, the Chicago, Rock Island & Pacific bought the Rock Island & Peoria and brought both railroads into its system. However, the Rock Island wasn't interested in much of the rural line and leased the original Rock Island & Mercer County route to the Rock Island Southern (incorporated on April 25, 1905). The Rock Island Southern (RIS) was designed to be an interurban company, and it already owned the former Western Illinois Traction line from Monmouth to Galesburg.

According to the February 1, 1910 *Rock Island Lines List of Officers, Station Agents, Etc.*, the line from Rock Island to Peoria was the Peoria Line, while the former Rock Island & Mercer County west of Milan was the Sherrard Branch, even with it under lease to the Rock Island Southern. By 1910, the RIS had built a connecting line from Southern Junction southward to Monmouth to consolidate the system. As with most interurban railroads, its business declined during the middle of the 1900s. It was shut down in February 1952 and abandoned on June 30, 1952.

The former Rock Island & Peoria route was also abandoned, with the route between Coal Valley (a few miles east of Milan) and Orion being removed in 1941. The route between Milan and Coal Valley remained to serve the coal mines in that area. The remaining track in the Rock Island and Milan area remained a part of the Chicago, Rock Island & Pacific until the company folded and was eventually sold to the Iowa Interstate.

Today, BNSF and Canadian Pacific both use the first mile of the Milan Branch to access the Crescent Mississippi River Bridge. From there south, the Iowa Interstate operates over the line as needed, often daily. The largest customer on the line is the steel warehouse at the end of the remaining Rock Island & Mercer County line, known as the Andalusia Spur or the Sherrard Branch.

Milan Branch

The mileposts on the Milan Branch are today based upon the distance from Chicago. However, the Federal Railroad Administration still shows most of the grade crossings with mileposts from Peoria. The mileposts from Chicago, as used by the Iowa Interstate, will be used, but some of the Peoria mileposts will also be quoted.

181.2 ROCK ISLAND – Located at 3031 5th Avenue is the former Rock Island passenger station. Details on this station and yard are found on page 112. The FRA shows this location to be Milepost 92.2.

181.4 IAIS TERMINAL JUNCTION – This is today's milepost for the switch to the rail yard at Rock Island. It was shown as Milepost 91.7 for the Peoria Line, the former Rock Island & Peoria Railway. Later FRA reports show this as Milepost 92.0.

Milan Branch

181.8 24TH STREET BRIDGE – The railroad passes under this bridge that crosses Sylvan Slough, a part of the Mississippi River, to reach Arsenal Island, once known as Rock Island. The bridge eventually connects with Government Bridge on to Davenport. The FRA milepost is 91.6.

182.1 20TH STREET – The Rock Island Southern Railway Company had a passenger depot here, listed as Milepost 90.7 in 1910. The first depot in Rock Island was actually once in this area, located at 2nd Avenue and 20th Street to the south. It was built in 1854.

The area to the south was once a maze of railroad stations and tracks. This was the west end of a large eight-track yard. On the south side of the tracks was the Peoria Branch 20th Street depot with a small attached freight house and covered platform. Just to the south was a much larger CRI&P freight house. A block further to the south and located on the southeast corner of 20th Street and 2nd Avenue was the CB&Q passenger depot and freight house. This area today is now the Spencer Towers and a large parking lot.

On the southwest corner of 2nd Avenue and 23rd Street was another railroad-related structure, the Tri-City Railway Company Electric Power Station.

The FRA shows this location to be Milepost 91.3, so some changes in milepost locations have taken place over the years.

182.3 SCHWIEBERT RIVERFRONT PARK – This area along the Mississippi River is part of the redevelopment program of Rock Island. In this area is the Schwiebert Riverfront Park and the Modern Woodmen of America building. Parts of the original Rock Island downtown are to the south. 17th Street and 18th Street both access this area and have grade crossings with the railroad.

Just south of the 17th Street grade crossing, the Chicago, Milwaukee & St. Paul (later Chicago, Milwaukee, St. Paul & Pacific) had a passenger station with a fifty-foot clock tower. Just to the south was the Milwaukee Road freight depot. In this area today is the BNSF Switch to their river bridge. Next to 1st Avenue is a small yard that eventually leads into the Dohrn Transfer facility. The area where the Dohrn complex now stands was once the Rock Island Plow Company.

IAIS 707 westbound in Rock Island, Illinois. Photo by Barton Jennings.

182.5 CENTENNIAL BRIDGE – This bridge, used by U.S. Highway 67 and located at the end of 15th Street, crosses the Mississippi River. There is a small yard with a BNSF office building under the bridge.

In this area, three railroads operated side-by-side during the early part of the Twentieth Century. Alongside the river was the Chicago, Milwaukee, St. Paul & Pacific. Just to the east was the Chicago, Rock Island & Pacific, with the Chicago, Burlington & Quincy further to the east. Toward the west end of today's yard, located between 12th and 13th Streets, the CB&Q had a diamond with the Rock Island to reach the bridge across the Mississippi River.

183.0 BUZZI UNICEM SWITCH – Next to the river is a small cement facility operated by Buzzi Unicem. In this area was once a turntable and nine-stall roundhouse, shown by Sanborn to not be used by 1906. There was also a six-track yard just to the south of the roundhouse.

183.2 ROCK ISLAND RIVER TERMINAL – There is a track into the barge loading dock in the Mississippi River terminal.

183.5 RETIRED SIDING – Located to the east between 4th Avenue and 6th Avenue is a retired short siding once used to serve the adjacent warehouse.

183.9 SIDING – To the east and located north of 1st Street is a short siding. There was once a track that curved off to the west to serve a small Mississippi River barge facility.

184.3 CENTENNIAL EXPRESSWAY – The railroad passes under this road built as a higher speed, limited access road to assist with getting traffic in and out of Rock Island. It is also Illinois Highway 92 in this area.

184.6 E&J METAL SPUR – To the west, just north of 24th Avenue, is a spur into a small scrap yard.

185.6 SARA LEE SPUR – To the west is a spur track into the former Sara Lee bakery. Carloads of flour and other baking ingredients used to be delivered to this facility.

185.7 ROCK ISLAND LIVESTOCK AUCTION SIDING – To the east is a short siding that decades ago was used to serve the stockyards. This cattle auction facility has been the site of regular sales dating back to the 1930s when cattle were delivered from across the country by rail. Local meat packers and feeder farms kept the barn busy until the past decade. The auction barn closed in 2015 and then reopened under new ownership in 2016.

186.5 ROCK SPUR – Located just south of 49th Avenue is a track to the east often used for rock distribution.

186.7 SEARS – David Benton Sears arrived in the Moline area in 1836 and built a dam and mill on Sylvan Slough. Sears was busy over the next decade, having platted both Rock Island and Moline. His work and development reportedly attracted John Deere to the community. After the federal government took over his property, he moved to the Rock River and built four dams on the river. One was here where the railroad would eventually cross the river, and Sears built a five-story flour mill on the south side of the dam and river channel by 1868. Nearby a number of other industries developed along 1½ miles of riverfront controlled by Sears, including papermills, sawmills, woolen mills, and a cotton mill. With this development, a town grew up known as Sears, or Searstown. Searstown was annexed by the City of Rock Island in 1915.

By 1907, most of the Sears mill complex was gone and a new project was underway. In that year, Samuel S. Davis established the Rock River Navigation and Water Power Company to build a hydroelectric dam on the Rock River. While never as large as originally planned, the S. S. Davis Water Power Company and its Sears Powerhouse was the third largest electric company of 63 waterpower dams on the Rock River in 1949. In 1958, the family heirs donated the powerhouse to Augustana College, which operated it until 1966. The powerhouse was closed and stripped, and then donated to the State of Illinois.

In 1980, Mitchell and Melba White leased the real estate and water rights from the State of Illinois through their White Hydropower Company with plans to rehabilitate the powerhouse and again produce electrical power. This was accomplished by 1985. In 2008, the City of Rock Island bought the power plant and upgraded it for local use.

186.8 NORTH ROCK RIVER BRIDGE – This bridge consists of three lattice through truss spans built in 1894 by Lassig

Milan Branch

Bridge & Iron Works of Chicago, Illinois. However, this is not their first location as they were moved here about 1930. These spans used to be part of the CRIP mainline bridge across Sylvan Slough leading to the Rock Island Arsenal and the Government Bridge across the Mississippi River. The bridge is about 470 feet long with each span being about 155 feet long.

This bridge crosses the north channel of the Rock River. The south end of the bridge is on Vandruff Island. The Rock River, approximately 300 miles long, starts in Fond du Lac County, Wisconsin, and wanders along the Wisconsin-Illinois border before entering the Mississippi River in the Quad Cities area, just a few miles downstream from here. Sources say that the Sauk and Fox Indians called the river "Sinnissippi," meaning "rocky waters."

187.0 SOUTH ROCK RIVER BRIDGE – Like the bridge across the north channel, this bridge also was moved to here from the Sylvan Slough bridge from Rock Island to Arsenal Island. Several of the piers have markings indicating a construction date of 1930, but the three lattice through truss spans here are also 1894 spans built by Lassig Bridge & Iron Works of Chicago, Illinois. The total length of the bridge is about 420 feet long with the longest truss span being 150 feet long.

187.1 HENNEPIN CANAL – The railroad once crossed the canal here. Today, the canal still exists, but the railroad uses a fill to cross the canal channel. The canal was built to connect the Illinois and Mississippi Rivers, but funding didn't become available until 1890 and the canal wasn't completed until 1907, reducing the distance from Chicago to Rock Island by 419 miles. However, by the time it was finished, the cost of shipping by rail had decreased (and was faster) and barge sizes and freight loads had increased making the Hennepin nearly obsolete. However, it did achieve some fame. It was the first American canal built of concrete without cut stone facings, and some construction techniques were used on later, larger canals such as the Panama Canal. Because of this, the canal is listed on the National Register of Historic Places.

187.5 MILAN – The old Milan depot is at 4th Street and 4th Avenue in Milan, Illinois. It sits in the center of a wye where to the east the line used to pass through the coal mines at Coal Valley and eventually went all the way to Peoria, but the track was cut back in the 1950s. To the west is the former Rock Island Southern trackage that extended to Monmouth, once known as the Sherrard Branch.

The yellow and red wooden depot is now the Whistle Stop Java Shop, a popular coffee shop that has used the building for years. The depot was built in 1917.

188.0 INTERSTATE 280 – The railroad passes under I-280, an auxiliary highway between I-80 and I-74 around the southwest side of the Quad Cities. Under the bridge is a switch into Cedar Creek lumber and building materials. This is approximately Milepost 85.3 based upon the FRA.

188.1 END OF TRACK – There is just enough track south of I-280 to allow a train to make the switchback move to serve Cedar Creek. The grade beyond here is now covered by numerous buildings and roadways.

Andalusia Spur

0.0 MILAN – The 1917 Milan depot is at 4th Street and 4th Avenue in Milan, Illinois, and is used by the Whistle Stop Java Shop.

0.2 MILAN SIDING – There is a short siding here to allow trains switching local customers to run around their freight cars.

Milan Branch

Former Milan depot. Photo by Barton Jennings.

0.5   **INTERSTATE 280** – The railroad passes under I-280, an auxiliary highway between I-80 and I-74 around the southwest side of the Quad Cities.

0.8   **ANDALUSIA ROAD** – The railroad crosses this east-west running street and then runs alongside its south shoulder to the end of the line.

1.4   **SPURS** – To the south are several track spurs into the facilities of the Interstate Chemical and Brandt Construction facilities.

2.2   **SPUR** – To the south is a spur track that ends at Metal Sales Manufacturing. Just to the east is Hasselroth Park with its small fenced dog park, and the Campbell Sports Complex and its four lighted softball fields.

2.8   **SPUR** – A short spur track heads south into the Miller Container Corporation complex.

3.0   **SIDING** – There is a siding between Centennial Expressway (Milepost 2.9) and 42nd Street West (Milepost 3.1).

This is the last chance for a train to run around its freight cars to switch local customers.

Just west of 42nd Street West the railroad curves to the south. There is a short siding here used to hold coiled-steel freight cars for the shipper at the end of the line.

3.4 END OF TRACK – The railroad runs through the Steel Warehouse Company and ends several car lengths south of it. The company was founded in 1947 and remains a family business that stores and modifies steel for its various customers.

IAIS 704, Milan, Illinois. Photo by Barton Jennings.

Prairie City Line
Altoona (Iowa) to Mitchellville Station (Iowa)

This line was originally the Des Moines Valley Rail Road, the first railroad to Des Moines, Iowa. It arrived in Des Moines on August 29, 1866, but was never anything more than a secondary railroad. The Des Moines Valley Rail Road actually started on September 1, 1853, when it was organized as the Keokuk, Fort Des Moines & Minnesota Rail Road. Construction started in 1854, but was halted in 1861 by the Civil War. Construction started again in 1864 when the railroad reorganized as the Des Moines Valley Rail Road. The line eventually built as far north as Fort Dodge, but went bankrupt in 1873. The company was split in two and the track east and south of Des Moines became the Keokuk & Des Moines Railway, incorporated on January 6, 1874. On May 14, 1878, the railroad was leased by the Rock Island and later acquired. The K&DM extended from Keokuk in a northwest direction to Des Moines, consisting of "162.285 miles of first main track and 28.008 miles of other tracks, or 186.293 miles of all tracks."

This line was known as the Keokuk and Des Moines Valley Branch in the *Central Division Time Table* of the Rock Island of October 30, 1966, and the Keokuk and Altoona Branch in the *Illinois Division Time Table No. 9* of August 21, 1977. When the railroad closed down in 1980, the 104 miles of track from Pella to Keokuk was abandoned but the line from Pella to Altoona became part of the Iowa Interstate. A major reason for this was that Pella Rolscreen Corporation, maker of Pella windows and doors, was one of the railroad's original backers.

However, Pella soon stopped shipping by rail and the line between Pella (115.6) and Otley (123.6) was embargoed on October 6, 1996, due to poor track conditions. IAIS received formal permission to abandon the trackage on August 7, 1998, and the rails were gone by early 2000. The track between Otley and Prairie City (135.0) was approved for abandonment on November 21, 2000, and the track quickly came out. This left service to the Heartland Co-op in downtown Prairie City.

In June 2014, the railroad applied to abandon more of the line, this time from Prairie City to milepost 145.75 near Nobleton.

The railroad reported that there had been no shipments over the line since 2008 and that the line had been primarily been used for car storage. The abandonment was made official on September 17, 2014, and the track was removed in 2015 east of NE 116th Street, also known as Center Street. Almost immediately, several groups began bidding against each other to replace the line with some sort of hiking or biking trail. Today, the rest of the line is generally used for car storage.

151.3 ALTOONA – This is the connection with the mainline of Iowa Interstate's Newton Subdivision. This branch runs to the southeast for about six miles, although it once went much further. For the first ten miles, the railroad crossed a series of low ridges, creating short grades of as much as 1.06%.

147.6 LITTLE CAMP CREEK BRIDGE – This was Bridge 350.2 on the old CRIP Eldon, Iowa, to Altoona, Iowa, branch line. Rock Island records show that it consists of three deck plate girder spans, two that measure 41 feet long, and one that is 19 feet long. It was built in 1900 by the Lassig Plant of the American Bridge Company.

146.7 CAMP CREEK BRIDGE – This was Bridge 349.3 on the old CRIP Eldon, Iowa, to Altoona, Iowa, branch line. This four-span deck plate girder bridge was built in 1903 by the American Bridge Company. There are four spans, each 44-feet long, held up by tall timber piers.

146.0 NOBLETON – Some maps show this location to be Mitchell or Mitchellville Station, named for Mitchellville on the Iowa Interstate mainline about a mile to the north. This made sense when this line was a competitor with the Rock Island Railroad. Photos from the 1950s show a station sign, but no station or extra tracks. There are a few houses here today as well as several tall radio towers.

145.7 END OF TRACK – For the original railroad, this location was known as Mitchellville Station as stage coaches ran from here north to Mitchellville. When the railroad abandoned the track on to Prairie City, this became the new end of track, located at NE 116th Street, also known as Center Street. This keeps the line entirely in Polk County in Iowa. When the track was abandoned from here to Prairie City, service to two former stations was lost. Zachary's was at Milepost 141.9, while Prairie City was at Milepost 138.3. The first settler in Prairie City was William Means in 1851, but the community was originally named Elliot after the second settler: James Elliot. James and his wife established a town here on June 7, 1856, and named it Prairie City. The town was incorporated on August 7, 1874.

Earlier, the line was abandoned through Fairmount (133.5), Monroe (129.1), Otley (123.6), Otley Passing Track (122.5), and Pella (115.6). The name Pella came from the Hebrew word meaning "a city of refuge." Pella has two founding dates – June 6, 1848, and its date of incorporation of April 10, 1868. Pella is the home of Pella Rolscreen Corporation, maker of Pella windows and doors.

Iowa Interstate Railroad: History Through the Miles

Photos by Barton Jennings.

Grimes Line
Des Moines (Iowa) to Grimes (Iowa)

The Grimes Line, known sometimes by the Iowa Interstate Railroad as the Grimes Spur, was once part of the Milwaukee Road's entrance to Des Moines. The line left Des Moines and split at Clive, with one route heading north to the Omaha-Chicago mainline and then on north to Boone, Iowa. The second route departed at Clive and headed west before turning north and going to Spirit Lake, Iowa.

Frederick Hubbell, Jefferson Polk, and several other partners that included Grenville Dodge and James Clarkson, editor and publisher of the *Iowa State Register* (the predecessor of the *Des Moines Register*), formed the Narrow Gauge Construction Company to build railroads. Three railroads were eventually built, two that created today's Grimes Spur. These were the Des Moines North Western Railway (110 miles from Des Moines to Fonda, what eventually became the line to Spirit Lake) and the St. Louis, Des Moines & Northern Railway (40 miles of track from Des Moines to Boone). The third line was the Des Moines & St. Louis, which operated a 68-mile line from Des Moines southeast to Albia.

Jay Gould was somehow involved with the company, and he soon leased the railroads in 1881 through his Wabash, St. Louis & Pacific Railroad Company. It was this partnership that also led to the creation of the Des Moines Union Railway. A few years later in 1884, Gould's railroad went bankrupt and the narrow gauge railroads returned to the control of Polk & Hubbell. These were eventually combined and sold to the Chicago, Milwaukee & St. Paul Railroad in 1898.

The St. Louis, Des Moines & Northern Railway Company was incorporated on May 21, 1881. According to local newspaper reports, the St. Louis, Des Moines & Northern Railway Company had been finished in August 1892 from the depot between Fourth and Fifth Streets in Des Moines to Boone. Reports indicate that the narrow gauge lines were standard gauged by 1891, the same year that the lines were consolidated as the Des Moines, Northern & Western Railway Company. The Chicago, Milwaukee & Saint

Paul Railroad acquired control of the lines in 1894 and fully purchased them in 1899.

When the Milwaukee Road went bankrupt, these lines were abandoned in 1980. However, Norfolk Southern acquired the line to Grimes and restored service. Some Grimes trackage was abandoned in 2012 by NS, which had no route of its own to Des Moines. Because of this, Iowa Interstate is contracted to work the line. The primary customers on the line are Pitt-Des Moines (a steel fabricator) in Clive and Beisser Lumber in Grimes.

The following mileposts are those that are along the line today that relate to the Wabash mileposts installed by Norfolk Southern. These newer mileposts were used by the Surface Transportation Board when it approved the abandonment of track between Milepost 353.0 and 354.7 near Grimes, Iowa. However, Milwaukee Road documents, and the Federal Railroad Administration's grade crossing data base, use different mileposts. These older mileposts are also mentioned in the route guide.

343.0 GRIMES LINE JUNCTION – This is the switch with the mainline of the Iowa Interstate Railroad. The railroad curves to the north to follow Walnut Creek. The Milwaukee Road milepost for this location is about 3.2.

Originally, the railroad had its own route into Des Moines, but today has a new junction on the former Rock Island mainline to reduce the trackage in the area. On Milwaukee Road maps, the area around the grade crossing at Milepost 3.8 was known as Coaldale.

345.0 WALNUT CREEK BRIDGE – This stream starts to the west of the Interstate 80 belt on the west side of Des Moines. Walnut Creek has one of the most urbanized watersheds in Iowa, with approximately 60 percent urban land use and 40 percent agricultural land use. Walnut Creek flows into the Raccoon River to the south.

The bridge consists of a 105-foot through truss, also called a Pony truss, span. The bridge was built by the Carnegie Steel Company. There is a short span trestle on each end of the bridge, making it a total length of 142 feet. There is a

345 Milepost sign at the end of the bridge. This bridge is at Milepost 5.0 on Milwaukee Road documents.

To the south is Grand Avenue. In a 1948 Milwaukee Road track profile, there is a note stating that there is an "Electric Line Grade Xing" on the north side of Grand Avenue. This would have been the West Des Moines line (also known as the Southwest Ninth or Fort Des Moines line) of the Des Moines Railway Company. This company started as the horse-powered Des Moines Street Railway in 1867. The company operated their first electric streetcar (a converted horse car) on December 19, 1888. In 1889, the Des Moines City Railway Company was created by the consolidation of the Des Moines Street Railway, the Broad Gauge Street Railway, the Rapid Transit Company, and the Sevastopol Street Railway. The system was bought in 1929 and became the Des Moines Railway Company. In 1940, the system was using 100 street cars, 31 trolley buses, and 37 gas buses. However, the last street car operated on March 5, 1951.

North of the bridge, the railroad crosses 1st Avenue/63rd Street at grade. Then there is a switch for a spur track to the west and then one to the east. In 1948, there were a number of tracks in this area, but no name was shown on railroad documents.

346.1 INTERSTATE 235 – The railroad passes under I-235, which forms an urban loop from West Des Moines east to downtown Des Moines, then north to a junction with I-35 and I-80. These two interstates loop around Des Moines on the north and west side and I-235 provides freeway access to downtown. The Milwaukee Road milepost for here is 6.1.

346.5 WALNUT CREEK BRIDGE – The railroad again crosses Walnut Creek. This bridge also consists of a 105-foot long Pony truss span with trestle spans on each end, this time for a length of 162 feet. Reports state that the bridge was built in 1902 and that the piers were rebuilt in 1943. This bridge is at Milwaukee Road Milepost 6.5.

347.5 CLIVE – In 1948, there was a siding on both routes at Clive. A track profile also mentions stockyards and a station here. The line that once went on to Spirit Lake continues straight here for a short distance. The junction is at Milwaukee Road Milepost 7.5. The mileposts continue up the line to Grimes.

According to *A Dictionary of Iowa Place-Names* by Tom Savage, Clive was established by the Union Land Company of Des Moines on January 18, 1882. The Union Land Company was incorporated by Hubbell, Polk and others to develop depot sites along their railroads. Clive was one of these communities, as was Grimes. Reportedly, five thousand acres of land was bought for the company by Nathan C. Towne, who also bought five thousand acres for himself, meaning he was quite wealthy. The Union Land Company of Des Moines was listed as an Iowa corporation at least until 1918.

There are numerous stories about where the name Clive came from. One states that it was named for the railroad foreman who built the line through the area. A second states that it was named for Robert Clive, a British general in charge of much of the colonization of India.

348.5 SWANSON BOULEVARD – The line has split and the main stem curves to the north and crosses Swanson Boulevard at former Milwaukee Road Milepost 8.5.

348.7 PITT-DES MOINES – This is the end of the line. This Pitt-Des Moines is a privately held company, established in 2010 to do fabricated plate and boiler shop work. It replaced the historical Pittsburgh-Des Moines Steel Company (originally the Des Moines Bridge and Iron Company) which dated back to 1892.

Clive to Woodward Jct. Line

This line once went north as far as Boone, Iowa. By 1948, Milwaukee Road documents showed that the line was still in to

Grimes Line

Granger and then up to the east-west mainline at Woodward Junction. It was known logically as the Clive to Woodward Jct. Line.

347.5 CLIVE – This was Milwaukee Road Milepost 0.0 for the line to Woodward Junction. In 1948, there was a siding on both routes at Clive. A track profile also mentions stockyards and a station here. The line to Grimes swings to the north, crosses Swanson Boulevard (Milepost 0.3), and passes between neighborhoods and a number of small businesses. Heading north, the railroad faces grades of as much as 1% to near Rider at Milepost 350.9.

348.4 U.S. HIGHWAY 6 – The railroad crosses the highway, also known as Hickman Road, on a bridge consisting of four deck plate girder spans. The Milwaukee Road milepost here was 0.9.

349.5 SPUR TRACKS – Located just south of the grade crossing with 100th Street are several short spur tracks. These tracks do not appear on a 1948 *C.M.St.P.&P. Condensed Profile for the Iowa Division*, but would have been at Milepost 2.0.

349.8 SIDING – There is a short siding here to the west of the mainline. Milwaukee Road Milepost 2.3 was located here.

350.9 RIDER – In 1948, there was a short house track to the east at Milwaukee Road Milepost 3.4. Today, a McDonald's and Pallet Recyclers of Iowa occupy this area.

351.2 INTERSTATE 80 – The railroad passes under I-80, a transcontinental highway that runs from downtown San Francisco, California, to Teaneck, New Jersey. It is the second longest Interstate Highway in the United States (after Interstate 90), and closely follows the route of the historic Lincoln Highway, the first road across America.

For a few miles in this area, Interstate 35 also uses part of I-80. I-35 is the ninth-longest Interstate Highway and the third-longest north-south Interstate Highway. It stretches 1568 miles from Laredo, Texas, to Duluth, Minnesota.

351.7 BEISSER LUMBER SPUR – To the west is a spur into this large lumber yard. To the east is a short siding. This location is just to the south of SE 37th Street at Milwaukee Road Milepost 4.2.

353.1 SW 19TH STREET – Heading west, this road becomes Meadow Drive, also known as 250th Street. It is located at Milwaukee Road Milepost 5.6. In October 2010, the Surface Transportation Board approved an abandonment request north of here to Milepost 354.7. The request was made by Norfolk Southern, the track owner, as well as Iowa Interstate.

353.8 SE 6TH STREET – This was once Milwaukee Road Milepost 6.3, but is now not even a grade crossing after the 2010 abandonment. The switch to the former 3377-foot long Grimes Siding was just south of this location. In 1948, there was a stockyard and station at Grimes.

Grimes was created when the St. Louis, Des Moines & Northern Railway built through the area in 1882. Grimes was incorporated as a city on May 7, 1894. The City of Grimes was named for James W. Grimes. Grimes moved to what became Burlington, Iowa, in the early 1800s. He soon became involved in politics and served as a member of the Iowa Territorial House of Representatives 1838-1839 and 1843-1844. Grimes was the Governor of Iowa 1854-1858, and then served in the U.S. Senate from 1859 to December 6, 1869, when he resigned due to his health. Grimes died in 1872.

Atlantic Spur
Atlantic Junction (Iowa) to Harlan (Iowa)

The Atlantic Spur departs the mainline near Atlantic at Milepost 440.8, once known as Audubon Junction. When the Iowa Interstate was formed and bought the line, this spur was known as the Audubon Branch, Subdivision 4B. The line was built by the Atlantic & Audubon Railroad Company, incorporated on June 20, 1878. The railroad was incorporated "to construct and operate a line of railroad from a point on the Chicago, Rock Island and Pacific Railroad at or near Atlantic in the County of Cass in the State of Iowa, in a northerly direction and in the valleys of the Nishnabotna River and Blue Grass Creek, to some point in the County of Audubon in said State." Completed in December 1878, the line went north 25 miles from Atlantic to the community of Audubon, Iowa. Soon after construction ended, the company was sold to the Chicago, Rock Island & Pacific Railroad Company.

The line was never a major route and the business at Audubon was split between this line and a Chicago & North Western line, built south from Manning to Audubon using their Iowa South Western Railway Company in 1882. The C&NW line was abandoned in 1952. By the 1970s, the track condition was so poor that the railroad couldn't move cars reliably. In the mid-1970s, a group of shippers along the line created the Audubon-Atlantic Branch Line Improvement Association, loaning the railroad trustee $100,000 to upgrade the branch. More money came from the State of Iowa making for a total of $750,000, all with the goal of making the line good for 20 miles per hour service. With the improvements, the Rock Island set a goal of 1000 carloads of grain annually on the line by 1976. However, only 327 cars moved in 1977, basically the same as a few years earlier.

During the late 1980s, this branch received some national fame as the home of the Purple Martin steam-powered tourist train, based at Lorah near Interstate 80. The equipment sat there for many years after the owner died until being auctioned off in June 1995. When the Iowa Interstate was created in 1984, the line to Audubon was included with the purchase. However, with the purchase, traffic levels didn't change and the line was abandoned from Milepost 445 near Atlantic to Milepost 465.20 at Audubon in late 1995. The abandoned part of this line is now the T-Bone Trail, named for the cattle moved over the line to the Chicago market.

Records show that the Iowa Interstate has changed the mileposts on the line, starting with Milepost 0.0 at the mainline.

0.0 ATLANTIC SPUR JUNCTION – This switch is just west of the East Nishnabotna River bridge at what was once Milepost 440.8. The line immediately makes a 90-degree turn, going from northwest to northeast, as it heads toward Audubon. To the east of the track and towards the center of the curve is the Frank Chapman Pellet Memorial Woods State Preserve. Frank Pellet moved here in 1907, but worried when many of his favorite childhood flowers couldn't be found. In 1908, he created a 20-acre wildflower preserve containing 8 acres of native woodland. After his death, the Iowa Horticultural Society and the Iowa Beekeepers Association continued the project. Eventually the land became the Pellett Memorial Woods, owned by the State of Iowa and managed by the Cass County Conservation Board since 1987.

0.2 LANDUS COOPERATIVE – Almost immediately on the line is a track to the east for this fertilizer terminal. Most of the fertilizer appears to be liquid products, common for the production of corn. The milepost here was once 441.0.

Until recently, this was the Atlantic Fertilizer Terminal. In late 2015, the members of the Farmers Cooperative Company of Ames, Iowa, and the West Central Cooperative of Ralston, Iowa, approved a merger between the two cooperatives. The merger became effective on April 1, 2016, creating the Landus Cooperative, the seventh largest grain company in North America based on storage capacity. The Cooperative states that it has approximately 7000 member-owners and has facilities in more than 70 communities in Iowa and Minnesota. The new cooperative has shuttle-loading facilities on all seven major Iowa rail lines, and is based in Ames, Iowa.

0.5   ELITE OCTANE – In 2017, construction was well underway on one of what has been described as "only a handful of first generation ethanol plants to be built in the U.S. since 2008." Plans have been underway for several years to build this ethanol plant, which includes a six-track rail yard further to the north. Scheduled to open around the middle of 2018, the plant will produce about 120 million gallons of ethanol per year. According to the Iowa Renewable Fuels Association, this will make the plant one of 21 of just more than 40 Iowa ethanol plants that produce at least 100 million gallons per year in Iowa.

New ethanol plant near Atlantic, Iowa. Photo by Barton Jennings.

2.1   MOORMAN – Moorman was located just north of the grade crossing with Echo Road at Milepost 442.9. There were several families with the name of Moorman in the area. Little is known about any track or station here except that one used to exist and that bagged feed was delivered in box cars.

2.7 HARLAN ELEVATOR – This location was once at Milepost 443.5. The elevator complex was built in 1990 by Farm Service Cooperative (FSC), and later became a part of a limited liability company (LLC) which FSC had with ADM. In 2008, FSC sold its interest in that LLC to ADM. This facility handles both grain and fertilizers for area farmers. ADM is described as being "one of the world's largest agricultural processors and food ingredient providers, with more than 32,300 employees serving customers in more than 160 countries." The company has 428 crop procurement locations like this elevator, 280 ingredient manufacturing facilities, 39 innovation centers and the world's premier crop transportation network which includes railroads, a barge line, ocean vessels, and a large private truck fleet.

At one time, this elevator was switched by a GE 45-ton locomotive with side rods, numbered ADM 4441.

Grain cars heading to yard on Atlantic Spur. Photo by Barton Jennings.

3.2 END OF TRACK – This is the location of the end of Iowa Interstate track at what was Milepost 444.0. It was abandoned beyond here in 1995. Communities that lost service in that year included Lorah (446.7), Brayton (452.0), Exira (455.7), Nishna (463.0), and Audubon (465.1).

Hancock Spur
Hancock Junction (Iowa) to Oakland (Iowa)

The line through Hancock was built in two parts. The route to the north to Harlan, Iowa, was built by the Avoca, Harlan & Northern Railroad in 1878. Within two years, the railroad was leased to the Chicago, Rock Island & Pacific Railroad Company, then sold to it on March 16, 1899. The line to the south was built to Carson, Iowa, in 1879 by the Avoca, Macedonia & Southwestern Railroad. According to the Board of Railroad Commissioners of Kansas, the railroad was legally consolidated with the Chicago, Rock Island & Pacific on June 2, 1880.

The route from Oakland to Carson, where a connection was made with a CB&Q line, was abandoned in December 1953. In 1973, Rock Island employee timetables identified the remains of this line as Subdivision 5-C of the Des Moines Division. A track chart also showed it to be the Oakland Branch, stretching from south of Oakland (Milepost 12.52) to Avoca (Milepost 0.00). Within a few years, this changed as the line northward from Hancock (Milepost 6.4) to Avoca was abandoned in December 1979. This left a small agricultural facility in Oakland, and Scoular in Hancock.

Over the past decade the line was basically here to serve the Scoular elevator, and the 4.5-mile long line south to Oakland was generally used for car storage. A challenge with the line is that various mileposts have been used to describe locations along it. For example, the FRA still uses the mileposts from the 1970's era of the Rock Island Railroad. This has Avoca at Milepost 0.00 and Oakland at Milepost 12.52. However, many Iowa Interstate records show the mileposts as "Between MP 0.4 and MP 4.5." Then, in January 2016, the Iowa Interstate received permission to abandon the line from the end of track near Oakland (MP 469.59) to near Hancock Junction (MP 467.77). This makes the remains of the line simply an industrial line to serve the Scoular elevator.

6.0 NORTH END OF TRACK – The railroad was officially abandoned from Milepost 6.4 at the Scoular Hancock elevator. In reality, the track was kept north to Milepost 6.8 to provide room for loading unit trains.

6.4 SCOULAR ELEVATOR – This elevator is the major regional unit train loader for the company. Grain comes in from eleven other Scoular locations by truck for these movements. The company estimates that 25 to 30 million bushels of grain move yearly through the Hancock facility, and the Griswold and Corley locations. Because of the volumes moved, the elevator has its own locomotive. In 2017, the locomotive was SCOX 5004, formerly owned and operated by Canadian National.

Scoular was founded in 1892 by Scottish immigrant George Scoular and remained under the ownership of his family until 1967. In that year, a team of grain industry executives acquired the company, setting it up as an employee-owned agricultural business. The firm has offices in North and South America, as well as Asia, producing nearly $6 billion in sales yearly.

Switcher at grain elevator in Hancock, Iowa. Photo by Barton Jennings.

Hancock

The construction of the Avoca, Macedonia & Southwestern Railroad opened up the land in this area to development, and F. H. Hancock took advantage of it. Owning a great deal of land at what is today Hancock, he laid out a town in late 1880. A house, coal yard, blacksmith shop, and grocery opened by the end of the year. F. H. Hancock opened a grain dealership and the first rail shipment was made in December 1880. Hancock finished building a 25,000-bushel grain elevator by June 1882 and had already shipped 325,000 bushels of corn. Several other grain dealers were also active in the area.

By the mid-1880s, the community was growing with several saloons and general stores, an insurance firm, a lumber yard, a hog dealership, drugstore, hotel, church, I.O.O.F. Lodge, and several restaurants. At the time, its population was well over 100, enough to obtain a post office. Hancock was officially incorporated on May 16, 1891.

According to the *History of Pottawattamie County, Iowa, Volume I, 1907*, by that year, Hancock had grown to more than 300 residents. It had two elevators, the Des Moines and the South Branch, "three general stores, one hardware and implement store, one furniture and one drug store, one hotel, one livery stable, one bank, two blacksmith and machine shops, two churches, Methodist and Presbyterian, graded school, with principal and two assistants, one harness shop, one jewelry store, barber shop, one machine shop, one meat market that does its own killing, one opera house, two lumber yards, one cement block works and one cannery."

Today, the population is smaller at about 200, but the grain elevator is larger than ever. A major attraction at Hancock is the Botna Bend Park on the West Nishnabotna River. This park includes river access, camping, hiking trails, day activities, and a nature park that features elk and bison.

6.7 HANCOCK JUNCTION – This junction connects the former Carson to Avoca line which passes under the Rock

Island mainline. The connection is designed for eastbound mainline trains to head north to Hancock on the branch, and was known as the Hancock Northwest Wye. This track was shown to be 0.51 miles long and had two side tracks in 1973. Today, the wye connection has only one siding.

7.0 IOWA INTERSTATE MAINLINE – The former CRI&P mainline passes above the Oakland Branch. It is in this area that the 2016 abandonment starts. Heading south the railroad follows U.S. Highway 59 through open farmland.

7.3 TRACK OUT OF SERVICE – The track is out of service starting at this small bridge. South of the bridge, the track is not maintained and has quickly been taken over by brush and trees.

8.7 SOUTH END OF TRACK – This was the end of track before the 2016 abandonment.

Iowa Interstate – Cedar Rapids Interchange Yocum Connection (Iowa) to Cedar Rapids (Iowa)

This line became the route of interchange between the Iowa Interstate and the Cedar Rapids & Iowa City (CRANDIC, reporting mark CIC) when the connection at Yocum was built. It became even more important with the construction of the new IAIS yard and shops at South Amana. Initially, the Cedar Rapids & Iowa City operated their trains from Cedar Rapids to Yocum Connection and then east to Iowa City. This changed in 2004 when the Iowa Interstate began to operate the interchange trains. Today the Iowa Interstate operates trains to Smith-Dows Yard from their new South Amana yard for interchange business. Reportedly, this route is the largest single source of business for the Iowa Interstate, and unit trains of grain and coal are not uncommon on the line.

This line mainly consists of the former Sixth Subdivision of the Milwaukee Road's Iowa Division. In 1981, CIC acquired the former Milwaukee Road's track between Cedar Rapids and the Homestead (IA) area, which became known as their Third Subdivision. The line originally extended between Cedar Rapids and Ottumwa (IA), and was built in 1884. From Ottumwa, the line was extended to Kansas City in 1887 in response to the CB&Q building into the Twin Cities. However, this hilly line could never compete with other Kansas City to Chicago lines, and in 1903, the line was downgraded when the Kansas City Cutoff was built between Muscatine and Rutledge (just north of Ottumwa).

The former Milwaukee Road route was connected to the original Cedar Rapids & Iowa City route by a new line from the wye at ADM westward to what is today Smith-Dows Yard. In many ways, this new track is today the heart of the Cedar Rapids & Iowa City, for this is where much of the ADM traffic is handled and interchanged with Union Pacific and Iowa Interstate. With dozens of tracks in several yards, there is almost never a time that a CIC switcher can't be found working in this area.

With the 2004 change that had the Iowa Interstate coming to Smith-Dows Yard to handle the interchange, IAIS power is now a common sight in the area. They operate at least one morning freight train to Cedar Rapids, and often a second later in the day when traffic is heavy. In addition, coal and grain trains are often delivered by the Iowa Interstate to the local railroad. With volumes increasing on the line, the Iowa Interstate became the primary carrier. Reportedly, during September 2010, the track between Fairfax and Yocum Connection was assigned to the IAIS, becoming known for a while as Iowa Interstate Subdivision 3B. With that change, track warrants for train movements over this route are now issued by the Iowa Interstate Railroad.

4.3 EDGEWOOD ROAD – Until recently, Edgewood Road crossed both the Union Pacific and CIC mainlines at grade. However, in 2009-2010, new bridges were built across both railroads, creating some great railfan photo locations. This is the east end of Smith-Dows Yard and their small yard office is just to the west of the bridge.

The Cedar Rapids market may be growing quickly for the railroads involved. In 2016, the Iowa Department of Natural Resources was awarded a $25.7 million grant by the U.S. Department of Transportation to build a transload and intermodal container yard in southwest Cedar Rapids. The total cost is estimated to be $46.5 million with the rest of the money coming from private investors. The terminal is to be located west of the ADM-Corn Sweeteners plant near Edgewood Road on 75 acres of land, with service provided by the Cedar Rapids & Iowa City.

The terminal is a result of a 2014 study of Iowa's freight transportation network. The study suggested the construction of a container intermodal terminal, a bulk commodities transload facility, and a cross-dock facility for consolidating and redistributing truck loads. The report stated that the facility would be the only one in Iowa with all three capabilities. Construction was expected to begin in the spring of 2017.

4.5 SMITH-DOWS YARD – Generally known as the 900 Yard, it was named for the Cedar Rapids & Iowa City's co-founders Isaac Smith and Stephen Dows. The Iowa In-

Iowa Interstate - Cedar Rapids Interchange

terstate makes at least one trip a day from Iowa City to interchange cars with the CIC at this yard. The yard was built as part of the Cedar Rapids & Iowa City's merger of the former Milwaukee Road line into the rest of the system. It consists of seven tracks, with wide access roads next to each track to allow cars to be inspected and repaired as necessary, and to speed up switching.

The Iowa Interstate uses the station code "CR" for the Cedar Rapids area, with most trains and traffic interchanged in this area.

5.3 OLD BRIDGE ROAD – Old Bridge Road is located at the railroad south end of Smith-Dows Yard. Two tracks cross the road, connecting Smith-Dows Yard with the Fairfax and West 900 Yards. The name of this road apparently comes from the pin-connected, 6-panel Pratt through truss bridge over Prairie Creek just to the north of the tracks. The bridge was built in 1906 and rebuilt in 1989.

West 900 Yard was started in 2010 when ADM built their ethanol plant in Cedar Rapids. It started with a 9000-foot track built just west of Old Bridge Road, allowing the interchange of unit trains with the Iowa Interstate. Today, there are two such tracks on the south side of the mainline, each with access roads to allow for the inspection of the trains.

5.9 FAIRFAX INTERCHANGE YARD – *Railway Age* described the Fairfax Interchange Yard in their March 2005 issue. "A new 1.9-mile, double-track interchange with Union Pacific was completed in six months to facilitate the movement of unit corn and coal trains in 135-car consists, vs. four-to-five multi-car cuts. Each track is more than 7,800 feet long, and was constructed with 6,750 concrete and 600 wood ties, as well as 3.4 miles of 133-pound rail. Not only are efficiencies created for the carriers, the interchange is free of grade crossings, enhancing public safety."

Iowa Interstate Railroad: History Through the Miles

7.6 **LEFEBURE ROAD** – Some maps show this to be Fairfax Road. This timetable location is used to hold trains out of the way of trains working the various yards to the east.

8.1 **FAIRFAX** – The Cedar Rapids & Iowa City line passes through the south edge of Fairfax at what was Milwaukee Road milepost 77.4. This community, established when the Cedar Rapids & Missouri River Railroad (later Chicago & North Western Railway, then Union Pacific) reached here in 1863, was named Vanderbilt to honor the owners of the land in the area. The site was officially surveyed on May 22, 1863, by County Surveyor S. W. Durham on the farm of George W. Vanderbilt. B. E. Vanderbilt had the contract to build the first railroad depot here, and immediately served as the station agent and postmaster. A small town began to develop.

However, a post office known as Fairfax (named after Fairfax County, Virginia) had been established nearby in 1852. In 1862, the post office was renamed Vanderbilt when plans for the railroad were announced, but was again renamed Fairfax late in 1863 after moving to the railroad station. Fairfax was incorporated in August 1930.

11.6 **WALFORD** – When the Chicago, Milwaukee & St. Paul Railroad reached this location (milepost 73.8) in 1884, a community by the name of Terry was established here. The community's name was changed to Walford on November 11, 1899, and the community was incorporated on April 15, 1954. The Walford family was active in the area for many years.

The CIC has an 1130-foot side track here. As the railroad heads to the south, the adjacent U.S. Highway 151 curves away and the railroad enters rolling farmland.

11.7 **COUNTY LINE** – Look for 1st Street North, also known as Linn-Benton Road. Linn County is to the east while Benton County is to the west.

Iowa Interstate - Cedar Rapids Interchange

Linn County was organized by the first legislative assembly of the Iowa Territory on January 15, 1839. Linn County was named after Lewis Fields Linn (1795-1843), a senator from Missouri. Linn was a champion of the Western Territories, and several midwestern and western states have a county named in honor of the senator. Today, with the town of Cedar Rapids, Linn County is the second most populous county in the state of Iowa.

Benton County was formed on December 21, 1837, from sections of Dubuque County. It was named after U.S. Senator Thomas Hart Benton of Missouri. Benton fought in the War of 1812 and was a noted attorney. Vinton is the county seat. Even though the first mention of Benton County was in 1837, the first white settlers didn't arrive until early in 1839, when several families named Wright, Smith, Scott, and Lockhart settled in different parts of the county.

With the beginning of white settlements in the area, the boundaries of Benton County had to be more clearly defined. Because of that, Section 9 of an act of the Territorial Legislature of Iowa, entitled "An act to establish new counties and define their boundaries in the late cession from the Sac and Fox Indians, and for other purposes," approved February 17, 1843, provided "That the following boundaries shall constitute a new county and be called Benton..."

13.3 **COUNTY LINE** – The railroad passes under Benton-Iowa Road, the county line between Benton and Iowa Counties. **Iowa County** was named for the Iowa River, which flows through the county. The county was formed on February 17, 1843. Iowa County is one of seven counties in the United States that shares its name with its state, along with Arkansas County, Hawaii County, Idaho County, New York County, Oklahoma County, and Utah County.

17.1 **EAST AMANA** – East Amana was established in 1859 by members of the Amana Society. East Amana, located on the hillside to the north, is east of the main colony of Amana, thus its name. It is probably the least touristy of the original colonies with no historic sites there listed by the National Park Service on their "A National Register of Historic Places Travel Itinerary of a unique historic communal society in eastern Iowa."

18.2 PRICE CREEK AND MILL TAIL RACE BRIDGES – The railroad crosses two bridges, one a mix of timber and steel and the second all timber. The northern bridge crosses Price Creek, which drains the area northeast of Amana. The Mill Race has a more interesting history.

According to the National Parks Service: "Between 1865 and 1869, the Amana Colonists built a seven-mile-long canal stretching from the Iowa River near West Amana, through Middle Amana, then through Amana, and into Price Creek, just past town, where it continued to the river. They dug it with human, oxen, and steam power so it could provide waterpower to the mills in Middle Amana and Amana. A dredge helped to complete the project. The colonists built a dam to divert water from the Iowa River into the canal. The water turned water wheels, which in turn powered the shafts for the machinery in the mills. This race provided waterpower for the two textile mills and one flour mill which the society operated."

18.6 AMANA – Technically, the road crossed here is 48th Avenue that leads to the small private airport to the south of the tracks. The old Milwaukee Road depot, built of wood in 1883 at Milwaukee milepost 67.0, still stands here to the north. There is a 1670-foot long siding at the depot.

Just to the north can be seen the Amana Woolen Mill, Iowa's only operating woolen mill. The Amana Woolen Mill has had a colorful history, surviving fires, floods and wind storms. In 1855, members of the group began their move to the Iowa River valley in Iowa and named their community Amana (which means to remain faithful). The mill equipment was moved and construction of a woolen mill in Amana was begun in 1857. The mill not only produced goods for the community's use, but gained a reputation nationally for their goods.

The History of Amana

The history of Amana is somewhat complex and the community's website does a great job of detailing it. However, here is a short version. The 1600s and 1700s was a time of major religious change. One of the religious movements was called Pietism, which advocated faith renewal through reflection, prayer and Bible study. Eberhard L. Gruber and Johann F. Rock were two of the noted leaders in this movement, and they were supported by the belief that God, through the Holy Spirit, may inspire individuals to speak. According to the history of the Amana Colonies, this "gift of inspiration was the basis for a religious group that began meeting in 1714 and became known as the Community of True Inspiration. Though the Inspirationists sought to avoid conflict, they were persecuted for their beliefs. Eventually the Inspirationists found refuge in central Germany settling in several estates, including the 13th century Ronneburg castle."

Religious persecution and an economic depression in Germany forced the community to begin searching for a new home. Many Community members left Germany for America in 1843-44, led by Christian Metz. The group acquired 5000 acres near Buffalo, New York, creating what they called the Ebenezer Society. The 1200 members adopted a formal constitution calling for a communal society where work and property was shared. While hoping for a rural life, Buffalo's growth soon edged onto their property and 26,000 acres of land in rural Iowa was acquired by 1855 to create a new community. Quickly, six communities were built in the Iowa River Valley, with each including housing, shops, factories, mills, schools, churches, and other structures needed for the Society to survive.

The villages were named Amana, Middle Amana, East Amana, West Amana, South Amana, and High Amana. A seventh, named Homestead, already existed and was bought by the Society to provide railroad access to national markets. The colonies were spread out across the 26,000 acres so that large farms could be operated within an easy travel distance for the workers. The Amana history states that each community "was laid out in classic, old-world style, resembling the German 'Dorf' of the Fatherland, with one long street and several offshoots. At one end were the barns and sheds, and at the other, the factories and workshops were gathered. On either side were orchards, vineyards and gardens. Each village had its own church, school, bakery, dairy, wine cellar, post office and general store." One noted feature of each town was the communal kitchen and dining hall where all the colonists dined. Today, these buildings still stand and are used for a number of other tasks.

The plan for the Society was to be self-reliant. They made their own tools and farm implements, as well as brick for their buildings. Soon, they were producing food and products for their own use, as well as to sell to national markets. Some of the better-known products that the Society sold were woolen fabric and products, furniture and grandfather clocks, baskets and brooms, potatoes and onions, and wines. The mills and factories that the Society built were some of the first built in Iowa. In particular, the woolen mills were widely known for quality and value.

While the Society was happy to sell products to outsiders, internally, the concept of private ownership was very limited. The Society developed a highly successful form of communism so that its members were free to worship in peace. Each member worked to produce goods for the Society, which then took care of all of their food, shelter and clothing needs. This plan worked as long as there were significant outside markets for their goods, bringing needed money into the Society. However, the Depression of the 1930s cut into this strategy. With problems arising, such as a lack of funds and younger members leaving the Society for opportunities elsewhere, the Society voted in 1932 to create "The Great Change," a move toward capitalism. A central corporation was created that owned many of the major holdings, with each Society member now holding shares that they could sell. Additionally, much of the rest of the property was sold to the members to do with as they wished. A final major change was an effort to attract tourism by opening the Amana Colonies to visitors.

Of all the changes, the tourism movement may be the most successful. Each year, more than 1.5 million tourists visit the Amana Colonies. All seven villages are listed as National Historic Landmarks, including more than 475 historical sites and buildings. A key part of the tourism is shopping, with most of the original factories and mills still producing products like hardwood furniture, clocks, crafts, woolens, meats, cheeses, breads, and wines. Restaurants are also a major part of the tourism industry, many featuring the family-style method of serving historic meals.

Here are a few interesting facts about Amana. When the Amana Colonies were founded in 1855, all musical instruments were banned, except the flute. Members of Amana's Community of True Inspiration were not buried side-by-side with family members, but in chronological order according to their deaths. Finally, the Amana Colonies claim to be the Bratwurst Capital of the World.

20.0 AMANA REFRIGERATION – Located to the north of the tracks, this is the only major manufacturing plant in the Amana Colonies. Employing over 2000 employees, the appliances made here have a fine reputation for quality. The original plant opened here in 1934, founded by George Foerstner as The Electrical Equipment Company. Located in Middle Amana, the plant was used to manufacture commercial walk-in coolers. The company was later sold to the Amana Society. In 1947, Amana Refrigeration began to manufacture upright freezers for home use, some of the first on the market. In 1949, it added a side-by-side refrigerator/freezer. In 1950, George Foerstner and a group of investors acquired the company and renamed it Amana Refrigeration, Inc.

With the ownership change, plans were created to expand the products sold. By 1954, air conditioners were being sold under the Amana name. The company was again sold, this time in 1965 to Raytheon, which had invented the microwave oven in 1947. This allowed the Radarange to enter the commercial market in 1954, and the consumer version in 1967. The consumer version was described as the first popular microwave designed for home use, and entered the market as an Amana product. More products such as furnaces, ovens, countertop ranges, dishwashers, and clothes washers and dryers were later added to the name.

In 1997, Goodman Global (now part of Daikin North America) bought Amana Refrigeration and then sold part of the company in 2002 to Maytag. In April 2006, Maytag was acquired by the Whirlpool Corporation. Today, the Amana Appliance Division still manufacturers home appliances.

This factory is on the south side of Middle Amana. With a population of about 600, Middle Amana also features a well-known bakery and the Communal Kitchen and Coopershop Museum. During the 1880s, Middle Amana reportedly contained a woolen mill (one of two in the Colonies), starch factory, machine shop, wagon shop, blacksmith shop, book printing and bindery, brick yard, general store, school, and meeting house. Middle Amana is also the home of The Old Creamery Theatre Studio Stage, one of several facilities for the oldest professional theatre company in the state of Iowa.

The East Refrigerator track is 2300 feet long. The West Track is long gone.

20.6 **IOWA RIVER BRIDGE** – The Iowa River is a 300-mile long tributary of the Mississippi River. It arises in two branches, the West Branch and East Branch. After the two branches merge, the Iowa River then proceeds roughly in a southeast direction, passing through the towns of Iowa Falls and Marshalltown, and then through the Amana Colonies. Just east of here, the river is impounded by the Coralville

Dam to create the Coralville Reservoir. From there, the river runs generally south and passes through Iowa City, merges with the English River and the Cedar River, and then flows on into the Mississippi River.

From south to north, this bridge includes two girder spans and two pony through truss spans, for a total length of about 315 feet. The pony spans were built by the American Bridge Company of New York in 1902.

There are two other long bridges in this area, one east and one west of the Iowa River bridge. These have been rebuilt to handle heavier train loads and to allow floodwaters to pass under the tracks.

21.8 YOCUM CONNECTION – On February 11, 2000, Yocum Connection, a full wye interchange between IAIS Subdivision 3, now the Iowa City Subdivision, and CIC Third Subdivision at Homestead (IA), was placed into service. Yocum would become the new primary interchange point for the two railroads, replacing the Hill Track in Iowa City (IA), a steep piece of trackage that extends out of the west end of IAIS's yard and is about as close to street running as you can get without being in the street.

A post office opened near here in 1852 with the name Homestead. In 1860, the community was bought by the Amana Society to access the railroad which was building through the site.

IAIS 510 westbound, Homestead, Iowa. Photo by Barton Jennings.

Hills Line
Iowa City (Iowa) to Hills (Iowa)

A description of this route is included since the Iowa Interstate operated it during the 2010s. In January 2012, the Surface Transportation Board (STB) approved a plan for the Iowa Interstate Railroad to lease and operate the Hills Line of the Cedar Rapids & Iowa City Railway Company (CRANDIC, CR&IC, or reporting marks CIC) for five years. This included 8.4 miles of track from Milepost 25.0 near Burlington Street in Iowa City, Iowa, to the end of track at milepost 33.4 in Hills, Iowa. The IAIS connects to this line near Milepost 26. According to the STB, there were three active shippers on the line and the CIC operated over the line one to two days per week. An issue was that there were no shippers on the Cedar Rapids & Iowa City line between Iowa City and Corn Sweetner Wye in Cedar Rapids, a distance of almost 25 miles, making it very time consuming for the Hills customers to be served, and the freight was often handed to the Iowa Interstate at Iowa City anyway. However, an October 4, 2016 decision by the STB noted "that CRANDIC and IAIS have agreed that the lease of the Hills Line by IAIS will terminate on October 26, 2016" and that the Cedar Rapids & Iowa City Railway Company will assume operations of the route.

The line between Iowa City and Hills is a former Rock Island branchline. CIC timetables from the 1990s show this part of the line to be the Second Subdivision but when the lease was made it was included as part of their First Division.

In 1879, the Burlington, Cedar Rapids & Northern Railway built a 66-mile branch via Hills from Iowa City to the coal mines at What Cheer, Iowa. According to the 1891 and 1892 issues of the *Annual Report of the Burlington, Cedar Rapids & Northern Railway Co.*, in 1891, the BCR&N Railway's Iowa City Division served What Cheer. In that year it carried 38,080 tons of coal, by far the most important commodity carried by that line. In 1892, mines along the BCR&N (all of which were in the What Cheer region) loaded 129,316 tons of coal. Obviously, coal was a growing source of traffic on the line in the late 1800s.

The tracks south of Hills to Iowa Junction, and then west to Montezuma, were acquired on February 22, 1974, by the Central Iowa Railway (formally named the Central Iowa Transportation Cooperative), based in the Amish community of Kalona. The railway was short-lived and it folded in October 1974. The railroad was probably best known for its unique locomotive. The Central Iowa operated a single 600-horsepower EMD SW1, painted blue and black, and numbered J33-3. The strange number came from verse 33:3 in the Book of Jeremiah in the Bible, which says, "Call unto me, and I will answer thee, and show thee great and mighty things, which thou knowest not."

In 1980, the trustees of the Chicago, Rock Island & Pacific Railroad sold the line between Hills and Iowa City to the Cedar Rapids & Iowa City Railway. Because of this, the mileposts shown on the line are from Cedar Rapids.

25.0 UNIVERSITY – This station is located just north of Burlington Street at the Main Library. Just south of here is a complex of tracks used to serve area customers and once used to switch trains for interchange with the Iowa Interstate. At the same location and beneath the Iowa Interstate mainline, the mainline curves to the east. There is a 1050-foot siding here also.

During late 2011, it was announced that the Iowa Interstate would lease the track south of here to serve the three customers on this line. With few freight customers on this line, the two railroads determined that it made more sense for the IAIS to handle these customers with their local switcher as opposed to the Cedar Rapids & Iowa City having to make a long trip down with their local.

25.1 IOWA CITY – Iowa City was originally located in May 1839 by a commission charged with selecting a capital for the Iowa Territory, fulfilling the desire of Governor Robert Lucas to move the capital out of Burlington and closer to the center of the territory. When statehood was announced in 1846 it became the first state capitol. The "Old Capitol'" is now a National Historic Landmark. Iowa City was Iowa's capital until 1857 when Des Moines was chosen as the new state capital.

Iowa City was officially incorporated on January 24, 1853. While it is no longer the capital of Iowa, it is the county seat of Johnson County. Not long after the capital moved, Iowa City became the location of the University of Iowa, which later became the first public university in the nation to admit men and women on an equal basis. Related to university life, the ACT, "America's Most Widely Accepted College Entrance Exam," is headquartered in Iowa City.

Heading south, there is a siding to the west for the next half-mile. Several industry tracks break off of the siding.

25.4 IOWA INTERSTATE BRIDGE – The Iowa Interstate's Iowa River Bridge also crosses over the Cedar Rapids & Iowa City line here. Just south of the bridge, the line curves to the east and the siding ends. Several blocks further to the east, the line curves back to the south, following the east side of Maiden Lane.

26.0 SWITCHBACK – Located at the highway intersection of Kirkwood and Maiden, there is a runaround track and switchback to allow trains to shove into the IAIS yard. This complex and tight interchange track, along with an enormous growth in business, caused the two railroads to begin using Yocum Connection and the new South Amana Yard as their primary interchange route.

The track from here runs up the side of Gilbert Court until it curves to the west at the west end of the IAIS yard, connecting to the mainline a block east of the former Rock Island station.

26.9 IOWA RIVER BRIDGE – This bridge has timber spans on the north end, then two through truss spans, then more wood to the south. Built in 1901, this bridge includes two different designs of truss bridges. One is a lattice through truss while the other is a more modern Warren through truss bridge.

27.2 GRINGER AG INC. – There is a loader hanging over the mainline. With the small amount of traffic on the line, cars have sometimes been unloaded here.

28.8 IZAAK WALTON – The railroad crosses Izaak Walton Road here. Just to the east is County Materials Corporation, a supplier of concrete construction and landscape products. This facility specializes in pipe and precast products. A short distance further to the east is S&G Materials, a quarry company and supplier of products like concrete sand, mason sand, river rock, black dirt, recycled concrete products, and asphalt millings. Both companies serve the regional market and do not use the railroad.

32.7 HILLS – Hills, originally called Hill's Siding, was named for local land owner Thomas Hill. The siding was installed in 1876, the town of Hill's was established in 1900, and incorporated as Hills in 1906. Today, this is the end of the line.

South of Hills is the Eldon C. Stutsman complex, a major rail customer on the line. In 1934, Eldon C. Stutsman started a milk route, and his neighbors soon asked him to bring supplies back from town. The requests kept coming and soon a company was born. Today, Eldon C. Stutsman, Inc., a family-owned business, is eastern Iowa's largest supplier of agricultural products, retail and wholesale.

Just a few miles to the southwest is Riverside, Iowa. Riverside was once a station on this Rock Island line. However, to some people, Riverside is famous as being the "Official Future Birthplace of Captain James T. Kirk." In March 1985, when the city was looking for a theme for its annual town festival, a member of the Riverside City Council suggested that Riverside should proclaim itself to be the future birthplace of Kirk, based upon a statement by Gene Roddenberry, the creator of Star Trek, that the character of James Tiberius Kirk had been born in the state of Iowa. Roddenberry agreed and the community hosts an annual Riverside Trek Fest, often with actors from the TV show and movies.

About the Author

For almost three decades, Barton Jennings has been organizing charter passenger trains and writing the route descriptions, both for planning purposes and for the enjoyment of the passengers. These trips have been from coast to coast, often covering operations that haven't seen a passenger train in decades. In addition, he has written a number of articles about various railroads for rail hobby magazines.

His basement has several rooms full of books, timetables and other documents about this and other railroads – important research items from a time long before today's internet. Today, Bart Jennings, after years working in the railroad industry, is a professor of supply chain management and teaches transportation operations. He also still teaches regulatory issues for the railroad industry, a way to stay in touch with the industry he loves.

This book is an outgrowth of all of these experiences. Much of the information comes from internal railroad records, government and public records, railroad workers, and conversations with old and new friends. It is hoped that you enjoy your adventure with the railroad and that this book is of assistance in some ways – *Iowa Interstate Railroad: History Through the Miles*.

The author, somewhere in western Iowa. Photo by Sarah Jennings.

www.ingramcontent.com/pod-product-compliance
Lightning Source LLC
Chambersburg PA
CBHW050624300426
44112CB00012B/1637